The *Iliad*, the *Odyssey*, and the Epic Tradition

CHARLES ROWAN BEYE is an Associate Professor of Classics at Boston University. Although his particular interest is in Homeric epic, he has also written articles on Euripides and Lucretius. The Archaeological Institute of America awarded him in 1963 the Olivia James Traveling Fellowship for a projected book on the geographical background of Greek poetry. Professor Beye is also working on a study of later Greek epic.

Professor Beye received his Ph.D. from Harvard in Classical Philology, and has taught at Wheaton College (Mass.), Yale, and Stanford.

The *ILIAD*, the *ODYSSEY*, and the Epic Tradition

CHARLES ROWAN BEYE

Second Edition

GORDIAN PRESS
NEW YORK
1976

Originally Published 1966
Reprinted 1976

Copyright © 1966 by Charles Rowan Beye
Published by Gordian Press, Inc.
By Arrangement With
Doubleday & Company, Inc.

Library of Congress Cataloging in Publication Data

Beye, Charles Rowan.
    The Iliad, the Odyssey, and the epic tradition.

    Reprint of the 1966 ed. published by Anchor Books,
Garden City, N. Y.
    Bibliography: p.
    Includes index.
    1. Homerus. Ilias. 2. Homerus. Odyssea. I. Ti-
tle.
PA4037.B503 1976   883'.01   76-10726
ISBN 0-87752-187-5

For Penny

PREFACE

Research into the Homeric epics during the past century has considerably enlarged our understanding of the *Iliad* and the *Odyssey* and the cultures that produced them. The two poems have been studied from every point of view by specialists in a variety of disciplines. Out of this material, I have attempted to draw information that is relevant to any critical understanding of the *Iliad* and *Odyssey* as poetry. Therefore, I have tried to give some account of the nature of oral poetry to help the reader formulate an aesthetic different from that which he would employ for literate poetry. I have described some details of the poems' setting over which Homer passes lightly so that the reader may perceive and imagine more clearly what Homer's audience took for granted. Moreover, I have discussed some of the common techniques of oral epic narration so that the reader may more easily notice when Homer is using these often routine devices for effects that are especially pertinent to his poem.

This book is principally designed for the non-specialist, particularly the many people today, both in college and out, who are discovering the *Iliad* and *Odyssey* in translation. Therefore, the poems have been treated as poems, not as documentary bases for hypotheses. Homeric scholarship is vast; much is cliché, much arguable, and much, by being overlooked, is repeated as original from book to book. There are no footnotes here. My learned reader will know the controversies and theories that stand behind my statements, and he whose interest is a critical understanding of the two poems possibly could not care. I have, however, added a brief section called "Further Reading" in which the reader will be directed to source material for my chapters, and which will enable him to begin a deeper, more pervasive study of Homer.

In the last three chapters I offer interpretations of the *Iliad,* the *Odyssey,* and—less thoroughly—the *Aeneid* (as a reflection and statement on the Homeric poems). These are my own; yet, frequently they, of course, depend on others' interpretations or share others' points of view. This is to be expected since an interpretation which departs radically from the consensus, an interpretation with which few could agree, does not seem to be a successful analysis of a work that is in itself common communication. Nevertheless, the interpretations should not be regarded as commonplaces of Homeric or Virgilian criticism (offered not as boast, but warning).

While lecturing on Homer in undergraduate and graduate courses, in translation and in the original Greek, for the past decade, I have learned as much as I have taught. I must thank collectively all the students who have asked the right questions or offered the perceptive responses that have guided me. Friends and colleagues have generously read all or part of the manuscript and generously criticized it. I should like to thank for this W. M. Calder, III, W. B. Carnochan, J. A. Coulter, E. J. Doyle, Ann Rosener and, most of all, Richard Sáez. My wife, Penelope, has read and criticized with the frankness that only a wife dares. It remains to say—in our own formulaic style—that whatever faults remain I owe to myself. One must be, I suppose, the arbitrary system of transliterating Greek names. I quite agree that it is high time to give up the Latin forms, so that Hector becomes Hektor and Hercules, Herakles. I cannot, however, be consistent since some transliterations seem to me to be odd. I have used Ajax: Aias is not Ajax to me and never will be. I have not followed logic but my instincts in these matters.

Finally, I should like to acknowledge my gratitude to my parents-in-law, Mrs. P. E. Pendleton and the late Admiral Pendleton, who have given me every kind of encouragement and assistance.

CONTENTS

The *Iliad,* the *Odyssey,* and the Epic Tradition

Chapter I

ORAL POETRY

Pierian Muses, who give glory through song come here, sing in me Zeus, hymning your father, by whom mortals are either unmentioned or mentioned, spoken of, made famous, or not by the will of Zeus.

Hesiod *Works and Days* 1–4

On us two Zeus set a vile destiny; so that hereafter we shall be made into things of song for the men of the future.

Iliad 6.357 f (Helen speaking of herself and Paris)

It is a paradox that the Old Testament and the Homeric epics, which are the most prominent and influential works of literature in the Western world, have such obscure authorship. Perhaps this is some sort of final justification of New Criticism because we are left with almost nothing but the texts themselves to consider. Greek historical thinking always insisted upon ascribing every act, no matter how general or sweeping, to the creation of a single person, and their tradition commonly maintained that the *Iliad* and *Odyssey* were composed by a certain Homer, a blind singer of poetry from the island of Chios, who lived at the latest in the ninth century B.C. The author of the Homeric-like *Hymn to Apollo*, whom we are to suppose was this Homer, at one point addresses his audience saying:

> Remember me later on when any man . . . comes here and asks you, "Who do you think is the sweetest singer that comes here? Who is he who gives you the most delight?" Then be sure to reply all in one voice: "He is a blind man and lives in rocky Chios; now and forevermore his songs will be the best." (166–173)

Whether the tradition ascribing the two epics to Homer's authorship developed from these lines, or whether there is more truth to it cannot be proved or disproved; the sensible course is to leave the matter here. Centuries of scholars have worried over the problem in vain. Even in antiquity it was a subject for scholarly inquiry. There is a clever essay by the ancient Greek satirist, Lucian, who describes his journey into Hades where he consults with the ghost of Homer on some of the disputed facts. Lucian certainly had the right idea. The only person who could satisfy our curiosity and lay our doubts to rest is Homer, and he is dead.

Authorship aside, the archaeological discoveries of the last one hundred years and the texts themselves have made possible various relatively reasonable hypotheses which extend our knowledge somewhat into the process that made these two epics. From a critical point of view this understanding is important because in the modern eye looking back to Homer there lies a mote in the form of the epic of the Latin poet Virgil, who created the tradition in which every epic writer since inevitably finds himself, even Nicos Kazantzakis, the author of a modern *Odyssey* which is a sequel to the Homeric *Odyssey.* Virgil's *Aeneid* is shot through with so many Homeric reminiscences and is so consciously Homeric in form and scale that it seems altogether reasonable to see Virgil as working in the very same tradition, simply refining and

Romanizing an essentially primitive Greek narrative technique. But there is apparently no basis for thinking that what in Virgil is full-blown is in Homer embryo. Their methods of composition were entirely different, as were their environments. Virgil was literate, a writer who spent ten years slowly fashioning his lines, often no more than a few a day. As an associate of Augustus Caesar in the early years of his rise to power Virgil watched the concept of society and government that was to be the Roman Empire come into being. Homer's manner and world, as we shall see, were quite otherwise.

Any scholarly and critical understanding of Homer today depends upon theories of oral poetry. These theories more or less inspire our notions of the poet's manner of composition. They also help to supply at best a tricky and unreliable index or gauge to the degree of originality in the poems. The *Iliad* and *Odyssey* take up relatively brief events within the context of what seems to have been an enormous enterprise, the attack by a federation of Greek cities upon the royal city of Troy in northern Asia Minor. Through the centuries credulity has alternated with scepticism in regard to this contest between the great Greek and Trojan empires. We shall never know whether or not such a war was ever actually fought, or whether Helen was ever first cause (how nice a thing to believe in an era of dispassionate war), but the archaeological investigations begun by Schliemann at Troy and Mycenae in the latter part of the nineteenth century and continued there and elsewhere to this day make it abundantly clear that at least the world of Homer's Achaians whom we call Mycenaeans did in fact exist. The epic then is not a fairy tale, nor altogether fiction. Somehow the saga tradition which had origins in fact had the means to maintain itself beyond the collapse and disappearance of this Achaian or Mycenaean world in the eleventh century B.C. into a time when a Homer spoke, even to the moment when what he spoke was written down. The writing is important since

what we have is only the written text which represents a
process and mentality scarcely earlier than three hundred
years after the Achaians were gone.

The Mycenaean world knew a system of writing which
has only recently been discovered to have been used for
the writing of Greek. This system, known as Linear B,
was a syllabary; that is, each symbol represented a syllable
—unlike an alphabet, which when used most efficiently
has a sign for every distinct sound. The syllabary is clumsy
since the possible combinations of vowels and consonants
making syllables are very many in any language. The number of symbols a writer must learn will be large, and the
urge to abbreviate is inevitable. Grammatical subtleties
are difficult or impossible to symbolize; vagueness is almost
inherent in the system. The Linear B script is hardly a
system of writing in which to create the close and
rhythmed texture of lengthy epic narrative. What we
possess of Linear B writing is archive records. This is
chance, of course, but it is eminently likely that no other
use was conceived for the Linear B syllabary.

As a matter of fact we have no proof that Linear B
survived the time when the Mycenaean Kingdom was
invaded and overcome by the Dorian-speaking Greeks in
the eleventh century B.C. The absence of inscriptional
evidence makes it likely that a period of illiteracy followed
the collapse of the Mycenaean Empire. The alphabetic
system of writing, which is the Greek script of the classical
period and still used today, was taken over and adapted
from a Semitic alphabet probably in the eighth or ninth
century, a considerable time later.

One is faced, then, with the existence of these two
lengthy epics describing or at least alluding to a world
which ended in the eleventh century together with the
fact that there was no system of writing or any system
capable of transmitting these epics to the time of the
making up of the texts we know. Some sort of oral tradition is the obvious solution, yet until this century few

scholars could believe that it was possible to carry in the head, not to mention pass on, something like the *Iliad*, which is roughly fifteen and a half thousand lines long. Scholars at an earlier time did not grasp the unique attributes of oral creation and tradition. Rote memory, verbatim repetition seem not to be important to oral poetry. Therefore the energies of the poet are engaged far more flexibly and creatively and far more lightly than scholars used to believe.

In the twentieth century a series of perceptive and detailed studies have demonstrated that such an oral tradition was possible. The means for this tradition and the stuff of epic recital were formulae. In ordinary human speech individual words which are each symbols of things are combined together to create a larger concept. In epic Greek, however, the minimal element is the formulaic phrase. Each idea or action may be described by a phrase which has a fixed metrical quantity. While for different metrical positions within a line there will be different phrases expressing the same thing, phrases of identical metrical quantity which say the same thing are very few. These phrases drastically reduce the effort of the composer because he is compelled to work out rhythms through far fewer free juxtapositions than would be the case if he were arranging each separate word. The absence of phrases which are at once metrically and semantically similar shows that over a long period of time a process of selection and economizing was at work, wherein generations of bards developed the best possible combinations, first to indicate precisely their meaning, second to ensure a flexibility in creating a line. Metrically parallel phrases describing the same thing would be an unnatural use of memory, just as two semantically identical words for "table" would be absurd. All but one of the phrases would disappear, while the intellectual effort was given to achieving different phrases which satisfied different metrical demands. A long process and a hard one, but one which finally made it possible for any one bard of great talent to carry in his memory a sufficiency of formulae out of which the variegated and detailed narrative of an *Iliad* or *Odyssey* could take substance.

The detailed analyses of the Homeric vocabulary which showed an economical use of formulaic phrases fit to every metrical situation immediately limited the earlier objections to the impossible strain of memorizing a lengthy poem. The poet built out of half lines or whole lines rather than words. He was not, then, compelled to remember verbatim the poem as he heard it, nor had he to create anew such a long poem word by word. The tendency of this line of research was to accentuate and to search for the mechanical elements of the epic tradition to which the poet was heir. The mechanics of the oral style are, as this chapter will demonstrate, of an obviously artificial nature; epic is ritual, contrived and unreal to a greater degree than most other art forms. Having first examined these, we shall be better able to appreciate that within the contrivance a strong and consistent mood of realism is accomplished that has allowed successive generations of man to appreciate Greek epic and identify with it. This theory of the creation of Greek formulaic poetry is, of course, an article of faith. It is, however, based on many accurate and penetrating observations of epic fact. The alternative is to believe that a series of ballads narrating short episodes were finally made into lengthy epics, our *Iliad* and *Odyssey,* when the discovery of writing removed the burden from memory. This is the basis upon which nineteenth-century criticism rested. Analogies of a sort were to hand; the Finnish epic *Kalevala* came about in this way, and Teutonic saga tradition revealed the same form. The *Iliad* and *Odyssey,* however, are each so obviously integral wholes, and so far superior to these other epics that this alternative theory is repellent, especially in view of the possibility of generations of memories, which retained phrases, motifs, and legends.

Upon this article of faith we can reconstruct a reasonable history of the oral technique which culminated in the *Iliad* and *Odyssey* as we know them. From the seventeenth to the eleventh centuries before our era there existed throughout the mainland of Greece some sort of political entity which had its seat of power in Mycenae. The glorious ruins of Mycenae and the extraordinarily rich and fine art objects from the graves there testify to a splendid civilization. Of the life at the central court we have no notion, although ample descriptions of local or provincial courts occur in the *Odyssey*. Perhaps the elegant palace of King Alkinoos on the island of Scheria is close to what Mycenae must have been like. Even the sophisticated Odysseus stared in awe at the splendor. One of the fixtures of these courts was the singing poet of whom Demodokos at the court of Alkinoos is the grand example. A blind man, he is led forth with great respect, his lyre placed in his hands, and he composes a song, on one occasion, of the events at Troy, on another, a rather saucy account of Ares and Aphrodite caught in adultery by her husband Hephaistos. The bard was no minor retainer, he held a high position. Agamemnon, according to the author of the *Odyssey*, left his court bard as guardian over Queen Klytemnestra, a task to which the poet proved to be unequal.

In the earliest times, then, epic poetry was a sung, or more likely chanted, account of the doings of either gods or men, performed by a professional. Amateurs too could try their hands at it, for we find Achilles and Patroklos in the ninth book of the *Iliad* taking turns in singing "the famous deeds of men" (189). The epic technique, nevertheless, seems too contrived and elaborate to have been taken up casually. Aristocratic young men could be trained to show some skill at it, but by and large it must have remained in the hands of men who spent their lives at learning the old themes and phrases and remaking them to their own view. It is hard to see, as some would like, any

connection between this highly stylized art and genuine
folk poetry. Not only is the style complex and sophisticated, but it is hard to discover anything in the epics that
is not sprung from or directed to an aristocratic conscious.
People of low birth do not appear on the scene. The concerns of the characters are those of the ruling classes. Even
the gods are those of a court, not of a simple rustic cult.

Very likely the famous deeds of men were always a
larger element of the epic recital than the affairs of gods.
In the sixth book of the *Iliad* there is a remarkable passage
in a conversation between Helen and her patient, not altogether unsympathetic brother-in-law, Hektor, when after
castigating herself for the misery she has brought upon
men, she suddenly remarks (357 f) that Zeus has brought
this evil fate upon her and Paris so that they should become the subjects of song among later generations. Likewise in the *Odyssey* when Demodokos has finished his song
of Troy, King Alkinoos expresses the same idea: "The
gods made this doom; it was they who fated this destruction for men, so that even among later generations there
should be a song of it" (8.579 f). These observations have
a strange logic. The sort of moral cause and effect which
we should expect is not there, unless one chooses to believe
that the epic was self-consciously educative. That is to say,
the gods and, of course, the poets create notorious examples of fortune and misfortune as moral guides to poster-
ity. Indeed, much of later Greek thought came to accept
this view, if not of historical causation, then of the manner of history writing, such as Plutarch, whose *Lives of
Famous Men* is nothing but a long string of instructive
examples of right and wrong behavior. But the epic poet
meant none of this by his statement. He is rather arguing
back from the fact of his saga material to describe the
source. Some men in past time have been so lifted up out
of the ordinary course of human events that they are remembered. It is mysterious, this mark that falls upon
some lives, and the bard instinctively and rightly assigns

it to the workings of the supernatural. By his reference to the gods the bard also manages to attach the greatest possible importance to his own profession. It is an awesome thing that a man's deed may be so grand that it can assume an imperishable reality beyond its commitment to become the common knowledge of later ages. It is an awesome thing that some men have the poetic skill to assure to the glorious deed its immortality. In an age without writing all this is the gift of Memory whom the early Greeks properly deified as wife to Zeus and by him mother of the Muses.

The language of the Mycenaean bards, we may assume, was the Greek that can be deciphered from the Linear B syllabary writing. The language of our *Iliad* and *Odyssey*, however, is an extraordinary amalgam of several different dialects of Greek, an artificial language that came about through wide circulation in many environments in the enormous political and social upheaval that followed the collapse of the Mycenaean Kingdom. Two contrary facts, isolation and commingling, are important. When the royal Mycenaean system of communications fell apart, the various areas of the mainland became isolated, and in this isolation the speech of the people began to grow distinct from the common speech and dialect variations came into being. At the same time an opposing process commenced. With the arrival of new peoples in the Peloponnesus, the older inhabitants were displaced. They migrated out of the area, out over the mainland to the east, and finally to Asia Minor, and for periods of time one dialect group mingled with another. In the centuries of long migrations and relocations of whole peoples the technique of saga telling which the professional bards at the Mycenaean court centers had begun became transformed. The bards moved away from the old centers in the general human flux of the times. As they met with different dialects, these bards made up formulae out of them. Some of these passed into the common stock when they were seen to be more congenial to the epic rhythm. This cross-pollination from dialect to dialect produced the hybrid language of the *Iliad* and *Odyssey*. It is difficult to describe the result to someone unacquainted with Greek; it is impossible to render its quality in translation, most unfortunately, for epic Greek in essence is a language totally artificial and totally alien to common speech.

Ancient Greek poetic rhythms were not primarily accentual as is generally true of English poetry. The distinction between long and short syllables was just what the terms imply: a long syllable takes twice as long to sound as a short syllable takes. Epic Greek was a dactylic hexametric rhythm, that is, six units each made up of one long syllable followed by two short syllables. The monotonous chain of rhythm was broken occasionally (sometimes frequently for a heavy effect) by the substitution of a long syllable for the two short ones, which did not upset the rhythmic lengths of time of enunciation. Early Greek fell naturally into a dactylic pattern because there are so many short syllables in the words that juxtaposing two of them to a long syllable was no effort. Long syllables, on the other hand, occur more frequently in Latin. The flowing dactylic hexameters of the *Aeneid* represent an extraordinary triumph on the part of Virgil over his predecessor Lucretius, whose *De Rerum Natura* is in dactylic hexameters which seem to be forcibly carved out of the spondaic Latinate rock.

The very great advantage to creating phrases that the epic poets discovered in mingling dialect variations can perhaps be illustrated by a somewhat absurd example from the English language. If one were to measure the time an Englishman, a New Englander, and a Southerner takes to enunciate the several syllables of the word "magnolia," he would very likely find that they could be schematized as măgnōlyă, măgnōlyēr, and māgnōlyă (I suppose that in reality no Southerner outside of the motion pictures says măўgnōlўa). Dialect variations are not an obvious

feature of written English because there is no attempt
made to spell phonetically. Mass communications are
rapidly diminishing any speech differences, and we have
no real American dialects as the Greeks did. But the
example will do to show that each variation has a different
metrical quality. In the epic, certain formulae could only
be achieved if a dialectal variant of the Mycenaean
Greek word were introduced. Once the formula came into
being and was accepted as the optimum phrase in terms
of semantics, meter, and aesthetics, it stood—there was no
alternative. The dialectal variation became a commonplace
of the epic language even though any given bard who used
the word in the traditional formula and perhaps even
made it the basis of creating new formulae might not in
his daily speech use that dialect.

Epic language was used only for epic purposes; it was a
thing apart from natural speech, an artifice, handed down
from the distant past, given over to describe the real in
unreal fashion, and thereby creating a very special world
and vision all of its own. It had the sanctity and grandeur
of aged obscurity that is akin to the qualities of the
English of the King James Bible. For this reason translators have sometimes put the Greek epics into King James
English, which, although emphasizing the feeling of the
unreal and of antiquity, can never manage to convey the
liveliness and simplicity of epic Greek. King James English
tends to be quaint in our time, whereas nuances of epic
Greek continued to be sounded in classical tragic and lyric
poetry, preserving epic diction as normal. On the other
hand nothing so rapidly achieves the banal as long
stretches of routine Homeric narrative done into modern
American English.

So much for the generations who created and continued
both the epic language, the formulaic motifs and themes,
and the systems of legend for which the language was cast.
The psychology of these, very likely, illiterate men was
such that the past gained permanence only through

memory. Eventually the Greeks gained the alphabet and with it quite another psychology, more or less that of our own time. Memory is released from her greater labors and that which gives man a permanence and coherence beyond the moment is the written word. And the written word gives total, unerring permanence. Contemporary field observation of oral poets in Yugoslavia and elsewhere shows that although the oral poets boast of reciting the stories exactly as they had learned them, they are in fact continually altering and, if adept, improving them. Half-consciously every bard must know that this is so, and know too the sobering thought that his own efforts are in part fated to perish. But the creator wants his work to be immortal. In the ninth century B.C. the discovery of writing must have been thrilling for the bard who realized its unique virtue.

Not that he himself could very likely compose in writing. The tradition that Homer was blind is perhaps symbolic of his illiteracy. A system of language and composition that depended upon an exquisite tension between intellect and memory, between originality and cliché, in spontaneous oral recitation could not be constrained to a medium wherein each word is the result of consideration and choice. Somewhat analogous to this is the best spontaneity of early Dixieland jazz compared to the written arrangements of Duke Ellington. There is, to be sure, a common idiom, but both in structure and details they are disparate musical ideas.

The bard, we will assume, could not use writing but could recognize its possibilities. The hypothesis which solves this dilemma is prosaic in the extreme, and yet by virtue of its resolving so neatly the gap between the spoken and the written word it is highly attractive: dictation. Ultimately it accounts normally for the fact that we possess a text of something essentially unwritable. We are free to imagine an oral poet, a superior one, the kind who would be quick to seize upon this innovation. He would dictate, recitating perforce more slowly than normal, having thus the time to work out the grand conception of an *Iliad* or *Odyssey*, more self-conscious than usual and struggling to give his finest performance, having what he had dictated before read over to him; in sum, transcending the limits of his art form in what would be the epic's swan song. For once become widespread, the art of writing destroyed the impulse to oral transmission. After the time of the *Iliad* and the *Odyssey* heroic oral poetry seems to have disappeared in ancient Greece.

This hypothetical account of the origin and development of Greek epic poetry provides for the view that one man was responsible for creating the *Iliad* and the *Odyssey*, but that he did so by the means available to illiterate oral poets, and that his language, his style, his story, indeed most of the elements of his epics were not original with him. The image of the poet as amanuensis agreed with much of the Homeric criticism of the nineteenth century which was influenced by studies of folk poetry and research into the heterogenetic development of the Pentateuch. Some Homeric scholars, who were aware of the formulaic nature of the epics, chose to believe that they were created over a long period of time by means of a general creative impulse of ballad singers, that the epics did not reveal the impress of any single intellect. A concomitant belief was that the epics were put together arbitrarily (although following the traditional plot) out of a number of shorter saga pieces much like the songs of Demodokos in the *Odyssey*. No final arguments may be brought against this point of view, although two compelling, and, for many, overwhelming arguments are that poets have always considered this conception of the *Iliad* and *Odyssey* to be nonsense, and that comparative studies have never discovered any group of ballads or pieced-together epics that could approach the masterly qualties of the Greek epics.

Tastes change, new vogues appear; most informed per-

sons today are convinced (as a matter of faith, necessarily)
that individual men created out of their own conception
the *Iliad* and the *Odyssey,* or that one man composed
them both. How far we may go in ignoring traditional
poetic elements when speaking of one man's having composed an epic is a delicate point. Are any of the elements
of style personal? The extraordinarily formulaic nature of
the epics, together with allusions to older things that are
not quite rightly understood by the poet and the occasional introduction of narrative that is not altogether apt,
yet seems to be something of a cliché—all this suggests
the mechanical repetition of tradition. On the other hand,
the absolute control of the plot and the well-developed
point of view consistently maintained throughout the story
suggest that the traditional material has been impressed
by one vision.

That two separate poets composed the two epics seems
more likely for a variety of reasons. The organization of
the plot of the *Odyssey* is far greater than the *Iliad.* It
describes a world that seems quite different from the
world of the *Iliad* (although this may be the result of the
essentially different spheres in which the action takes
place). Finally, the attitude seems different. The ancient
literary critic Longinus remarked that if Homer was the
author of both epics, the *Iliad* must have been the product
of his youth and the *Odyssey* of his old age. The central
preoccupations of Achilles are the honor due him, the
death of his friend, and the alternatives of a glorious death
in youth on the battlefield at Troy or a comfortable but
inglorious old age in his homeland of Thessaly. For
Odysseus returning home to his wife and son and regain-
ing his kingly possessions vie with his overwhelming
curiosity for mastery of his soul. Do these epics reflect
significantly different points of view? It is hard to be certain, yet one instinctively feels that this is so, although
the monolithic quality of the traditional devices of storytelling constantly obscure distinctions. A belief in two

poets does not favor the dictation theory because one is almost forced then to posit two separate occasions upon which this solution for permanency was discovered. Perhaps it is not much easier to imagine one man repeating the agony of dictating two such poems.

It is difficult to understand and assess the degree and kind of control which an oral poet exercises over his material. Traditional saga has an existence of its own, that may resist, in a way peculiar to it, being reorganized into one man's poetic expression. The opening lines of the *Iliad* and *Odyssey* reflect the peculiar nature of oral poetry. "Sing, goddess, the wrath of Achilles" begins the poet of the *Iliad*. In the relationship between poet and poem the epic bard saw a third element in the Muse. This goddess is not simply the Muse of inspiration whom later convention made the source of the *poetic* quality in the arrangement of words, although her manner is partly that of inspiration in the original sense of breathing into someone, as the first line of the *Odyssey* shows: "Muse, tell in me [or through me, we might say] the man of many turns." The Muse, as the daughter of Memory, is in addition somehow the informal personification of the entire body of epic tradition, that reservoir of legend and technique which generations of poets created as common property for anyone who has trained himself to the profession. In calling upon the Muse the bard is asking for strength of memory to sustain him throughout the thousands of lines of poetry ahead of him. He was obviously well aware of the effort of memory and he calls upon the Muses elsewhere in his epic, such as before the Catalogue of Ships in the second book of the *Iliad*. There in an expanded and fervent fashion he summons them before he attempts the truly difficult recital of the Catalogue which is more or less a census list studded with proper names and place names, the hardest sort of thing to remember. In Greek epic, between the poet and his Muse there is something of the relationship of cult priest to his goddess which reminds one of the epic poets of Ireland who were considered to be genuine seers and prophets, illuminators, however, of the past rather than the future. The characteristic anonymity of Homer is the poet's consciousness that he is, in one sense, no more than a vehicle for the Muse, and the re-creator of material not his own.

On the one hand we may try to assess the poet's originality; on the other, we must consider the cultural uniqueness of the poems. The Near Eastern epic *Gilgamesh* tends to belie the notion of a peculiarly Greek quality in the *Iliad* and *Odyssey*, because the three epics share so many ideas and plot details. The story of *Gilgamesh* has been pieced together out of fragments which come from a variety of areas and are written in different languages. This diffusion shows that *Gilgamesh* was widely known in the second millennium. It is a major story which some scholars believe was imported by the Phoenicians into Greek lands and there served as a model for the *Iliad* and *Odyssey*. To be sure, many motifs from *Gilgamesh* appear in the Homeric epics, but their refinement and their complete integration into the stories of the *Iliad* and *Odyssey* imply that the bards of Greece had long been practicing these stories. The common elements probably derive from a time in the second millennium when the Minoans and Mycenaeans had considerable contact with Asia Minor and the Levant.

Gilgamesh as a hero resembles Achilles. He is born of a goddess mother and mortal father: the same tension between superhuman powers intimating immortality and human frailty prophetic of death moves the story. *Gilgamesh* is essentially more tragic, more pessimistic. There is nothing in the story that sustains Gilgamesh once his friend Enkidu dies. Gilgamesh himself also dies and the story is retrieved from nihilism with a description at the very end of his funeral. It is grand, heroic and rehabilitative as is the description of Achilles' funeral in the twenty-fourth book of the *Odyssey*.

Enkidu reminds one of Patroklos immediately although his sexual relationship to Gilgamesh seems far more pronounced. He is a more complex being than Patroklos, made of clay, an innocent child of nature, achieving wisdom through sexual intercourse with a temple prostitute. The consequences are civilization and yet debilitation. The matter is complex. Worship of woman, homosexuality, and anti-feminism are all involved.

Heroic Gilgamesh, like Achilles, seeks fame and glory through adventure, after having been told that he would be a great king but never immortal. On this adventure Enkidu, like Patroklos, makes a magical error in opening a gate and so prepares the way for his doom.

The goddess Ishtar, who brings on Enkidu's death, is enraged because Gilgamesh has spurned her advances. Like Circe, she has transformed her lovers. As in the *Odyssey* women are suspicious, treacherous creatures, and sexuality is a way to power for Gilgamesh, as for Odysseus, even in wrestling with Enkidu, a scene that has strong sexual overtones.

Enkidu's death causes Gilgamesh to wander. Like Odysseus he inquires and learns much. Death confronts him everywhere, but there is a difference. He can never define his life because of the yawning vacuity of death. Hopelessness pervades the epic, a hopelessness utterly foreign to the *Odyssey* especially.

Gilgamesh is short. Since it is not an integral whole, but pieced together from several versions, any one interpretation is suspect. Yet certain themes are clear: the search for glory through heroic valor, a quest for life's meaning in terms of death's inevitability, the flavor of friendship won and lost, the enchantment of sexuality and of deity, the loss of innocence, and the search for truth through wandering. These themes appear significantly in either the *Iliad* or the *Odyssey* or both. A reading of *Gilgamesh* is in some ways a peculiar reverse illumination of the two Greek poems. Continually there are intimations, suggestions of similarity, but *Gilgamesh* is so short, so terse that the clues that would establish the relationship and define it are not to be found. *Gilgamesh* is more immediately spiritual, yet lacks altogether the grand design and the virtuosity that make the *Iliad* and *Odyssey* eternally real, living and profound. Considerably more study of *Gilgamesh,* however, would be fruitful for critics of the Homeric epics, for it would help to define certain basic underlying pyschological and spiritual tendencies that transcend cultures and poetic personalities. The parallels with *Gilgamesh* establish the probability that a common Mediterranean saga was widespread.

Within the Greek world alone the enormity of the body of inherited saga must have proved hard for any individual poet to control. Homer imposes a formal beginning and end in a casual way. When in the beginning of the *Iliad* he has asked his Muse to sing of the wrath, and filled a few lines in describing it, he continues, "sing from that point when Achilles and Agamemnon first began to quarrel." By directing his Muse to that place in the saga where he wishes to begin his story he reminds his auditors that the epic story is without beginning or end, that it is made up of an infinite complex of events and people, all equally familiar to epic audiences. This wealth of saga background gives oral poetry its extraordinary depth, but also allows for digressions and obscurities that are disallowed in other genres of literature. Behind the names of persons and places lie other stories which are somehow connected to our narrative. By contrast, lyric poetry, drama, and the novel in varying degrees continually focus on the moment in narration. In these genres it is not always sensible for a reader to consider events antecedent or sequel to the moment of action. For example, to concentrate upon Oedipus' killing of his father and marrying his mother completely distorts a reading of Sophocles' tragedy in which these events are very deliberately overlooked. This conception of structure does not apply to epic, however. The details of the foreground and the background are so equally well known that the logical priorities of narration can be ignored. As the bard chooses he may depart briefly or at length into the side avenues of the saga tradition. Often the digression has a mechanical motivation such as the brief, clearly traditional, description of Olympos to which Athene returns after appearing to the sleeping Nausikaa in the sixth book of the *Odyssey*. The poet wishes to effect a temporal transition from the night of Nausikaa's sleep to the dawn of her waking, and since the epic narrative is awkward at leaping over periods of time an interlude is introduced. The detailed description of Olympos allows for this, but it is more than that. Within the epic scene it is a reminder, hardly conscious, of the absolute infinity of human existence and its environment. While the central narrative unfolds we are forever being shown other scenes occupying another place in time or space so that the effect is a cosmic vision grasping the totality of experience. In this respect epic achieves a realism that the other forms of literature which narrowly restrict the scene cannot produce.

The saga background permits the poet to make allusions which are often obscure to us, but were very likely not obscure to his original audience. Having had the opportunity in the course of a lifetime to hear every episode of this almost endless chain of story, his audience could make clear sense of any chance reference. So, in the ninth book of the *Iliad* Phoinix's relatively scanty narration of the reasons for Meleager's behavior at the time of the siege of Calydon is enough to call forth the episode to the audience's mind. More would deflect attention from the analogy which the poet is making. The brief allusion to elements of the culture from which the epic poem derives became one of the hallmarks of literary epic. The emphasis changed from simple description to the mounting of symbolic meanings in the reference. The *Aeneid* is almost a compendium of Graeco-Roman civilization, as *Paradise*

Lost is a composite of Graeco-Roman and Judaeo-Christian learning. Much of the meaning of these two poems comes in the allusions. Only a knowledgeable person could have read them successfully. In our own time in the general absence of this knowledge only a pedant could read or compose *The Waste Land.* Homer was, however, expressing himself far more directly and he makes clear any significance that his brief reference might have for the central story. Beyond this the allusions are an adornment and a means to produce a completeness for the epic scene.

Because the epic story was so well known the bard was freed from developing the narrative in a chronologically reasonable way. Time sequences, the inevitable procession of cause and effect may be simply dismissed. Although the poet of the *Iliad* sets out to describe a relatively brief period in the tenth year of the Trojan War he has managed here and there to introduce all the important items of the entire venture. In the second book before a routine encounter of the two armies he describes in a completely formal manner suitable to the initial battle of the war the Greek and Trojan forces. In the third book he poses Helen and the Trojan King Priam upon Troy's walls, and she identifies formally some of the Greek leaders to the old king out on the plain below. The poet ignores the fact that in the course of ten years during truces, parleys, and the like (to one of which in fact the king is at that moment about to go) Priam must have met every major Greek figure.

In the hearing and rehearing of a great number of episodes, sometimes as the central theme, sometimes only a ramification to it, the exact relationship of the episodes ultimately becomes obscured. Since the familiarity has allowed the episode's legitimate causal relationships to be blurred the poet is able to introduce scenes in another way so as to imply several things. In the eighteenth book when Achilles' mother, the goddess Thetis and her retinue come to lament the death of Patroklos, Homer treats it formally and emotionally in manner far out of proportion to the meaning of his death. It has been argued that the scene of Thetis and her Nereids actually was taken by Homer from another epic which described the death of Achilles, to which occasion Thetis' grief and the magnitude of the scene would be far more appropriate. What may be meant by Homer's taking this scene over from another epic is not altogether clear. No doubt tradition had established the elaborate grief that Achilles' death would occasion, a tradition with which Homer was familiar. By introducing the scene here he achieves several things at once. Thetis and the Nereids are mourning Patroklos in the immediate, yet beyond this they are mourning the death of Achilles, which is now an apparent fact, anticipated by the audience, but actually beyond the scope of the *Iliad*, which ends with the death of Hektor. Patroklos' death motivates Achilles to return to the fight, in turn to cause his own death. In that sense Patroklos' death signals Achilles' death and the bard is inspired to a grander description of mourning. Achilles' action from this point through to the end of the *Iliad* may now be gauged as the behavior of a doomed, or to reverse natural time, of a dead man, for we have already had his funeral lamentation. The elaboration also points up the feelings of the participants to the scene. The ceremonial lament reflects the utter desolation and grief of the sorrowing Achilles. As a superb psychologist Homer conceived that Thetis in any case would be grieving always and only for her son. A few lines beyond this scene he has a mordant but sympathetic comment on feminine mourning which applies to Thetis equally well. "The women stood over the body mourning aloud, supposedly for Patroklos, but each in reality was lamenting her own misfortunes" (19.301 f).

Just as the temporal relationships within the epic have been reordered, so the temporal relationship of the epic story and its auditor is equally tenuous. We may say that the epics have been given a setting outside of time. The narrator, while notorious for giving no hint of himself, does not in any way relate the time of his action to any sort of relative or absolute chronology. These things have happened in the past (and even that does not always make a strong impression), but at what time we cannot say. The mechanical reasons for this are clear. The epic art began, we may assume, as a contemporaneous or nearly contemporaneous commentary on great events. Very likely the auditors' own memories were sufficient temporal correctives. As time went on, however, and memories grew dim, and succeeding generations of bards altered the saga material both by introducing new things and misunderstanding the old, the epic scene became less and less organically connected with time. The sense of the contemporaneous persisted, diffused with a feeling that the thing was past. The sensation is faintly melancholic, and this was perhaps reinforced by the chaos of the centuries during which the epic technique reached its maturity. The legends grew out of the centers of Mycenaean civilization and reflected their glory. Mycenae's collapse and the subsequent period of shock seem to be the source in the epic of an over-all wistfulness for something irretrievably lost. The bard is rarely specific in suggesting a comparison unfavorable to his time, beyond remarking that epic heroes had a strength that later times could not equal. But when he alludes to the coming destruction of Troy in the *Iliad* or when in the *Odyssey* many of the characters reflect back upon their past lives, whether it be Odysseus thinking of the war, or the swineherd slave, Eumaios, remembering his free and princely youth, there is never the slightest suggestion of an amelioration, of the potential substitution of anything better. That which had a glory and a goodness about it is gone forever.

While the phraseology of the poems seems often the most mechanical aspect of the poem's manner, this formulaic language too has its peculiarly realistic effect. Greek epic poetry, as was earlier remarked, is made up of phrases which seem to be the product of centuries of practice. The manner in which this phraseology was achieved is most clearly seen in the qualifying epithets with which almost every personal and place name as well as the more common nouns such as "sea" or "ship" are endowed. Many of these are familiar. Everyone knows swift-footed Achilles or the wine dark sea, but not every translator is faithful to their appearance so that the reader without Greek is often unaware of the very intricate system of metrical language which they substantially buttress. Greek, like Latin, is an inflected language and naturally every case form of the noun or every form of the verb will not be metrically alike. Analogies from English do not altogether work, but if we were to consider the English language in terms of time elapsed to voice each syllable it would be fair to say that the genitive form "man's" takes longer to utter than the nominative form "man." More obviously "drove" is quite different metrically than "have driven." Consider a language in which a noun could conceivably appear in fourteen different forms and a verb in well over one hundred, where some forms will be metrically similar, but the majority will not. The problem of matching grammar to metrics is magnified to the limit.

In developing a system whereby they could anticipate suitable metrical components for a line of verse when they subconsciously plotted the succeeding narrative, the bards made great use of the ornamental epithet as an element which when combined with a name could finish a line in a variety of ways. Epic speech is so thoroughly contrived that every name has a specific epithet to be employed for each grammatical case that is metrically different. The semantics determine the syntax, which in turn determines the form of the noun which finally determines the particular epithet used. In the *Iliad* Odysseus is generally "shining" in the nominative, "godlike" in the genitive, "great-hearted" in the dative, and "like unto Zeus in counsel" in the accusative case. While a great many epithets are common to metrically identical names, some are reserved to one character, such as "swift-footed" which with one exception is applied in both epics only to Achilles. These epithets either are more capable of characterizing or the personalities to which they belong are more individualized in the poet's mind.

The epithets recur so quickly and are, so to speak, so shopworn that they go unheard, in a positive sense, by the audience. Certainly Homer himself seems at times to be careless or less than sensitive in using them. That is to say, it seems as if he might have phrased the line another way so that the metrical necessity for the employment of a particular epithet would not have arisen. In the *Iliad,* Hera, the wife of Zeus and titular mother of the gods, can be called (in the nominative case) Hera of the soft white arms or Hera of the golden throne. Each is relative to one of her roles. The first book of the *Iliad* closes with the line, "Then up to bed went Zeus, and down beside him lay Hera of the golden throne." Certainly this is the moment to fashion the line so as to use the other epithet. A very famous instance of Homer's supposed nodding occurs in the first book of the *Odyssey* when Zeus singles out Aigisthos as a mortal who sinned in the full knowledge of what he was doing. "Zeus was angry in his heart" says the bard, "at blameless Aigisthos."

But perhaps the use of the epithet "blameless" here and the many cases like it are embarrassments only for later audiences. In a ritualistic, idealistic society which the epithet suggests perhaps Zeus can quite logically blame a blameless Aigisthos. For while it is true that Aigisthos had in his seduction of Klytemnestra behaved in a way that rendered him culpable both to men and gods, it is also true that Aigisthos was by birth, training, and environment an aristocratic person. One of the ideal attributes of such persons is their goodness, their blameless quality, and the epithet "blameless" is frequently attached to the noble warriors of the epic. This quality is inherent in Aigisthos regardless of his personal and particular culpability. Homer is merely paying homage to the ideal in using the epithet, not consciously, but from the instinctive heroic viewpoint.

The use of epithets tends to attribute to men and objects eternal, immutable ideal qualities that the exigencies of the moment cannot alter. When this is so, what matter if ships rotting on a beach are called "swift" or the sea on a summer's calm is called "hoary with white caps"? The epic invokes a world peopled with objects that are changeless and timeless. Nonetheless, it is the consummate artistry of the epic tradition to be able to introduce an element of the singular and specific and so to avoid creating unreal generalized abstractions. The epithets, while having reference to ideal attributes, are sufficiently narrow in focus —because they remark upon only one of many possible attributes—that they do not idealize or generalize the object or person to which they are joined. They bring to the fore only a facet, and from the constantly changing facets which the bard displays in his epithets there is created the illusion of change and of the unique, both of which go to make up the sensation of variegated reality.

The common events of the heroic environment occur often enough that the epic poets have created whole formulaic lines to describe them. These, if they are less than a whole line, must be joined to some other expression, and conform to the metrical requirements of the joining. The bard knew that when he wished to describe the dawning as an isolated and complete fact he would say, "Dawn rose from bed, from the side of illustrious Tithonos, so that she might bring light to immortals and mortals"; but whenever he wished to co-ordinate the dawning with something else, he would say, "when early-born rosy fingered Dawn appeared." The necessity for the temporal conjunction "when" in the latter quotation completely alters the metrics of the line.

The ornamental nature of these expressions will not bear repeating for an audience of readers who savor each word and know that they can look back if memory boggles or interest is piqued. The reading audience wants variety or nothing in successive expositions of the same idea. The audience of an oral poet, however, makes no such demands; the spoken word has at best a very brief past or future, and the voiced statement scarcely lives but in the moment of utterance. In addition, the hearing of a normal person misses about half of what is said, the mind filling in the lacunae unconsciously from a knowledge of the language and the presumed intent of the speaker. Cliché expressions are therefore essential to any sustained session of listening. In accounting for the continued enjoyment that Greek epic gives to generations of men whose temper and manner are more or less alien to the epic style, the formulaic element is an important consideration. In a poetic manner which is in so many ways artificial and unreal, the ornate ritual lines, depicting in clichés common events such as eating, sleeping, rising, or leave-taking, come to be an apt counterpart of the real action, which, being frequent and common to all human experience, must itself be in some way a cliché.

Roughly one third of the Homeric epics consists of repeated lines, many of them of the sort that have just been discussed. Many more are routine one-line descriptions of the maneuvers in hand-to-hand fighting. Some repeated passages consist of a speech which is delivered to one person who in turn relays it to another. Neither a summary of the speech nor a simple reference to it would be in keeping with oral technique, which must ever accommodate itself to the fact that everything which has been said no longer exists. The sort of paraphrasing that Homer tries is ultimately not really paraphrase at all. When in the first book of the *Iliad* Achilles recounts to his mother, Thetis, the events that led up to his quarrel with Agamemnon, the poet uses line for line some of his earlier description of the event, omitting simply the intervening speeches of the priest Chryses and of Agamemnon.

Some passages of greater significance are repeated and definitely make an impression upon the reader; he looks for a motive, for intended irony, or the like. Is this search legitimate? Being trained to symbolism, do we not read in a more studious way than many authors had intended? For an auditor how many lines of spoken verse can separate like passages before the memory of the first one is thoroughly blurred? Does epic poetry attempt to direct the attention either back or forward, and, if not, would an auditor have the instinct to remember more than the plot? These are hard questions to answer. It is harder still to assign to the epic poet some subconscious motive for repeating exactly when and where he does.

Consider the passage at the end of Book Six of the *Iliad* (506–511) where Paris is compared to a horse galloping forth into a pasture, freed of his stable. The same comparison, in exactly the same language, is made of Hektor in the fifteenth book. In the case of Paris the simile is excellent. The scenes involving Paris in Books Three and Six have established him as a sexual artist and athlete, who owes his special nobility to a splendid body and the natural use which he brilliantly makes of it. As Paris dashes forth from the palace to join Hektor on his way to the battlefield, all the qualities of masculine sexuality well used are evoked by the simile. He has obviously come from Helen's bed ("having been well fed in the stable"); he experiences the freedom and vigor that is the aftermath of sexual intercourse ("breaking his rope he races over the plain"); he will wash away the sweat of love-making in the sweat of the battle ("being accustomed to wash himself in the river"); he is proud and happy in the knowledge that he is good in bed ("proud, he holds his head high . . . trusting in his brilliance, he moves with ease . . ."). So successful is the simile that we must with Hektor forgive Paris for being an indifferent soldier, a selfish prince who is bringing ruin on Troy; Paris is too magnificent not to be appreciated.

The simile occurs again in Book Fifteen. Hektor, who is lying upon the ground dazed and bloody, is given renewed strength when Apollo speaks to him and rallies him on. When his strength comes back and he rushes forth to fight, he is compared to a horse exactly as Paris was. While the general point of the comparison is sound in this passage, the separate aspects of the comparison have less meaning: the feed in the stable, the washing in the river, the pride and joy of the body may be applied to Apollo's rally and Hektor's subsequent joyful sensation of a return to strength. Psychologically, however, the comparison is more superficial. To a reader the repeated simile is irksome because it fit so well the first time; something is spoiled if a greater meaning cannot be worked out of the repetition. But none can. Homer did not wish this to be an ironic commentary on Hektor, who, compared to Achilles or Paris, seems to come off second best in the *Iliad* in any performance of the human body. Homer had forgotten or overlooked the earlier passage or he instinctively assumed his auditor would have. The simile is essentially so good that in a long oral piece it deserves repetition.

Sometimes when exact repetitions occur in passages which are formally very similar the matter of interpretation is made difficult. Compare a speech of Agamemnon to Menelaos after the latter has been wounded in the deceitful breaking of the truce in Book Four of the *Iliad* with Hektor's farewell to Andromache in Book Six.

AGAMEMNON TO MENELAOS

4.155 Dear brother, now it seems that it was your death
          that I was forging in the truce,
       setting you out in front of the Achaians to fight
          the Trojans alone,
       since the Trojans have attacked you and trampled
          on the oaths we trusted.

But the oath and the blood of lambs are not at all
in vain,
nor the libations of unmixed wine and the right
hands which we clasped in good faith.
160 For even if the Olympian has not immediately
brought the consequences,
soon he shall, and they will pay greatly for this,
by their own lives, their wives, and their children.
*For this I know full well in my mind and in my
heart:*
*There will come a day sometime when holy Ilios
shall perish,*
165 *and Priam and the people of Priam of the strong
spear.*
Zeus, son of Kronos, in his high throne, dwelling in
the sky,
he himself shall shake his threatening aegis at all of
them,
angry at this deceit. And these things will not go
undone.
But for me there will be a dreadful ache because of
you, Menelaos,
170 if you should die and accomplish the term of your
life,
and I were to return blamed and despised to thirsty
Argos.
For the Achaians will immediately begin to think of
their homeland,
and we would leave to Priam and the Trojans their
triumph,
Helen of Argos, while the earth will rot your bones
175 as you lie in the land of Troy, your goal unreached.
And some one of the exulting Trojans will say,
jumping upon the tomb of glorious Menelaos:
"Would that Agamemnon might vent his anger in
this fashion always,
he, who led an armada of Achaians here,

180 and now has gone home, back to his dear fatherland
with empty ships, leaving the noble Menelaos."
Thus sometime will someone speak. But when that
happens let the wide earth open for me.

HEKTOR TO ANDROMACHE

6.441 I too, my wife, am thinking of these things. But
dreadfully
shamed would I be before the Trojans and their
long-gowned women
if like a coward I were to slink away from battle.
Nor does my spirit allow it, since first I learned to
be courageous
445 always, and to fight in the forefront of the Trojans,
gathering great glory for my father and for me as
well.
*For this I know full well in my mind and in my
heart:*
*There will come a day sometime when holy Ilios
shall perish,*
*and Priam and the people of Priam of the ashen
spear.*
450 But it is not so much the grief that will come to the
Trojans that moves me,
nor that of Hecuba herself, nor of Lord Priam,
nor that of my brothers, who many and noble
have fallen in the dust at the hands of enemy men,
as your grief, when some one of the bronze-clad
Achaians
455 leads you off in tears, taking away your days of
freedom.
Then perhaps in Argos you will work the loom for
another woman,
and perhaps carry water from the spring Messeis or
Hypereia,

much forced, and heavy necessity will lie upon you.
And then sometime someone seeing you crying may
say,
460 "There goes the wife of Hektor who used to be the
finest warrior
among the horse-taming Trojans, when they fought
over Ilios."
Thus someday will someone speak. For you it will
be yet a new grief
bereft of such a man who could have warded off
your slavery.
But may the earth, heaped up, cover me dead
at least before I hear the sound of your cries and
your being led away.

The two speeches have many similarities. Both are
speeches of compassion delivered by the stronger of two
persons most immediately concerned. Roughly the same
length, they begin by acknowledging one point of view
(155–157; 441) but preferring another (158–162; 441–
446) for the same reason (the italicized identical lines).
After a few more lines, the concern of both speeches turns
to the person being addressed (169 ff; 454 ff); a situation
in which each is humbled (Menelaos dead; Andromache a
slave) is envisioned, imaginary remarks delivered at each
in their humbled state are evoked (178–181; 460–461). In
both cases the imaginary remarks reflect back upon the
speaker (Agamemnon; Hektor). Both speeches end with a
prayer for death if the alternative is to witness the misfortune being conceived.

The logic that calls for the introduction of the parallel
lines is quite obvious in the case of Agamemnon's speech.
Troy's wrongdoing in having broken the treaty is only another outward manifestation of the moral inevitability
which shall destroy the city. Hektor brings in the lines
somewhat awkwardly, but the logic must be that since
doom is inevitable vigorous fighting is the only possible

course of action. Strategic retreat (which Andromache is advocating) has less glory in it, and under the circumstances would accomplish nothing. The speeches therefore are integral unities; there is no need to consider the possibilities of an interpolation in Hektor's speech.

The speeches are separated by roughly one thousand lines, which makes it likely that the similarity is not conscious. On the other hand the speeches are so similar, yet do not, on the basis of other speeches in the epic, appear to be simply stock speeches. The *Iliad* devotes so much attention to the inexorable processes of the cosmos that one is inclined to see the two speeches as conscious representations of two aspects of Troy's doom. The exactly repeated lines would be a definite mnemonic signal. Whether one may make these assumptions upon the basis of the oral theory is an individual's critical decision. To the least suspecting auditor of an oral delivery of the *Iliad,* there must at least have occurred some sort of startling and paradoxical sensation of the *déjà vu.*

The occasionally puzzling nature of the repetitions, which seem at first sight to be poetic nonchalance, if not downright carelessness, arises from an almost exclusive concern with the narration of the moment and the use of formulaic language. Seen in this way the carelessness may be called a mechanical effect of the epic way. It is unlikely that it caused any conflict, considering the normal manner of hearing. However, what may have begun as largely mechanical could be adapted by a poet for effect. Like the playwright demanding of his audience a suspension of disbelief, an epic poet could expect of his audience the toleration of inconsistency.

The toleration of inconsistency may appear to be a peculiar aesthetic principle, since it seems to be immediately an assault upon the human intelligence. All criticism of Homer, however, must come to grips with the inconsistencies. The nineteenth-century Homeric scholars were engaged in an heroic effort to discover the origins of the *Iliad* and *Odyssey*. Proceeding upon the assumption that no works of such length could be a product of oral tradition but must be rather an amalgam of far shorter pieces, they worked at discovering the original limitations of the individual shorter pieces. The single most important criterion which came to them out of their association with the nineteenth-century novel was the presence of inconsistency. This, they said, revealed different levels of the *Iliad* and *Odyssey*, or if not that, then the artlessness of the persons who organized the separate pieces into a whole. However, it seems absurd to assume that anyone who was objectively putting together an *Iliad* or an *Odyssey*, fully conscious and possessed of leisure, would not have been equally aware of the inconsistencies, and sufficiently determined to remove them. Far more reasonable is it to assume that the inconsistencies were altogether consonant with epic art, and that those of our *Iliad* and *Odyssey* are traditional and organic. If this be so, we may call them a stylistic device when the poet seems to have introduced them consciously. Otherwise they are a perfectly natural concomitant of spontaneous oral presentation.

For example, in the sixteenth book of the *Iliad* Patroklos beseeches Achilles to return to the fight or let him go instead. Achilles replies angrily, bringing up all the elements of his original quarrel with Agamemnon and his determination to stay away from the fight until it comes finally to the neighborhood of his own ship. In his passionate denunciation of Agamemnon he seems to have forgotten completely the conversations in the ninth book, when Odysseus brought him Agamemnon's formal plea for reconciliation and promise of generous compensation. It is as though the very crucial dialogues of the ninth book had never taken place. How can we resolve this?

Very briefly we may say that Achilles' refusal to accept Agamemnon's conciliatory gestures in the ninth book put him in the moral wrong (as Phoinix's speech in the ninth book shows). Achilles had gone too far in his anger. But

Achilles is the hero of the *Iliad* and once it is established
that he is exceeding himself the poet evidently sees no reason to reinforce this idea in Achilles' speeches. If the
speech in Book Sixteen had been designed as a complex
analysis of every aspect of the present situation Achilles
would seem a shabby person, indeed, in the face of Patroklos' humane and heroic request. Passion must be met with
passion, not petty legal maneuvering, so Achilles replies
with vehemence, in an uncomplicated view of the quarrel
and his wrath. In the sixteenth book the poet does not
want our sympathy for Achilles to be diminished. We remember simply that Achilles has stepped over the line,
and Patroklos' death will reinforce this. On the theory that
the *Iliad* is an oral composition the complexities of this
inconsistency would probably not have been noticed since
several thousand lines separate the two scenes.

Athene's directions to Telemachos in the first book of
the *Odyssey,* offer a more complicated state of inconsistency. The instructions in effect offer a direction for the
plot in the next two or three thousand lines. As a program,
they may be followed, or, for purposes of suspense and sur-
prise, they may be overturned. But her directions are so
muddled that no action could possibly accrue. Athene tells
Telemachos to summon the suitors to a public meeting, to
tell each to go to his home, to send his mother home to
her parents who will arrange a new marriage for her; then
she tells him to sail to the mainland to seek news of his
father, and if he hears that Odysseus is dead he is to return to pay funeral honors to his father and to give his
mother a new husband, and finally after all this is done to
consider the means to kill off all the suitors who throng
in the palace. The orders are plainly contradictory, and
must be accounted for. The traditional solution is that a
later composer joined the first book to the second and in
so doing took from the speeches of the suitors in the second
some of the contrary advice which Athene offers in the
first. Again this solution fails to come to grips with the

mentality of a copy editor; he is devoted to bringing order out of confusion, clarity out of obscurity. Editors have an objectivity that creators rarely possess. Why must we assume that they were so unaware of what they were doing? If inconsistency is the characterizing feature of these hypothetical editors who certainly could not be far removed in time from the supposed authors of the poems, why is it not likely that they had simply discovered that inconsistency was one in the bag of epic tricks?

Athene's advice is the poet's doing and he had his reasons. In a legend well known every conceivable opportunity for suspense must be explored; in so long a poem some sort of outline of the plot ought to be offered to the auditor, which at the same time offers some freedom to the poet. The poet of the *Odyssey* has managed to introduce these things in this speech. Athene's arrival at Ithaka upsets the status quo and sets the action going; the poet, however, wishes to introduce a sense of crisis on the human level. All the remarks in the first two books alluding to Penelope's impending remarriage do this; time is running out for Telemachos and for Odysseus, and the son has got to do something. Thus the assembly and the plans for his trip are overhung with a real sense of urgency.

At the same time the voyage of inquiry is made suspenseful, because on its outcome somehow the fate of Telemachos and Penelope will be decided. And finally there remains in the background the tantalizing fact that the suitors may be killed. Upon reading Athene's speech over anyone can say that its contradictions nullify any emotional impact it might have. The poet, however, had no intention of its being read over; he certainly would not even have considered repeating it orally. Each successive item may contradict; but there is no going back to be sure. An atmosphere of uncertainty, of crisis, of suspense, and of expectation is generated by the speech. The plot is launched emotionally and several possible solutions are ready. Beyond this the audience is left in the dark and must pay attention to find the answers. The relatively glaring inconsistency is an insult to the intelligence of a reader; to an auditor, especially to a seasoned auditor of epic recital, it is an element of style that demands toleration of inconsistency, *if*, indeed, the inconsistency were noticed, as the rhythmed train of language continued.

We have discussed two kinds of realism that the epic style achieves. One is the formulaic language used to describe without variance the common elements of human behavior. As life itself shows eating, sleeping, and the like to be immutably arranged phenomena, so the ritualism of the language exactly mirrors this. The other is the frequently occurring digression offering glimpses briefly or longer upon other moments in time or space which continually break down the artifice of an arranged view of action; the world is seen to be as vast, as complex, and as spread out in time as we know it to be.

Perhaps nothing is so real as the paratactic style into which the language is cast. Parataxis is the term used by the Greeks to describe a system in which each idea is contained in a separate sentence. These are then juxtaposed with a simple conjunction, or nothing at all. Our own sentence structure appears generally as syntaxis, wherein certain ideas are subordinate to the central idea in clauses of time or cause, or relative clauses. The difference between the two can be seen in the following: "It was raining and we stayed home" is parataxis; "Since it was raining, we stayed home" is syntaxis. In the first the two ideas lie side by side equal in their value; in the second our staying home is given priority. Ernest Hemingway is a modern example of paratactic style; Edmund Burke of syntactic style.

How the paratactic style produces a kind of reality in the Homeric epic may be seen in the following simile. Menelaos has just been wounded in the thigh by an arrow.

Straightaway   the   dark   blood   flowed   from   the

wound. Just as when some woman stains a piece of
ivory with purple, a Maionian woman or Karian, in
order to make a cheekpiece for horses, and it lies in a
chamber, and many are the horsemen who long to
carry it, but it lies there to be an adornment for some
king, both an ornament for the horse and a thing of
glory to its rider. Just so, Menelaos, your thighs were
stained with blood. (*Iliad* 4.141 *ff*)

The immediate comparison is excellent, but the act of
staining the ivory has a reality, a history, a vitality of its
own, and we are made to move farther, from the shouting
moment at Troy to the quiet of a woman's chamber, anywhere in the eastern world—two places are suggested—
then to the living desire which the beautiful object engenders, and finally we are reminded of its universal and
ideal function, its inner virtue—an ornament for the horse
and a thing of glory to its rider.

The example makes clear the Homeric disinclination to
subordinate human experience. Every experience is of
equal value, one placed against the next, a progression of
equivalence. We may say that this is in essence the highest
realism, for it is true that in the daily living of our lives
no editor cuts out or shapes anything; we must experience
each thing and live each moment, and it remains true
when all is said and done that the consummation of a great
love affair can often occupy far less time and command far
less concentration than the picking of one's teeth.

Chapter II

THE POET'S WORLD

Then upon this much nourishing earth still another
  generation, the fourth,
did Zeus make, more just and nobler
a race of heroes, godlike, who are called
demigods, the race previous to our own upon this
  boundless earth.
> Hesiod *Works and Days* 157–160 (in his
> description of the generations of man)

Centuries elapse between the time when we assume a tradition of oral heroic poetry first sprang up in the great Mycenaean palaces and the time when some one or two master poets created our *Iliad* and *Odyssey*. It is the nature of formulaic verse being passed more or less objectively from mouth to mouth to assume constantly the audience's knowledge of the story's background. Consequently the heroes move through a social, political, and material world that is never explained, because Homer felt too familiar with part of it and did not understand the rest.

As has often been observed, there is no greater difficulty than trying to infer anything from the epics relevant to their presumed historical epoch and vice versa. Neither really explains the other. The poems, however, do offer the necessary foundations, I believe, for certain generalities about the social, political and philosophical life of the times. Furthermore, the historical events of the period in the broadest fashion seem to reveal themselves in the poems. Consequently, I shall attempt to set forth in this chapter various observations and quasi-facts in the hope that the general reader of the *Iliad* and *Odyssey* will have the scope of his imagination enlarged—or at least better furnished—when Homer describes his story's background too briefly.

The poems represent a curious amalgam of different historical periods. The strangeness of the matter is compounded by our lack of knowledge about the periods involved, so that we cannot accurately sort out the anachronisms, or determine exactly to which historical period the general tone of each poem belongs, although by and large we may assume that the flavor was contemporary, that is, eighth century B.C. For example, allusions to the richness of the Egyptian city of Thebes must go back at least to the fourteenth century, which was the last time that the Achaians had direct knowledge of her glory. The description of the boar's tooth helmet that Meriones gives to Odysseus in the tenth book of the *Iliad* is an interesting heirloom, for it describes an item made in part of perishable material which held the teeth together. Such a helmet could never have survived the end of the Mycenaean period, and yet the description is so exact that archaeologists can easily figure out from the remaining fragments of these helmets found in graves how to reconstruct them. This is an excellent example of the manner in which the language and formulae hold fast to elements that were contemporaneous several centuries earlier, but by the date of the final recitation were objects beyond the experience of the bard.

This point is interesting, too, in that it shows that the poet need not have the kind of control over his material that we generally expect. In some ways, I believe, the poet's ability to handle objects beyond his ken is analogous to the psychological phenomenon of word association when a subject talks freely and spontaneously, developing ideas and images and associations between them that he does not at all immediately comprehend. He allows no intellectual restraint over his verbalizing. Likewise the way in which the Homeric poet can develop scenes out of dissonant materials seems not the tour de force of someone patching but rather the positive thrust of formulae, tradition, and memory imposing a life of its own on elements not otherwise logically or organically combined.

It is possible to describe a boar's tooth helmet without knowing one and be in little trouble. Homer gets involved in more complicated confusions in battle narrative where changing styles in battle equipment cannot be reconciled. The differences between fighting in the Mycenaean period and in the period in which Homer lived are not too many, but they do sometimes affect the battle descriptions. Although I will take up later in this chapter the Homeric representation of fighting, I might introduce here a few details that will illustrate the author's confusion.

Shields, for instance, in the Mycenaean period were large, covering the entire body, suited to hand-to-hand combat between individuals. Later fighting had become a feat of the group, in a kind of phalanx, for which small round shields were suitable. As a rule epic poetry had converted to the new shield, although one can discern the other often clumsily lurking in the line. When Hektor in the sixth book of the *Iliad* leaves the battlefield to return to Troy, he is described as going the whole distance with a shield that "bumped as much against his ankles as his neck," obviously a large body shield, and hardly necessary since he was going through friendly territory. Homer brought forth a description that would increase the stature of Hektor's return to Troy (at best an ill-motivated scene), ignoring the fact that elsewhere Hektor is always described with a small shield and that the line here implying a body shield is ridiculous.

The change from the heavy spear used in Mycenaean hand-to-hand fighting to the two, lighter throwing spears carried by the contemporary phalanx fighters is sometimes not resolved by Homer. In the duel between Paris and Menelaos they cast lots to see who will use his throwing spears first, but then Paris is armed with one thrusting spear, which he proceeds to throw. Similar confusion exists in the fatal encounter of Hektor with Achilles in the twenty-second book of the *Iliad*. On the contrary, the fight between Telemachos, Odysseus and the suitors, which seems to begin as a contest in throwing spears but ends as hand-to-hand combat with thrusting spears, suits well the confined and impromptu circumstances of the encounter, even if an understanding of the difference in spears makes the passage illogical.

Nonetheless, without any accurate time sense or knowledge in depth Homer is aware of the time that has passed since the events he narrates might have taken place. When Diomedes once picks up a rock to throw at the enemy, Homer describes the rock as "a big thing, which not even two men could carry, such as mortal men are nowadays" (*Iliad* 5.303 *f*). Twice again Homer describes other stones, one lifted by Hektor, one by Aineias, that his contemporary men wouldn't be able to budge. This sort of observation is made only in the *Iliad*—which is perhaps logical since the *Odyssey* is pervaded by a sense of contemporaneity and lacks the heroic distance of the other.

There are occasions when Homer even seems to be making real use of this long passage of time in his narrative. Once when Zeus is rebuking Hera for her constant hot hatred of Troy he promises to destroy a favorite city of hers someday, to which she answers:

As you well know there are three cities by far my favorites, Argos, Sparta, and Mycenae with its wide streets. Destroy these, whenever they become hateful to you in your heart. (*Iliad* 4.51–53)

Can we imagine a chill running through that part of the audience who knew that Mycenae stood in their time as a magnificent hill of ruins? Further on, in the twelfth book of the *Iliad,* Homer describes the future destruction of a protective wall around the Greek ships which were at this point being seriously threatened. As long as the war lasted, he says, the wall stayed, but then Poseidon and Apollo through the agency of flooding rivers and high tides washed it away, returning the great beach to its appearance before the war began (*Iliad* 12.12–18). The poet seems anxious to square events with a real landscape, or perhaps to dissolve again quickly the whole notion of the wall that he knew full well was never part of Troy's tradition. The mind of the antiquarian concerned with historicity breaks through, and in keeping with that mentality, Homer goes on in this passage to refer to the men who died at Troy as a race of men half-divine. Numbers of scholars have objected to this passage because of that appellation, since nowhere else does Homer suggest that his heroic figures are materially different from his flesh and blood contemporaries except in being considerably stronger. But the objection is not valid, because Homer so rarely considers the passage of time analytically that generally, we are made to feel contemporaneous with the action of the narrative. Here, however, Homer steps back and acknowledges the great change since epic was young. In Hesiod this dimly felt sense of change is made into history.

Hesiod, a poet more or less contemporary with the composition of our *Iliad* and *Odyssey,* has a famous description of the ages of man in his *Works and Days* that reflects again the mind of the antiquarian and the historian. In describing man in terms of metals, he acknowledges the anthropological fact that man moved from the use of bronze to the use of iron, although, being a poet and wishing to establish several transitional moral categories, Hesiod elaborates the image, creating earlier ages of gold and silver. After the Age of Bronze and before the Age of Iron he inserts a nonmetallic epoch, the heroic age in which lived a godlike race of heroes, called demigods. Hesiod is dealing with poetic ingredients that are often just as commonplace as Homer's; here I think we can see an idea, a classification that was perhaps generally understood by the poets of the time. They understood from the oral tradition, from random graves accidentally uncovered, that there was an age when bronze was the common metal. They knew that in their own time iron had replaced bronze. The ruins of the Mycenaean buildings would also demonstrate that there had been another earlier culture in their land. Bridging the gap was the oral tradition of heroic saga, ever being sung again and slowly but surely recast into a more contemporary mold. Hesiod's insertion of the age of heroes is acknowledgment of this changing, evolving, quasi-historical description. Where Homer is subjective with his narrative, he can do the same thing, as the passage in the twelfth book shows. And, indeed, throughout the *Iliad* Homer consistently introduces bronze weapons in order to refer the action essentially to the past, to the period of the Mycenaean Empire although in proverbs and metaphors he accepts the existence of iron in his own day.

The second millennium before Christ saw the rise and fall of several great cultures, among them the Minoan and Mycenaean empires. The former, centered on the island of Crete around the palace at Knossos, is still very much visible today. Although in ruins, its size and complexity are revealed through the excavations and restorations which Sir Arthur Evans made in the early part of this century. The site produces a kind of thrill that few others do. The Mycenaean Empire emerged on the Greek mainland, centered in a number of palaces throughout the area, but dominated (perhaps only in our minds) by the large complex of buildings at Mycenae. Hence the name Mycenaean; these people are Homer's Achaians. They are thought to have been Greek-speaking peoples, a branch of the people who originally lived together perhaps in the Caucasus speaking a language that is ancestor to most languages from India through Europe. This hypothetical language, called Indo-European, was broken up into dialects as great bands of people dispersed, leaving the original site. Distance and the passage of time turned the dialects into separate languages, just as the Romance languages evolved from Latin. In the second millennium as the Greeks came into the Greek mainland, the Hittites moved into Asia Minor, and the Phrygians came into the area of Troy. All originally spoke the Indo-European language. While Homer always ignores any linguistic difference between the Trojans and the Greeks, this does not reflect probably any linguistic consanguinity that he recognized, but is simply a natural literary convention. He does not, for that matter, even indicate that much of a cultural difference exists between the two warring parties. The Trojans are vaguely described as being ethically and morally different. Paris in the *Iliad* uses a bow and dresses himself in animal skins. If not a cultural difference, it is at least a different way of looking at things. The heavy masculine martial façade of metal is absent, and using a bow (while it seems really far smarter) avoids the ritual heroic encounter of two men and spears. But they worship the same gods, and understand the same conventions (although one cannot really imagine a Greek living as King Priam does in a domestic arrangement including fifty sons and twelve daughters, children of a wife and several distinguished and respectable concubines).

The Achaians or Mycenaeans moved into the fertile plains of Greece and over the centuries built palace centers and elaborate roads connecting them. Pottery finds dotting the whole of the Mediterranean area show that their trade grew to be extensive. Their relations with the Minoan Kingdom in Crete are hard to clarify. The evidence suggests that for the most part neither culture at first dominated the other, but that considerable interchange took place. The Minoans were the older culture and they seem in many things to have been the teachers. Pottery finds reveal an interesting reversal. In the outlying islands for centuries Cretan and Mycenaean pottery seems to have been used in equal amounts, then toward the end of the millennium Cretan pottery becomes scarce and Mycenaean pottery common. About 1400 B.C. Knossos was destroyed—at whose hands, no one really knows. The theory is that finally the growing power of the Mycenaeans caused rivalries in the matter of trade and that Mycenae had to suppress Knossos. The myth of the Minotaur perhaps unconsciously encourages scholars in this view. Monster offspring of Queen Pasiphaë's strange union with a bull (the omnipresent Minoan cult symbol), nominally son of Minos, the Minotaur stands for Cretan power, and as the Minotaur demanded a yearly offering of Athenian youths, we can imagine that Knossos demanded protection money from Mycenae for the right to pursue trade in the Mediterranean. Theseus, the young heir to the Athenian throne, who goes to Crete, kills the Minotaur, and becomes the symbol of Mycenae's emergence as not only a rival but superior power. In the last decade the discovery that the curious writing found at Knossos and Mycenae (among other places) called Linear B is very likely a system for writing the Greek language shows that finally the mainland came to dominate the island. The Minoans were not Greek-speaking, and when the palace records at Knossos came to be kept in Greek we may imagine a class of Mycenaean overlords who managed the island's economy.

It is a pity that these Linear B tablets do not tell us much about the Mycenaeans. The tablets, made of clay, were for the most part meant to be very temporary records of trade transactions and census statistics. Those found today survived only because they happened accidentally to undergo firing when the archive rooms burned. This happened at Knossos and on the mainland at Pylos where the vast majority of tablets have been found. So they very rarely go beyond lists of names or products. What they do tell us is that the Mycenaeans had an elaborate bureaucratic structure, that they carried on extensive trade, and that the great palace centers were primarily commercial headquarters containing both records and stock rooms.

Excavated graves on the other hand bear striking testimony to the very high quality and great quantity of works of art, especially gold jewelry, daggers, cups, and the like. The descriptions in Homer corroborate this. Everywhere in the *Iliad* and the *Odyssey* we are met with descriptions of furnishings and jewelry that reveal a highly developed sense of ornament. The references to inlay and varieties of materials show how evolved it was. And the amount of gold recovered gives a hint that the Homeric depiction of the glitter and the grandeur of his heroic world was not fiction.

On cups, breastplates, sword hilts, and gravestones there often occurs a kind of decoration that seems immediately like the subject of so many Homeric similes. That is the natural world, but especially the lion in pursuit, or the bull, or any kind of hunting themes that were central, evidently in both the poems and the Mycenaean world. Since lions were not a part of Homer's actual world his frequent use of them in similes very likely came from a long tradition. Homeric similes, however, because they contain a number of word forms that linguists classify as late, and because they often contain references to objects from Homer's era, are generally thought to be definitely not a product of the Mycenean period, but rather a stylistic innovation in the long tradition. They have been linked stylistically with geometric art, which appears in the Greek world from about 1000 to 700 B.C. The comparison derives from the similar manner in which a geometric vase painter and a creator of the simile use a very few details to suggest the entire scene, hence not a naturalistic style, but an abstract one. For example, in the short three-line simile (*Iliad* 14.361 *ff*) comparing Apollo destroying the Achaian wall to a boy destroying his sand castle: Apollo's colossal size is implied in the relation of the boy to the castle, a god's unreasonable and irrational way is a boy's, men are god's toys, the scene both times is the beach, and the irony of the innocent pleasure derived from destroying what men broke their backs to build—all these ideas are called forth from the bare lineaments of description. Similarly scenes are established on Greek geometric vases with a minimum of drawn lines, offering a few details that illuminate the imagination and amplify it.

Perhaps the similes involving rapacious animals, especially lions, form a distinct class, and are earlier than the others. Their animal subject matter reflects Mycenaean art work (actually a Minoan import—at least Minoan inspiration lies behind much of the animal motif). The lion seems to be a Mycenaean heraldic symbol, for over the great entry gate at Mycenae stand two majestic lions. Similes of lions occur most frequently in battle narrative so perhaps those parts of the *Iliad* can be understood as more direct inheritances of the Mycenaean world, symbolic references to Mycenaean power.

Mycenae's first known major expedition was against Egypt in the thirteenth century b.c. Mycenae's great trade empire makes the probable motive an attempt to remove potential rivals from desirable areas of trade. The *Iliad* and *Odyssey*, however, continually imply that war's motive for these people was almost solely plunder. If this be so then the eventual decline of the Mycenaean world can be understood as the failure to find new people to exploit. But the epics probably reflect a later, more unsettled period than that in which a powerful Mycenae dominated, a period in which plunder would be inevitable. The collection of plunder and its distribution is a major concern for the heroes of the *Iliad*. Much of their stature derives from the quantity of their loot. The *Odyssey* shows a metamorphosis of the urge to plunder in the obvious pride and delight which Menelaos and Odysseus, for instance, take in accumulating gifts from their several hosts when homeward bound. One is hard put to account rationally for the extraordinary generosity, shown especially by the Phaiacians toward Odysseus. This gracious custom of bestowing considerable wealth on a visiting stranger reflects perhaps a more sinister reality in which peaceful peoples offered protection money to wandering pirates and plunderers so as to be left alone.

Mycenae's final expedition seems to have been the war against Troy, also in the thirteenth century. Excavations at Troy reveal that in the same period the city of Troy was sacked and burned, and she was never the same again. However, the Achaian victors did not enjoy their supremacy long because within a hundred years their power was beginning to be eclipsed. The Greeks of the historical period used to speak of "the return of the Heraklidai"; to us it is the Dorian invasion, that is, the arrival of large numbers of Greek-speaking people of another dialect—the Doric. They were ancestors of the inhabitants of Sparta as well as most of the rest of the Peloponnesus; as such they have generally been endowed by modern scholars with a brutishness and thickness that seems to have been true of their descendants, the fifth-century Spartans. Thereby springs an analogy between the destruction of wise and beautiful Athens by hard, insensitive Sparta in the Peloponnesian War in the fifth century B.C. and the destruction of glorious and rich Mycenae by presumably an earlier version of the Spartan beasts. All rather romantic (classicists are!); the over-all archaeological evidence however, does not support the theory of a hostile invasion. It is probably more accurate to assume that part of the existing population was assimilated while the majority moved out as the whole population expanded. The Achaians who didn't move up into the mountains migrated eastward in the direction of Athens. The Mycenaean Empire was gone, art (the constant index to events in a prehistorical period) became more lineal, in a sense less refined, less free, and certainly busier. Archaeologists style the new age the Geometric Period.

We do not have too clear a picture of this period. Linear B tablets no longer exist. What little literacy there was in Mycenaean times seems to have gone. The pottery styles no longer show a universal standard that formerly the large, well-organized and coherent Mycenaean Empire produced. There is a good deal of movement, migration spreading eastward, finally across the Aegean Sea to Ionia, the west coast of present-day Turkey. The oral poets moved, of course, with their people, receiving new influences. One can see it in little ways in the epic, as, for instance, when a bird is being described (*Iliad* 14.291) Homer says it is a bird which the gods called *chalcis*, but men call *cumindis*. The latter is a non-Greek word, picked up very likely in Ionia in mingling with non-Greek people. The most significant effect of this period of wandering and migration was, as we discussed in the first chapter, the mingling of dialects in the poets' phraseology. The subsequent fragmentation of the Greek people in the classical period more than anything else made the *Iliad* and *Odyssey national* poems. There alone within the various dialects could each man find something peculiar to himself and his city, yet part of a common whole.

After the passage of a few centuries men had retreated into cities each in its own fertile valley protected all around by hills or mountains. The dream of empire was past; the era of the city-state was soon to begin, solidifying dialect differences, mutual suspicions and finally centuries of war between Greek and Greek, until the Romans brought to Greece sanity and boredom in their imperial embrace.

The insecurity of the period of the wanderings is a part of the epics. In the *Odyssey* in the Underworld Achilles laments his death by saying (11.489 *ff*), "I'd rather be alive working for hire, a laborer, for another man, even a poor one . . . than be lord over all the dead." The person he describes, a *thetes*, is clearly the poet's idea of the most miserable form of human existence. Like the American migratory farm worker today whose lot is more awful than most can comprehend, the *thetes* was lower than a slave, because he had no place, no status in the society. He might be hired as Eurymachos offers Odysseus a job (18.357 ff), saying:

> Stranger, would you be willing to work for me, if I'd take you on, on an outlying farm; your pay would be a set figure—collecting stones for walls and planting tall trees?

But there was no security, for as Hesiod says in the *Works and Days* (601 f): "But when you've set your [harvest] all snug inside the house then let your *thetes* go . . ." (crueler still in the Greek; literally, "then make your *thetes* houseless," which is to say once you've housed your wintertime provender, your food, you've no room for the inconsequential, the human being who is not of your family, so he must get out to make room for the harvest). And Achilles in the *Iliad* (9.648) describes how Agamemnon treated him "like a migrant who has no rights." This is the insecurity that lies behind the lust for home, place, and stability that animates much of the *Odyssey*. The man who left his own town could get no reception in a neighboring one. He was meant to die in the town in which he was born; his accent and manner would always betray him elsewhere. The misery of the late years of the period of wandering and migration belonged to the ones who were still outside of the developing stability. If one can talk of a folk conscious, surely the attendant anxiety of this period of general homelessness left a psychic scar on the Greek culture, manifesting itself in a compulsion to total identification between the individual and the city-state, which has had a long history from Plato's *Crito* to Mussolini's theories of state, and beyond.

The political system as Homer describes it is another example of what seems to be the blending together of different periods. The hierarchy of the *Iliad* is thought by and large to reflect Mycenaean conditions whereas the kings of the *Odyssey* are the lesser, more local men whom Hesiod attacks in his *Works and Days*. Some of the tablets from Pylos now deciphered offer immensely helpful clues in attempting to establish a notion of Mycenaean government. At the head there seems to have been a king, *wanax*, a term used often in the Homeric epics to mean king or leader, and nicely enough most frequently in the epithet phrase *wanax andrōn*, almost always coupled with Agamemnon, who holds the top position in the epics. Next a *lāwāgetās*, "leader of the people," very likely the army leader. In Homer there is no such figure; Agamemnon takes the field himself.

A lesser but still important title is *hepetēs*, literally a follower, obviously meaning someone in the royal retinue, an intimate of the king (not unlike the title "count" coming from the Latin *comes* meaning companion; hence originally a count was an intimate of the king). While the title does not occur in the Homeric epics, the verb "to follow" appears often enough describing the relationship of various people in situations where any literal sense of following is impossible so that perhaps the concept remains imbedded in the formulae.

Less important are a number of minor officials with the title of *basileus*, which became later in classical Greek the standard word for "king" whereas *wanax* grew to mean no more than "leader" (or "lord" when addressing a god in prayer). This has caused some confusion through the centuries in interpreting Homer, because there seemed to be such a liberal sprinkling of kings (*basileis*) who for unaccountable reasons were obeying Agamemnon. Now, however, we have some evidence that the *basileus* in the vicinity of Pylos is not a king but a feudal lord. This makes the interpretation of Agamemnon's relationship to the other major figures easier to understand in the *Iliad*.

In the *Iliad* Agamemnon, who is king of Mycenae, seems

to have some superiority to the men of his council, who
are in turn the leaders of the separate contingents from
each area. The epic is ambiguous on this point because no
such political unity existed in the fragmented world of isolated city-states when Homer sang. Homer's contemporaries lived in a kingless age when each city was autonomous,
led by an independent first family, or first families. Later
Greek tradition created the legend of the oath of Tyndareus to resolve this confusion. According to that legend all
the suitors of Helen, Tyndareus' daughter, had to swear to
go to the defense of whichever man was finally chosen as
her husband if any harm ever came to Helen. So they all
followed Menelaos to Troy—Menelaos, who was, as the
Iliad makes plain, subject to his brother if for no other
reason than a basic mental and psychic inferiority to him.
The *Iliad* has nothing so contrived as the legend of the
oath. Agamemnon, Nestor tells Achilles, must be obeyed
because he is "more kingly," or "more powerful." The dis-
respect and hostility shown to Agamemnon by his followers
from time to time, and his indifferent qualities of leader-
ship do not necessarily fortify Nestor's appraisal; but
Homer has simply left it at that. This confusion is a source
of dramatic tension in the *Iliad*. Achilles' rebellion against
his overlord is not an absolute open and shut case of lese
majesty, because the varying dimensions of Agamemnon's
and Achilles' power are not well understood by the author.
So that free will, choice, and the power to act function in
what would otherwise be a mechanical political situation.

Although the decipherment of the Linear B tablets
points out the distinction between the king (*wanax*) and
what we may call the noble vassal (*basileus*), it does not
help us to translate the relationship between the king of
Pylos and the vassals in the surrounding towns into the
relationship between Agamemnon, king of Mycenae, lord
of the whole Mycenaean Empire, and the rulers of the
Greek cities who were his vassals. This is the relationship
which the *Iliad* implies, but the tablets do not supply evi-

dence for this. For instance, the Linear B tablets from Pylos *never* mention any place name outside of the immediate vicinity of Pylos, and this silence raises questions about the relationship of Mycenae to Pylos. Furthermore, in the Argolid the presence of the fortified citadel of Tiryns only a few miles from the fortified citadel of Mycenae implies hostilities, and tends to deny the immediate and over-all hegemony of Mycenae. It is very curious when one visits the area: Why was Tiryns built so close to Mycenae and why fortified? It seems to be the fortified castle of another great overlord. But its proximity to Mycenae makes that seem impossible. Very odd. Only the pottery styles show that the influencing dominant force everywhere was Mycenae. Could it have been an aesthetic rather than a political hegemony, one wonders.

We shall accept the uncertainty that our evidence and Homer give us as an underlying fact in our notion of Agamemnon's position, and proceed to describe him as overlord of the Mycenaean Empire. His was an hereditary kingship bestowed on the family by Zeus, as Homer makes clear in his chronology of the royal scepter made by Hephaistos, given to Zeus, who gave it to Hermes, who hands it on to the family of which generations later Agamemnon is the heir (*Iliad* 2.100 *ff*). His power is considerable. He can give away a large piece of land containing a number of towns in a part of the Peloponnesus far from Mycenae and hardly under his immediate and personal power. They lie near "sandy" Pylos and thus constitute part of Nestor's domain, yet the old man hears Agamemnon's plan to give them to Achilles without demur. The situation is analogous to that of the feudal kings of Europe.

Agamemnon's power is not, however, absolute. Western ideas of liberty, due process, and balance of power already appear in the *Iliad* and *Odyssey*, and perhaps they represent an inheritance from the social and political arrangements of the migrating, nomadic Indo-European peoples. Surrounding Agamemnon is his retinue, his companions.

These are the kings of the cities second to Mycenae throughout Greece. They constitute the major characters in the *Iliad,* and Agamemnon does little without consulting them. The Linear B tablets talk of a council of elders, to which this group would correspond. These men are responsible to Agamemnon and he to them. He gives nightly banquets that are as symbolic of his role as father and shepherd as Versailles was of Louis XIV's control over the nobility. Many of the suitors at Ithaka are—in terms of the social hierarchy—the natural retinue of the absent King Odysseus. As such their right to banquet at the palace is established, a fact to remember when judging their excessive behavior. They were not unnatural in their presumptions.

In addition to the council of major heroes was the assembly. Its membership was open to any fighting man in the *Iliad,* but as the *Odyssey* shows it was also a peacetime civic institution. Any hero could convene it—as Achilles does in the first book of the *Iliad.* Anyone who was nobly born could speak out in the assembly. When Thersites tries to speak in the second book of the *Iliad,* he is beaten. The assembly's democratic energies were strong, few could control it as is demonstrated in the second book of the *Iliad* when a mass flight to the ships commences after Agamemnon's announcement that they might better quit Troy than stay on. Odysseus alone manages to reverse the popular swell, offering an aphorism now famous:

> We Achaians can't all be kings here. Many kings is not a good thing. Let there be one ruler, one king, to whom Zeus has given the scepter and the power to judge so that he can make decisions for the people. (2.203 ff)

Whatever may have been the peculiar position of Agamemnon, there certainly was in no sense a court, as it was conceived in Europe after the model created by Diocletian, nor do we find one anywhere in the *Odyssey.* His council, the heroes who surrounded him, his retinue as I have called them, are grouped informally. They are his companions. Each one of them in turn is usually described as having a "companion" whom Homer alternately terms "servant." He means, of course, only that the companion acknowledges some modest inferiority and is pleased to serve the major hero. The relationship is one of a man to his wise and affectionate valet, except that the companion is far more an equal, a kind of alter ego, perhaps. In substance this is the relationship of Patroklos and Achilles, closer than brothers, closer than father and son, a union just this side of the sexual. The Greek tragedian Aeschylus wrote a tragedy (now lost) based on the homosexual love of Achilles and Patroklos. To read that into their relationship in the *Iliad*, however, would be to miss the subtle emotional and psychological ramifications of the relationship between hero and companion-servant. To understand the companion-servant as an alter ego far better brings out the peculiar dependence each has on the other in the relationship, a dependence between males that would in our society definitely be considered sexual, even if not overt. The relationship is mystical, on small scale a reflection of the mystical bond that holds the entire group together in Homer's description of the Trojan War. This relationship is also a staple of the greater saga tradition since it appears also in *Gilgamesh* between the hero and Enkidu.

King Alkinoos in the *Odyssey*, in contrast to Agamemnon, has very little power. He seems to be first among his equals in ruling over the Phaiacians rather than superior. As he says, "There are twelve pre-eminent lords (*basileis*) among the people and I am the thirteenth" (*Odyssey* 8.390 f). One senses a change of attitude from the *Iliad* to the *Odyssey* in the society for whom the bard sang. The aristocracy has grown strong enough to challenge any king's pretensions to absolute power. Hints of this already lie in the arrogance af Achilles and the sternness (sometimes masking disgust) in Diomedes. On the island of

Scheria the change is an accomplished fact. Nausikaa perhaps can say: "I am the daughter of greathearted Alkinoos
from whom derives the Phaiacian strength and power"
(*Odyssey* 6.196 f), but Alkinoos seems careful to defer to
the counselors, the elders of the island, the heads of the
first families. He joins them in assembly, they station
themselves as a kind of constant king's council in an outer
hall of the palace where Odysseus finds them offering libations to Hermes. When Alkinoos entertains Odysseus he
decides to summon a still larger representation of the eld-
erly male aristocrats. While this assemblage of aristocrats
has considerable influence on Alkinoos, he and they are
not on the other hand concerned with the feelings of the
people. After having given Odysseus a number of gifts,
Alkinoos is moved to a new height of generosity and says
to the body of first citizens:

> I say, let's each of us give him a large tripod and a
> caldron. Then we shall recover the sum for ourselves
> by collecting it from the people. After all, it's very
> hard for one man to be generous without reimburse-
> ment. (13.13 ff)

Although he shows little concern for the people here, his
dependence upon them is obvious. One cannot imagine a
king in the heroic style of the *Iliad* needing to go to the
people to maintain the richness of his generosity. Or is it
indeed a question not of needing, but of admitting the
need? Those scholars who insist upon separating the composition of the *Iliad* and *Odyssey* by some distance of time
because the *Iliad* seems so much more archaic are perhaps
overlooking the possibility that the poet of the *Iliad* was
not only consciously archaizing but trying to be consistent
with the heroic motives that fill the *Iliad*. Certainly the
Odyssey seems to have a more realistic—even cynical, at
times—understanding of human behavior, more like Hesiod's. Such a vision, however, would not adapt itself to
heroic action.

Homer describes the royal family at Scheria curiously from our point of view. On the one hand we have a lengthy portrait of the palace as Odysseus approaches it. Certainly this palace is the most glorious, rich, and important of any in the two epics. The gold and silver alternating with bronze, the intricacy of decor, the breadth of view and the logic of its plan cause us to fall silent in contemplation much as Homer says Odysseus was affected. Yet on the other hand Homer describes Nausikaa and her father engaged in the simplest domestic arrangements, she going to the stream to wash the royal clothes, he personally directing a slave to hitch up a wagon for her. Somehow we have a country squire in a principal palace. The author of the *Odyssey* describes the Phaiacians as living more or less in the Never-Never Land; however real he may imagine the behavior of the people to be, he can allow his descriptions of the place to move into the fantastic. One feels that in his description of this wondrous palace he is using elements in the saga tradition that are a reflection of the great palace at Mycenae, or another rich Mycenaean center. From the vantage of his world where very likely aristocratic girls did go out to wash the noble linens, such a palace would seem properly fabulous.

Telemachos' position in Ithaka reveals the power of the aristocracy. Obviously the throne was inherited, and, since Odysseus was king before, Telemachos could expect to succeed him. He was, however, a youth, and evidently the conception of a regency was not tolerable to Greeks of the period. Clearly the king's family was not that sacred. Whoever fulfilled the function of king had primarily to be kingly, to be able to rule. Age had evidently made Odysseus' father, Laertes, incompetent. The aristocracy, because they understood that the king was no more than *primus inter pares*, quite rightly realized that unless there were someone immediately ready to succeed a dead king the throne could perfectly easily pass to another aristocratic house. Out of respect for the principle of an hereditary monarchy the vacant throne passed to the man who married the widowed queen. The same practice lies behind the story of Oedipus, who after killing the Sphinx, gets as his prize the widowed queen, Jocasta, and when he has married her he becomes king of Thebes. One wonders if there lurk here vestiges of reminiscences of an aspect of a matrilinear society in which the continuity of the generations passed through the women. This practice reaffirms again that the suitors were quite rightly pursuing the queen, and were understandably affronted at her lengthy delaying tactics. Furthermore their relatively pleasant manner in talking to Telemachos is not impossibly contrary to their subsequent designs to assassinate him. Well as they may like the boy, as potential heir apparent he will soon reach adulthood and thwart the plans of their years of waiting. Clearly he is something to remove.

It is at Ithaka in the *Odyssey* that one sees best how life was lived by the Greeks of that time. The *Iliad* describes the battlefield where there is no place for normalcy. Men live in huts, most of them with concubines, and they eat at an army mess. While huts are huts, Achilles' place is rather grand, fitting his rank, and the fact of ten years' duration—high-ceilinged, thatched over, surrounded by a courtyard marked with a palisade the door of which has typically heroic dimensions, including a bolt made of a single tree trunk that took three to put in place.

In the *Odyssey,* however, domestic life can be observed. The house in which Telemachos and his mother live seems clearly enough the Mycenaean palace which archaeological excavations have uncovered several times. Probably the clearest and most informative site is Pylos in the southwestern Peloponnesus near Navarino Bay. From the remains there as well as from other excavations archaeologists have made a fairly confident reconstruction of the kind of house that existed in the Mycenaean age. Many would argue that Homer living so far after the period most likely has quite another kind of house in mind, that one is

mishandling evidence to attempt to find an equation between Homeric descriptions and archaeological data. Certainly Homer *is* much later; certainly he never lived in or
saw the kind of house the Mycenaeans inhabited. Nonetheless, one can argue that the rigidity of the oral tradition would retain a memory of this house. In any case the
correspondence seems real enough. Homer never gives a
full description of the houses in which Menelaos, Nestor,
and Telemachos live, houses similar in plan and aim if
not in quality. His modest descriptions imply either that
he assumes that his audience is fully conversant with the
style of house or that he is sufficiently confused as to the
true nature of the traditional house to pass over it quickly.

The architects who made Hektor's palace created, we are
told (*Iliad* 6.316), *thalamoi, doma,* and *aulēs.* Except that
for *doma* one much more frequently encounters the word
megaron, we have here the three principal elements of a
house of that time.

The *megaron* or *doma* is the large hall. More than anything else the *megaron* characterizes this style of domestic
architecture. It is thought by many, in fact, that the classic
temple developed from a *megaron* or large central hall
with the two side supporting walls extending somewhat in
front to create a porch. The *megaron* was the center of
life in the palace and the architectural focus for the addition of rooms. A large room, the *megaron* was often broken
by columns which held up a roof, probably raised over
the *megaron* into some kind of tower to allow clerestory
windows for light and some means of evacuating the
smoke. For the central object of the *megaron* was the
hearth. The honored seats were between it and the
columns. Arete works by the light of the hearth; Demodokos sings leaning against a pillar. The public life of the
palace took place in the *megaron.* Archaeological excavation has revealed the remnants of exquisite decorations
in these great halls, but the presence of the great hearth

should remind us that they must have been very smoky rooms.

Adjacent to the *megaron* is often a corridor off which are innumerable storerooms reminding us that the palace had a commercial nature in addition to its domestic and courtly personalities. The storerooms were located so near because the *megaron* was a public room for commercial transactions as well, we may suppose. The multiple functions of the palace made it truly a center for the people, so that houses came to be clustered around the palace, the beginnings of the city culture so peculiarly Greek.

The term *thalamos* is used for the private apartments, the reverse of the *megaron*. At Pylos there are bedrooms and bathrooms for both the king and queen on the ground floor, but the *Odyssey* describes Penelope on the stairs so often we assume that her *thalamos* was above. On the other hand, Odysseus' bed, made of part of a live olive tree, must have been located in a ground floor room. Homer hardly had a floor plan or its equivalent in mind, and he probably cared little that his auditors or readers could or would work out the room arrangements. Penelope's rooms are logically placed upstairs to avoid trouble with the suitors. Homer sometimes speaks of women coming out of a *megaron* that is not the central hall of the palace. Therefore, we can understand, I should imagine, that in the queen's apartments was a central hall, a common room for her and her attendants. The *thalamoi* were private rooms, and off bounds in so public a place as a Mycenaean palace.

The *aulē* is a courtyard surrounding the palace, perhaps in the more elaborate palaces landscaped into outdoor areas that are the equivalent of rooms. At Ithaka, however, it was rather unkempt. Within the courtyard were other *thalamoi*; for instance, Telemachos is lighted out from the *megaron* to his *thalamos* which is set in the *aulē*. Another interpretation of the Homeric allusions to domestic architecture has created a picture not unlike many modern resorts in which cabins (*thalamoi*) are set about in a park (*aulē*) dominated by the main lodge (*megaron*). This would account for the several descriptions of servants lighting persons from one place to the other, but if we can trust a correlation with archaeological facts Mycenaean remains show a more compact dwelling.

The primitive quality of Odysseus' palace must be remembered. The floor was of hard mud, which had to be watered down in order to prevent the fearsome dust that walking on such a floor would create. Cleaning it would be hard. Naturally with numbers of people eating there was an amount of spilling; hoes were used to get up really bad messes. The exposed wooden beams and the ceiling were black with smoke and the rooms themselves were smoky enough perhaps to be difficult to see in. Homer does not insist upon the inconveniences of this manner of living, and they do not really intrude upon the narrative. But as we can see here it was an underlying reality which the original audience used for setting the story in their imagination.

While the author of the *Odyssey* takes for granted the details of his characters' houses, the author of the *Iliad* assumes his audience's knowledge of heroic warfare. In the Mycenaean period fighting was very much an individual affair, sustained by those individuals who could command the equipment and retinue necessary for battle. The image of a few persons actually doing battle surrounded by groups of men formed the perfect context for the creation of notions of heroism. As in a tapestry, on a field of massed men there are picked out for notice a few glorious figures. These heroic chieftains were driven into the thick of battle in a chariot (not riding horseback, hence cavalry action seems not to have been practiced); their loyal friend-servant often managed the reins. Once at battle station they stepped down and hunted out a target for the spear which they carried.

Their armor consisted of a metal helmet, crowned by a

plume of horse hair that continually waved and nodded, a
fearsome thing adding considerably to the dimension of
the man beneath. The helmet came down to cover the
vulnerable parts of the head; in front the full cheekpieces
created slits above for the eyes, contributing further to a
grim war look. The chest was covered by a metal breastplate, beneath which the man wore a corselet of metal or
tough leather to help protect the parts of the torso exposed
by the necessary joints of the breastplate. On his legs he
wore greaves of metal, protection against hostile blows;
these were confused in Homer's mind with the much older
shin pieces that gave protection against the inevitable
chafing produced by the large Mycenaean tower shield.

As I mentioned earlier there is a definite confusion in
the *Iliad* on the matter of shields. The Mycenaean shield
was large, covering the whole man, having a kind of in-
dentation resembling a wasp waist in the middle between
the top and the bottom. From this point the man could
peek out to seek his enemy. Such a shield is cumbersome,
and very heavy, perhaps accounting for the exclusive use
of chariots. No man could go far on foot with such a
burden (again demonstrating the absurdity of Hektor's
going all the way from the field of battle to Troy with
one), nor could he manage one from horseback. He and
his helpers set him up with his shield and he became
more or less immobile.

Later, however, the mode and dress of battle changed.
Everyone was armed, they fought together, moving about
on foot in a phalanx pattern. They used throwing spears
and also their swords more, because a fluid random hand-
to-hand encounter had replaced the quasi-duel of Mycenaean times. Their protection consisted of a much
smaller (easily portable) round shield. This together with
the shields of his neighbors gave each man security. It was
this shield that called for greaves and breastplates. The
tower shield gave ample protection for the whole body;
the smaller round shield, on the contrary, was meant to

ward off obvious direct blows, and left much of the body exposed. Homer conflates the two traditions, but so confidently that his battle narratives seem whole to all but trained archaeologists.

Those are the elements in the background to the narrative of the *Iliad* and *Odyssey*. With facts that were consistent with his own time Homer could assume a knowledge in his contemporary audience, and avoid any detailed exposition that would intrude the person of the narrator too much into an otherwise objective narrative. Facts that were remnants of another era handed on in the tradition were often so imperfectly understood by the poet that he naturally omitted any detailed reference to them. He was striving to portray human action and experience; therein he achieved all his consistency and so directed his audience's attention that the background stayed where he planned it—in the back.

One other aspect of the Homeric world remains to be mentioned, that is, the role of the gods, or ideas of god as they come to us through the medium of the poems. The subject is not easy to define because Homer uses his deities very much as an integral part of the poem; therefore, we cannot speak of some such abstraction as religion that stands unassimilated into the context of the story. Furthermore, insofar as the representations of the gods in the *Iliad* and *Odyssey* relate to religious ideas, the bards probably took their notions of deities both from oral poetic tradition and from cult practice and mingled them indiscriminately over a period of time. Archaeological excavation tells us more about cult ritual than about attitudes in matters of religion so that one can less easily discern elements old and new in the poems. Some examples can be brought, however, to show a range of time within which the tradition formed. For instance, when the disguised Athene leaves Odysseus at the palace of Alkinoos and returns, as the poet says, to Athens and enters the house of the king, Erektheus (*Odyssey* 7.78 *ff*), we have a reference to a Mycenaean religious practice. During that period very likely no distinction was drawn between king and city, so that any city cult of the goddess would be equated with the royal cult, the king would serve as high priest, and her shrine would be in his house. This passage is to be compared to Helenos' advice to Hektor (*Iliad* 6.86 *ff*) to return to Troy to encourage the women of the city to assemble, form a procession, and go to the temple of Athene where they are to lay upon the lap of the seated statue a new dress for the goddess. In this passage the temple, the seated statue, and the offered dress are, as archaeologists know, religious events to be dated to the eighth century B.C., several hundred years later than the practice observed in the passage from the *Odyssey.*

Ancient Greece never knew a priestly caste. Because of this there was no dogma, no theology that was the exclusive creation and possession of the priests. The idea of godhead was worked out by all those who had a stake in religion. Naturally poets were major contributors because the mythologies which formed their subject matter centered on the supernatural and the divine. Herodotos, the Greek historian of the fifth century B.C., said that Homer created the pantheon of gods, that more or less constant group of major deities whom most Greeks reverenced, deities who constituted a means for the poets to symbolize and comprehend the manifold elements of the universe as it impinged on human kind. Almost to our day the Homeric pantheon has remained a fertile means in all the arts of defining the universe. Homer probably did not entirely himself create the complex conceptions of the various deities who appear in the two poems. The *Iliad* and the *Odyssey* do, however, emphasize certain features of these many faceted beings which seem to have remained significant in the history of Western letters.

The major deities in the *Iliad* and *Odyssey* are in many ways the most human characters in the story. They are more prominent and better delineated in the *Iliad.* Zeus,

known as the father of men and gods, can be considered
superior to all other beings, as a kind of first principle.
While he did not, in fact, father all the gods, he is in an
ethical sense the father of the members of the pantheon,
and Homer describes him often in the emotional role of
parent. The numerous stories of his seducing mortal
women are not meant to reveal a decadent godhead, but
show the natural inclination of noble families to trace
their bloodline to divinity by means of the fabled seduction of an ancestress. Furthermore, his sexuality, anthropomorphized naturally to fit the poet's story, is entirely
consistent with the generative force that any first principle
should possess. As king of the gods his position is that of a
Mycenaean king ruling over his often petulant vassals—
vassals who sometimes seem to be trying to establish that
he is only *primus inter pares*. He wields great power, however, and reigns from an inherited throne.

His wife, Hera, is also his sister. As the Ptolemies well
understood, no one but a truly close blood relation could
become a rightful consort in a world where no other dynastic line seemed even the near equal to Egypt's throne.
Hera is rarely Zeus' sexual interest, but that is immaterial.
The titular mother of the gods and wife to the king and
father of the gods must be as much *uno in carne* as possible. The divine incest here bears intimations of mono-
theism, because the two, as brother and sister, husband
and wife, father and mother, establish themselves as a
common principle with different aspects. Beyond this,
Hera has the personality of a difficult wife—a shrew, hard-
hearted, shrill, and often cruel. Homer never suggests any
redeeming qualities. Her terrestrial counterpart is Hecuba
as she is portrayed in the twenty-fourth book of the *Iliad*.
Hecuba's grief at the death of Hektor, not to mention
countless other sons, has given her rage and resentment
which make her especially ferocious. Hera alone one could
imagine saying as Hecuba does: "I wish that I could attach

myself to [Achilles'] innermost liver and feed on it"
(*Iliad* 24.212 f).

The god Apollo seems to be most powerful after Zeus.
Perhaps this is because he seems to have a remote and
little delineated personality, or perhaps because he seems
to command great respect from his divine family. He
speaks little in the *Iliad,* not at all in the *Odyssey,* and
holds himself aloof from human affairs generally. As a
consequence, he does not display the human emotions so
often exhibited by his siblings. Therefore, he seems more
readily to possess the kind of goodness and moral authority
that we moderns understand in a deity.

Apollo's sister, Artemis, is almost equally remote, although this impression is due more to her relatively infrequent appearances in the poems. Virginity is an important
aspect of her conception. She is the goddess who presides
over nature, wild things, and growing things. As such, she
is fresh and intact.

Quite another sort of virgin goddess is Pallas Athene
who is the most prominent deity in the two epics. Her
briskness and astringent aggressiveness are always with her
as she enters the action time and again. While she is
closely identified with war, her association is that of a
problem solver rather than a juggernaut. The emphasis is
on her aggressive cleverness; she was born, springing forth
from her father's head, fully matured, product solely of
his being. Her emblematic intelligence seems to be the
feminine principle mingled in masculine strength and
virility.

The other side of war is represented by Ares, titular
god of killing, of blood, of guts spilled on the earth. Homer
portrays him as stupid, heavy, and hated by all the gods
on Olympos. While Ares' human personality is better delineated than most of the gods, he is most frequently
used as a quick metaphor, usually of war at times of death.

The sometime wife of Hephaistos, golden Aphrodite,
with whom Ares is once discovered in bed, is the goddess

of creation, of sexual pleasure, and of the grace and peace of mind that sexual intercourse alone can bestow. She is called "laughter-loving"; the Greek word for this is only a few sounds different from "genital-loving," from which it was perhaps moralistically changed by prudish mythographers. Either suits her personality. She combines all the attributes of Botticelli's Venus as well as those that derive from the primitive story of her birth in which it is said that she sprang forth from the foam and sperm of the god Ouranos' amputated penis.

Poseidon, Hermes, and Hephaistos are portrayed by Homer as important and comfortable members of the divine family on Olympos, but they are not actually prominent in the action of either poem. Poseidon, a brother of Zeus, belongs to the older generation. In the inheritance from their father, Kronos, Poseidon received the ocean as his kingdom. Heavy, temperamental, and demanding, he suggests an older order of deity. Hermes is a messenger god and as such he conducts the dead to the underworld. The highly comic and mischievous personality with which he is endowed in the roughly contemporaneous *Hymn to Hermes* appears occasionally to have motivated the conception of him in the epics. Hephaistos, the artisan god, is also touched with humor, although not his own, but the author's who views him. Perhaps because he is the worker god amid aristocratic deities who have less well-defined functions, he seems to demonstrate less finesse and less style. Velásquez has perfectly conceived his rough, simple personality in the Prado painting "Apollo at the Forge of Vulcan" which shows the moment when Hephaistos is told that Aphrodite is in bed with Ares.

Capsule definitions such as these do not show that the gods are more complex than any simple idea. Homer portrays them as much more. While they at times seem the source for the workings of the universe, and keepers of man's destiny, elsewhere they are the foundation for moral absolutes, or again personifications of the forces of nature, or symbols of ideas and conceptions, or a means to comment on the human action somewhat after the manner of similes.

The Homeric gods differ from man in being first of all immortal, then ageless, and finally superhumanly powerful. Otherwise they seem capable of any emotion or impulse that mortal man can devise. Truly the Greeks created god in their own image. Actually it was not long after the time of Homer that objections began to be raised against the epic tradition's view of god as capable of every crime and perversion that mortal mind knows. Later ages failed to understand Homer's brutal objectivity. His conception of god accounts for a world that is flawed and he will not accept a first principle or a supernatural being or an absolute free of error. Evil is as natural as good, although goodness may be more desirable.

God is all things. So Homer can describe Hephaistos in the first book of the *Iliad* as a laughter-provoking cripple who is patronized and tolerated, as a frightening ball of fire in the twenty-first book's account of Achilles' battle with the river, and as the exalted, supernatural craftsman, maker of all things beautiful and complex in the eighteenth book's description of his making of the shield. Again in the *Odyssey* after describing in the most amusing way how Aphrodite is caught in the middle of the act of sexual intercourse with Ares by a metal trap that holds her in that position while all the other gods come to laugh and comment on the scene, after this humiliation, this touch of the common, when Hephaistos has let them loose from the trap, Homer restores her to her majesty with these words:

> Laughter-loving Aphrodite went to Cyprus, to Paphos, where her precinct and fragrant altar are. There the Graces washed her and anointed her with immortal oil, the kind that covers the gods who exist

forever, and then dressed her in beautiful clothing and she was a wonder to behold. (*Odyssey* 8.362 *ff*)

Similarly Homer plays with complexity in depicting Hektor's death at the hands of a deceitful Athene, or Patroklos dying when Apollo beguiles him. One tends to invest the god's action with cruelty and treachery. Man, however, gains glory falling victim to a god, whereas god is untouched by human kind. As Apollo the most awesome and least human of the deities says to his brother god:

> You would consider me to be without sense, if I were to fight with you for the sake of mortals, wretched things, who are like leaves, at one moment flourishing in burning colors, eating the fruit of the land, the next minute fading away into death. (*Iliad* 21.462 *ff*)

Apollo does nothing wrong in bringing Patroklos to his death, since the event was fated anyway. The bull who is brought to his death by the greater bullfighter is ennobled by it. Patroklos' death is translated into greater significance by the god's presence.

Even away from the battlefield the awful and fatal majesty of a god is displayed. The famous incident in the third book of the *Iliad* when Aphrodite draws up a chair for Helen to sit in is an example. Since antiquity this scene has drawn objections from those whose concern is theological propriety, because goddesses do not act as handmaids. But Homer is much more interested in showing how very much Helen is Aphrodite's creature. Shortly before this moment the goddess, whom Hera once describes (*Iliad* 14.198 *f*) as controlling all men and gods through love and desire, has suddenly dropped her laughter-loving mask when Helen begins to remonstrate with her. She points out to the unhappy adulteress that if she were to remove her protection from Helen the Trojans would destroy her. So Helen must perforce do as

she is bid—here, to make love with Paris. The hovering
goddess then is not simple ornamentation but in this scene
a chilling threat as she arranges Helen's chair.

In neither epic does Zeus appear in any earthly scene.
He is vaguely felt to be less human, more aloof, approxi-
mating the notion of godhead, not taking sides. Yet one
of the most compelling scenes in the *Iliad* is the moment
when Zeus looks down from Olympos at the fatal progress
of his son Sarpedon in battle with Patroklos, wishing to
alter the fate of the death, crying from the impotence
that only the separation of the species and the inexorability of fate can produce. Partly Zeus must lament at this
moment that he himself will never die, a melancholy fact
of god's existence that sustained the Greeks in much of
their tragic theater.

While Zeus remains in Olympos, free of human en-
tanglement, and thereby more godlike, the poet always is
careful to indicate which of the other gods is involved
in any particular action. When, however, any one of the
human characters wish to ascribe an event to a god's
agency, invariably he speaks of "a god," "a spirit," or "the
gods." The obvious reason for this is, of course, that
Homer, like any author, is all-knowing and can identify
the gods, whereas the characters cannot and must simply
speak of "a god." In any case, man cannot properly speak
of a specific god intervening, for it implies that man is
privy to divine mysteries. He becomes too intimate with
the divine. Perhaps also the growing scepticism of the
time did not tolerate a character having so anthropomorphic an understanding of god.

Frequently, of course, god is personification of human
action. This can work in a very dramatic way as in the case
of Athene staying Achilles' hand when he is about to draw
his sword on Agamemnon. Common sense comes to his
rescue; Athene was simply a poetic attendant, an expression of psychic intervention. Sometimes a popular pro-
verbial way of speaking seems to be behind the line, for

instance, "Zeus put this thought in my heart" (*Odyssey*
14.273) for "it occurred to me" or "[at dawn] the nymphs
. . . roused up the goats so that my comrades could eat"
(*Odyssey* 9.154 *f*) for "it was daybreak; consequently the
goats proceeded to appear; as a result my comrades had
something to eat." In the very long battle which stretches
from the twelfth to the seventeenth book of the *Iliad*, we
are specifically told that Ares is not fighting (13.521 *ff*,
15.113 *ff*), yet he is described as entering Hektor and filling him with ardor (17.210 *f*). Again he is a personification of the martial spirit, rather than the divine being who
is part of the story.

The gods make infrequent appearances in the *Odyssey*.
The two councils on Olympos are their only real scenes.
The conclusion of the plot is much thwarted by Poseidon,
to be sure, and Odysseus loses his crew because of Helios,
the sun god; nevertheless, in very few major scenes do we
encounter the gods. This has been attributed to the
absence of battle scenes which require attendant deities as
part of their heroic dimension. A mechanical explanation
will not do, however, because certainly the goddess Athene
is often present. And she functions in an unusual way in
the *Odyssey*.

As a whole Athene implicates herself in the workings
of the plot, as well as develops an emotional relationship
with the major characters. Athene matters to the story in
a way that no deity does in the *Iliad*. Her sustained appearances are natural because her interest in Odysseus'
good fortune inevitably must extend itself to the fortunes
of his house, as they are in turn maintained by his wife
and son. Hence her concern for their welfare, too.

Until Odysseus begins to describe his travels, Athene
appears as herself only twice in the narrative, both times
in divine council meetings on Mount Olympos. Otherwise
she appears in disguise, as a stranger, as Mentor, as a
maiden, and so on. On each occasion she gives a person
in the story the impulse to act. She is acting through a

disguise, and because the disguise takes on considerable life of its own each time (since the formulaic language cannot really adapt to create "Athene speaking as Mentor," or whatever), the goddess *qua* goddess cannot be said to have entered the human plot at all in the earlier portions of the *Odyssey,* as, for instance, she does, although briefly, when she appears to Achilles in the first book of the *Iliad.*

In describing his travels Odysseus never once mentions Athene. The poet feels this sufficiently awkward to force him to break his objectivity to account for it (13.318*f*, 341 *ff*). He says that she respected Poseidon's hostility for Odysseus and refused to help Odysseus until the gods were prepared to see him reach Ithaka again. There are any number of theories for her absence, but the most likely is that the stories of the wanderings involve magical situations and fairy tale stories. In this setting Odysseus does not seek heroic solutions to the fairy tale problems set him so that he doesn't need an Olympian deity to give glory to his actions. Furthermore, Athene would be awkward on Kalypso's island or Polyphemos' cave. There is simply no place for her in the travel stories.

Once he is in Ithaka she reappears but in a changed fashion. Gone are the disguises, except at the very first when she appears as a young man to Odysseus. When he lies in answer to her question, "the goddess bright-eyed Athene smiled, and caressed him with her hand; in form she came to appear like a tall and beautiful woman, skilled in beautiful handiwork" (13.287*ff*).

Before his eyes there occurs an epiphany of the goddess, changed into her true divine shape, an unusual event, and one that marks the assertive entry of the goddess into the story. Her transformation with Odysseus as actual witness marks the intimacy of their relationship, augmented by the caress, the smile, and most of all by the extraordinarily mocking and familiar tone of the following lines, the only occasion in Greek literature known to me when Athene sounds somewhat sexually interested. One almost feels that the best translation would begin "Odysseus, you sly puss . . ."

From this moment on she is thick in the plans and plots to murder the suitors, always acting on human terms, ignoring the divine power at her command, until the final moments when Odysseus and Telemachos set upon the suitors. Then she changes into a bird and flies to the roof beam. In this so human epic she cannot intervene in the contest of human strength and human skill. Finally she becomes goddess manifest to all at the very conclusion of the story, bringing an end to the plot. As goddess she sets the seal on the action.

The *Odyssey* needs few deities to counterpoint the human situation because the three major characters are logically associated with the same god, Athene. The lengthy narrative of the saga hero lost in fairyland forces a completely human action upon Odysseus. The divine entourage does not follow heroes into that world. The largest part of the narrative is the complex story of a man's cunning in inserting himself subversively into a hostile environment, which by virtue of further cunning he destroys. There is no place for divine action here either. Among so many delineated characters who participate in a single plot rhythm, Athene is gradually evolved by the poet into a human character, though still very much a goddess, but a well-realized individual who matters in the plot. This is far from the *Iliad's* conception of god.

Another factor in the diminishing effectiveness of the Olympian pantheon in the *Odyssey* might very well be growing contemporary ideas of absolute and eternal justice. Hesiod's *Works and Days* and *Theogony* are both searching for something to fill the void that inspires the melancholia of the *Iliad*. The *Works and Days* talks of the rhythm of nature, the natural requital that all things in this world owe and pay to their environment. From this Hesiod develops a notion of justice, the compensation

for loss, equity, the sharing. The *Theogony* is a lengthy
cataloguelike history of the origin of gods and man. Two
generations of gods appear before Zeus. Ouranos and
Kronos are their kings, the former overthrown by the latter
who in turn is overthrown by Zeus. Unlike the god of
Genesis who precedes both the beginning and creation,
the Greek gods are born into this world. Therefore their
infinite power was questionable. As a foundation for
eternal moral absolutes, Zeus was a shaky figure. Hesiod,
in a passage (*Theogony*, 886 *ff*) which scholars have ques-
tioned, resolves this dilemma with the myth of the goddess who is pregnant by Zeus with a son fated in turn to
overthrow his father as Zeus had his own. In one stroke
Zeus alters the entire rhythm of the universe by swallowing
the pregnant goddess, thereby keeping his future and his
destruction forever in his belly. Eternity was won.

   That mood seems to dominate the *Odyssey*. Not so the
Iliad, where, in fact, Zeus stands in an ambiguous relationship to fate. Much of the *Iliad's* strength comes from
this confusion. Zeus is, to be sure, captain of the universe,
yet as we notice when his son Sarpedon must die, he is
helpless, or when he holds the scales over Hektor and
Achilles, fate, not Zeus, manipulates them. No one ought
to seek into this equation because the poet has left it
purposefully vague. Within a world of impersonal inexorable processes that make men lonely beings there vibrates
and moves the animation of anthropomorphic deities giving comfort and a mode of identification to man. Else his
despair would be too much.

Chapter III

EPIC TECHNIQUE

Mother of mine, why do you object to our trusty singer
giving delight in whatever way his mind inspires him?
The poets are not responsible for their subject matter
  but Zeus rather
who gives to each man what he will.
So attach no blame to this man for singing of the Greeks'
  sorry fate.
For men much more praise whichever song
comes newest to their ears.
                                        Odyssey 1.346–352

In modern times the elements of pre-historic Greece
have begun to come to light, but Homer grows no more
familiar. He remains "Homer," "the poet or poets of the
Iliad and *Odyssey*," "the bard," almost totally anonymous
because he so rarely reveals himself in his epics. We are
aware of the poet's existence at the story's beginning when
he calls out to the Muse for her gift of song. Thereafter
he disappears, simply the vehicle through whom the
marvelously wrought tale is transmitted. The poet of the
Odyssey emphasizes this in his first line, saying "O Muse,
sing *in me* of the man, . . ." Curiously the poet from
time to time breaks away from a totally objective style,
returns, so to speak, interjecting himself into the narrative.
He sometimes calls out to characters in the action. In

doing so he abruptly and surrealistically alters the grammatical person from the objective third to the subjective second. The prelude to Patroklos' death, for example, is made more lamentable and more personal in this fashion. As the hero begins the fatal encounter, Homer says:

> Three times thereafter he [Patroklos] made a charge, like swift Ares, shouting out fearsomely. Three times he slew nine men. But then when he rushed out the fourth time like a kind of god, then, O Patroklos, the end of your life showed forth. (*Iliad* 16.784 ff)

In calling out to Patroklos, the poet bestows tragic irony upon the moment, reminding us of the pitiable estate of chance and ignorance set within the inexorable, impersonal universe. There suddenly appears the larger world which oversees human action and knows the course of events that are unknown to the human actors. The poet's apostrophes to various characters do not, however, reveal him as middleman, the transmitting agent of story to audience, someone apart. They seem rather to situate him psychologically among the auditors, as though he, too, had no control over the action he is relating.

Twice in the *Iliad* the poet very briefly refers to his craft. Both occasions similarly illuminate the great effort of memory that strains the bard. Before the Catalogue of Ships, a particularly treacherous piece of memory work, he summons the Muse again to give him special help with all the proper names he is about to recite:

> I couldn't relate all that crowd or name their names, not if I had ten tongues, ten mouths, a voice that wouldn't break down, and a heart of bronze, unless the Muses, daughters of aegis-bearing Zeus, were to remind me who they were who came to Troy. (2.48 ff)

When he begins to describe the battle at the wall around the Greek ships he seems almost to grumble. For he commences with a line that is very often prelude to a thorough listing of names:

Some were carrying on the fight at one gate [of the wall] and some at others. (12.175)

He continues by saying, however:

It would be very hard for me to narrate all these things, as though I were some god. (12.176)

Elsewhere he apologizes for his description of the wall and the fighting around it. The unsureness at this point suggests that Homer here is not relying as much as usual on traditional material and is therefore insecure. But it is remarkable how rarely the poet does show himself in the *Iliad*.

The poet of the *Odyssey* is, on the other hand, obviously interested in his own function and status in the society which he served. He created two bards, one at Ithaka, named Phemios, and one at King Alkinoos' court, by name Demodokos. The latter is blind as Homer was supposed to have been. The author implies that blindness and the gift of song are natural complements of each other, saying: ". . . the good bard whom the Muse loved exceedingly. But she gave him both good and evil. She took away his sight but gave him sweet song" (*Odyssey* 8.62 *ff*).

The bard is shown to occupy a high position in the *Odyssey*. When Alkinoos plans a banquet his first thought is to summon the singer, Demodokos. As the poet himself has said earlier, "singing and dancing are the adornments of a feast" (1.152). Homer lingers lovingly over the details of Demodokos' entrance, his being assisted by a herald, the refreshment he is offered, and the richness of the appointments that surround him. When Alkinoos decides that everyone shall go outside for athletic contests, Demodokos is also escorted to the playing fields. As for Phemios, more than once the poet reminds us that he plays for the suitors only by force, implying that in more normal circumstances the bard is very much his own master.

We can get some idea as well of the atmosphere in which the bard performed. He seems to be listened to in relative quiet, for Homer describes the loud noise that starts up when he has left off singing. The audience does not, however, appear to be restrained after the fashion of modern concert hall audiences. People walk about, getting food for themselves and talking while the bard sings. True he is in the center area, near the hearth, against a pillar, whereas, presumably the talkers are off in a corner of the *megaron.* That kind of animation in a relatively small room probably reflects the actual conditions of oral poetic performance. It offers us the reminder that no oral poet wanted or expected a "close reading" of what he was putting together.

The poets whom Homer describes are never shown attempting anything so lengthy as the *Iliad* and *Odyssey.* Of course, these epics are both too long for anything other than a recitation of several days, which calls for a festival. Still, not even a mention of such an event occurs. The bards in the *Odyssey* seem to be ready to sing episodes from the Trojan saga. The audience could evidently call out for a favorite, as Odysseus does when he asks for the story of the Wooden Horse. Demodokos is versatile. He can sing pieces from the Trojan saga which we assume to be in the high heroic style. He also delivers (and our poet offers it in full) a witty and baroque story of Aphrodite and Ares caught in adultery. The mood and the description are far removed from a heroic context. We speak so often of the traditional, the formulaic, and the like in talking of Homeric epic that it is good to remember that the poet could use these techniques for invention. I believe that the poet of the *Odyssey* wishes to display his inventive powers in the story of Aphrodite and Ares, which in his version resembles in tone and structure a later stepchild of the heroic epic, the Homeric hymns, most specifically the *Hymn to Aphrodite* or the *Hymn to Hermes*. These hymns seem to be inventive in the very same fashion, that is, using the whole armory of traditional epic usage for the creation of non-epic effect.

The principle of novelty and the range of the bard's endeavors are suggested when Penelope rebukes Phemios for singing of the lamentable Trojan War, implying that he might sing any number of other things. Telemachos answers her by saying that men praise the song that comes most recently to the hearer. So the story of the Trojan War, or stories of parts of it, must once have had a new ring to them. In any assessment of newness or originality in the *Iliad* or *Odyssey* this must be borne in mind. One is tempted to believe that the poet means a contemporary reference when he speaks of the newness of the story of the ill-fated return of the Greek chieftains from Troy. Perhaps he is. Perhaps he is advertising in the first book of the *Odyssey* the newness of his version of the saga material which he worked out on the theme of the return from Troy.

To speak of fiction, as opposed to traditional saga material, in the Homeric epics is difficult, because it is honestly impossible to distinguish what might be the outright creation of the last poet or poets who worked over the ever changing body of material before it was somehow committed to the everlasting stability of writing. As a reaction there has grown up the tendency to consider the poet's material so traditional that he is essentially a transmitter rather than an innovator. One does not speak of Homer's "intent." Yet I am sure that Homer or at least the poet of the *Odyssey* understood his poems as something created, not given. We can even catch reflections of the poet's sense of his control. When Odysseus ends the story of his wanderings by catching up chronologically with his arrival at Scheria, he reaches the point which he has already described to the king and queen, that is, his meeting with Nausikaa. Here he says: "I don't like to tell again things that are already clearly said" (*Odyssey* 12.452 f).

Actually this may be some reflection on the continual repetition in the *Iliad,* that in turn probably is typical of much oral poetry that has not survived. It shows the poet's concern for selecting and organizing; in turn Odysseus' description of his wanderings shows the same conscious striving for artistry.

We gain perhaps a little more insight into Homer's life and purpose from a comment by the poet Hesiod, a poet vaguely contemporary with Homer. In his description of how first he got the gift of poetry, he says the Muses visited him as he and his comrades were in the hills shepherding, and they spoke to him. "Country shepherds, wretched disgraces, nothing more than bellies, we know how to tell many lies as though they were true, but we also know, when we wish, how to speak the truth" (*Theogony* 26 ff).

Hesiod, a farmer from the backwoods of Boeotia, speaks with a kind of Puritan fire in his poems, searching for something to justify the wretchedness of his existence and his consistent bad luck. In formulating notions of absolute justice the only poetic diction available to him was the dactylic hexametric formulae of high heroic oral poetry as well as traditional household and barnyard proverbs evidently also cast in dactyls. His combination of these two elements is often awkward, yet he has created a personal style.

Of one thing he is very conscious—the honesty and truth of his philosophizing. When he quotes the Muses' remarks to him he is acknowledging how disparate is his life, his manner, his habit of thought from the vision of the Muses who sang to the far more elegant, stylized, and probably socially superior heroic poets. But in the dichotomy between poetic truth and fiction which he introduces, Hesiod points first to the fact that what he has to say has a kind of objectivity and straightforwardness that we associate with prose. And then, he is demonstrating that the entire oral poetic tradition—with which he must have had considerable contact to have been able himself to create such poetry—is bound up in the creation of fiction.

Homer no doubt would have understood the Muses' speech to Hesiod, for he was probably fully aware that he could contrive and invent as well as pass on tradition. We are free then to look in the poems everywhere for meaning that an individual poet intended. We may assume that Homer naturally handled the elements of traditional epic poetry to create the over-all conceptions that animate the *Iliad* and *Odyssey*. But further we can look at the traditional techniques and motifs, at commonplaces, to discover in the details a contrived point of view that may be assumed to be Homer's. Many techniques in the Homeric epics, however, need to be examined simply because they often elicit responses from the modern reader that, while certainly genuine in themselves, certainly worth experiencing and remembering, are, as far as one can judge, responses that are false to the spirit of the original mood and intent of the poem.

Perhaps for this reason the *Iliad* often produces an unfavorable response on first reading. Several readings generally will convince one that it is the greater of the two poems, because the *Iliad* seems to portray human situations more fundamental and of considerably greater consequence than the story of the *Odyssey* develops. The idea of "several readings" almost suggests "brainwashing"; one ought not to forget that the *Iliad* can seem an unsympathetic poem. The way of the action, the exaltation of force and power, the central core of Achilles' psyche bordering on petulance, the (in some ways) stupid valor of Hektor, these are not necessarily of the same high quality as the extraordinarily civilized and clear-eyed behavior of Odysseus in the *Odyssey*. (For this interpretation one must set aside romantic prejudice to acknowledge civilization and civility as man's finest creation.) Again, the numerous awkward moments in the *Iliad*, sometimes confusing, sometimes boring, contrast with the general smoothness of the *Odyssey*. Why does the *Iliad* often seem to be, nonetheless, a better, more satisfying poem? The question demands a detailed answer, which probably lies in the numerous details of the narrative.

A Greekless reader is naturally at a disadvantage, but anyone who looks closely will see that Homer, like Shakespeare, amplifies the story with myriad little moments and pieces. Often a particular liveliness or the development of a point of view results from the way in which the poet alters what would otherwise be a mechanical and traditional theme. The garrulity of epic sometimes leads readers to the conclusion that much of the narration is simple decoration. Amplifications and digressions, however, are usually subjective commentary upon the central action of the *Iliad*. What follows is a series of discussions of elements of the *Iliad* and *Odyssey* that seem to me in need of elucidation. Since there is no rationale for the sequence the several topics for discussion are set apart and separately headed.

CHARACTER DELINEATION

In the first book of the *Iliad* a number of figures who play significant roles in the story make their initial appearance. Very few of them are given any real description. Achilles and Agamemnon are typical; called simply "shining" and "leader of men" respectively, they take their place in the narrative as though the audience knew them well. This, of course, seems very likely, since they were important in the saga tradition, or at least Agamemnon must have been.

On the other hand, when Patroklos is first mentioned he is identified only through the patronymic Menoitiadēs. Thirty lines later he is finally called Patroklos. Nothing descriptive is applied to him. Patroklos does not seem to be a major figure in the saga. His role in the *Iliad* is also limited to his relationship to Achilles and the responses this relationship engenders in the greater hero. One would imagine that the audience in this case needs identification. On the assumption that the ramifications of epic poetry are worked out, elaborated, and made complex as the poem grows spontaneously, it might appear that Homer has not yet really developed an idea of Patroklos when first he appears in the narrative. Or because he is not important in the first book, perhaps he need not be described.

Old Nestor is the first character for whom the poet stops the forward flow of action to offer a description. The circumstances imply that Homer's character descriptions are sometimes suited to the needs of the narrative moment rather than any logical exposition of the story's dramatis personae. Nestor comes on immediately after the scene of rage that builds up between Agamemnon and Achilles, coming to a climax in Achilles' curse, capped by Achilles hurling the scepter to the ground. The description of Nestor accomplishes several things. First Homer brakes the intensity with calm in Nestor's being "sweet speaking" and very old. Both qualities put him outside or beyond angry passions of vital younger men. The intrusion of calm allows for his speech that follows; it prepares for the rather intellectual and abstract quality of the speech. The second achievement of the description is to invest the speech itself with qualities that the language cannot develop, sweetness (in the sense of political gentleness, tact) and dispassionate aloofness.

A similar use of character description appears in the *Odyssey*. It is noteworthy first of all that Penelope's suitors are very sketchily delineated. These young men are not familiar figures of saga, in fact few of the characters in the *Odyssey* are. One would expect description when first they appear. So little identification is given to the suitors that two, Antinoos and Eurymachos, are suddenly set apart and made important by so innocuous a remark as "leaders of the suitors, who were by far best in terms of prowess"

(*Odyssey* 4.629). Where description appears is in the assembly called by Telemachos. The Lord Aigyptios rises to speak (2.15). He is described as weak with age, very wise, father of four sons, one killed by the Cyclops, one a suitor of Penelope, spending his time in the palace, and two working for him on his farm. The description is quite long, and symbolizes the situation at Ithaka which remains explosive throughout the *Odyssey.* Specifically Aigyptios' speech is flavored by this description. The loss of his eldest son (as yet unknown to the old man) is the great resentment-making void of his impotent old age; the outrageous behavior of his suitor son has great potential for ruin as well, whereas his farming sons mirror the stability and productivity that normalcy confers. The irregularity that Odysseus' absence brings to Ithaka is summed up in the old man's description. Much of the emotional intensity of the following speeches grows out of this. But still we have learned little about Lord Aigyptios.

Subjective capsule description by the poet helps give meaning to the immediate scene, rather than to the character. On other occasions the narration of action rather than any description tends to develop a conception of a character. Patroklos—only a shadow figure in the first book of the *Iliad*—begins to come alive in the ninth through Homer's description of his and Achilles' actions. In an episode filled with speeches Patroklos says not a word, yet his presence is felt. He first appears in the ninth book in silence, waiting to take his turn in singing after Achilles. He stands up to greet the new arrivals following Achilles' lead. When Achilles calls out to him, he is described as being nearby, "hanging around" as we would say. Patroklos' service to Achilles stems from affection as we may assume from the poet's saying "he obeyed his dear companion." Yet he is clearly in second place. He builds up the fire for cooking while Achilles gets the meat ready. He serves the bread while Achilles cuts the meat. Achilles bids him sacrifice to the gods, he asks him to direct the servants to make up a bed for Phoinix. Clearly he is Achilles' servant-friend. Yet the episode shows them working in a unison that is a closer bond than words can tell. The scene ends with their going to bed in the same tent, each with a concubine. The girl with Patroklos is a gift from Achilles, so that not only do the two men enjoy sexual intercourse in each other's company (one of the most intimate acts in any relationship) but Patroklos is supplied sexually by Achilles. Clearly Patroklos grows to be understood in the ninth book as Achilles' absolute alter ego, except for the fatal fact that this is, of course, not so in truth. Therefore, his death becomes imminent in the sixteenth book when he puts on Achilles' armor. He has not a similar heroic vigor, so he can not bear the potential of such armor.

When Patroklos comes to Achilles to ask his permission to lead out the Myrmidons in fight, Achilles notices his sorrow and says:

> Why are you crying, Patroklos, like some silly little girl, who runs along by her mother demanding to be picked up, clinging to her gown, and slowing her down as she goes . . . ? (*Iliad* 16.7 *ff*)

The simile is a perfect recapitulation of the relationship of the two men, the strength of Achilles, the dependency of Patroklos, and the deep, mystical, non-sexual emotional bond between them. When Patroklos dies, once again Homer describes him as Achilles' alter ego when Achilles mournfully remarks that he revered Patroklos over all other men, equal to his own life.

Only in the episode of the ninth book does Homer really define Patroklos. The situation again calls for that development, because he forms a kind of ethical-moral background to the action and to the speeches between Achilles and Odysseus, Phoinix and Ajax. What Achilles says and thinks in that scene about the value of life, the necessity of death, about commitment and obstinance, all these will be measured in Patroklos' death, especially because Patroklos' death can be seen in some way to be the death of Achilles himself. This identification is established by the description in the ninth book.

Ultimately, then, Patroklos comes to be described far more fully than many of the other more prominent characters, but never through speeches, nor through a subjective description by the poet. The realizations of Patroklos give considerable insight into Achilles' behavior, but do not necessarily make Patroklos stand out in the narrative as a personality. Certainly his counterpart in *Gilgamesh,* Enkidu, is a much more defined personality who exists apart intellectually and emotionally from the epic's hero. One has the feeling that Patroklos was created to serve dramatic ends: to help define Achilles and for nothing more.

Although the portraits which Homer develops of his characters are not usually made up of physical details, there are exceptions, such as the rather lengthy physical description of the rude boorish Thersites who rebukes Agamemnon so loudly in assembly. The length of the description depends on the fact, I think, that Thersites is an anomaly, an unheroic man speaking out before his betters. It must be a physical description. Thersites as a menial, a nonentity among dynastic aristocrats, has no other dimension to his being than his physical appearance. He would in any case be remarkable to a heroic audience since before the days of universal affluence the physically deprived tended to be ugly, often grotesque. The most common means of developing characters is through speeches. An example of this occurs toward the close of the fourth book, when Agamemnon goes to review his troops. As he encounters each leader he speaks to him and each responds to his chieftain in a fashion that we grow later to realize is characteristic of each man's personality. When, however, a scene has the potential of being developed in physical terms Homer carries this out subtly and to perfection. Such a case is the third book of the *Iliad* which is our introduction to Paris and Helen, both notable for their physical beauty and sex-

ual prowess. The book begins with the Trojans and Greeks
meeting in battle. Unlike the other warriors in their bronze
armor, Paris is said to be dressed in the skin of a leopard.
This unusual difference commands attention; he is a pretty
beast, an idea reinforced by Hektor's subsequent remarks.
Physical beauty is a leitmotiv continued in a reference to
Laodike, loveliest of the daughters of Zeus, and the implication of loveliness in Helen's shimmering robe. When
Helen arrives on the city walls old Priam asks her to identify the Greek leaders on the plain below. His questions
and her answers take up only their physical characteristics.
For instance, of Agamemnon he asks: "Who is the man
. . . so large. Others may be taller, but I've never seen
anyone so handsome, nor so noble in his bearing?" (*Iliad*
3.167 *ff*). Whereas when he sees Odysseus he asks: "Who
is that fellow shorter by a head than Agamemnon, but
broader through the shoulders and chest. . . . He seems
to me like a thick-fleeced ram . . ." (192 *ff*).

Nowhere else in the *Iliad* or *Odyssey* does one get such
a complete feeling for the physical attributes of these figures whom we eventually know so well. When, however,
Homer chooses to describe Helen in this scene he employs
an oblique device that has long been famous. Helen is
singularly beautiful. Men's sexual appetites being various,
no two would likely settle on an identical description of
the world's most beautiful woman. So Homer leaves it to
each man, but guides their imagination by describing the
effect she produces on the old men of Troy. They have in
turn just been described in terms of their quavering high-
pitched voices, like the sound of cicadas. Disembodied,
they are beyond sexual interest, yet when Helen appears
they can arouse themselves so far as to agree that no one
can blame the Greeks and Trojans for fighting over this
beautiful woman. So aroused are they, indeed, that in that
moment they can accept the death of their progeny and
the collapse of their entire world. Helen has never been
nor will be more formidably beautiful.

For metrical reasons, which were discussed in the first chapter, ornamental epithets, descriptive adjectives usually, accompany almost every personal name in the epics. When a given epithet is used almost solely in connection with one character's name, a minute facet of characterization is achieved. Achilles is called "swift of foot" in three metrically different, semantically similar epithets. The man of battle, the man of superb physical prowess, the fleet man (implying perhaps by extension even intellectual agility) are all implicit in that phrase. The fleetness of Achilles in pursuing Hektor to his death around the walls of Troy in Book Twenty-two of the *Iliad* is the symbol, blown up from the epithet perhaps, of the totally superior warrior overcoming his inferior. Hektor, in turn, is usually described as "having a shining helmet." This epithet does not really illuminate him; but then Hektor has perhaps less personality. The helmet, however, makes Hektor noteworthy, and the poet sees him in terms of it. When Hektor holds out his hands to embrace his baby son, "the boy shrank back . . . terrified as he saw the bronze and the crest with its horsehair nodding dreadfully, as he thought, from the peak of the helmet" (*Iliad* 6.467 *ff*).

As one might imagine, Odysseus, with more personality than any other hero, has epithets of a psychological nature that reveal more of him. All turn on one of two ideas— wisdom and endurance. The second idea, however, is expressed in Greek by a word that actually implies both endurance and daring, which are after all two sides of the same thing. The difference depends on how much freedom and will one brings to the experience. So that Odysseus by these capsule characterizations is the clever man who dares all and endures all.

The kinds of epithets scattered throughout both poems, used indiscriminately for a number of figures, present (superficially) the ingredients of the heroic being, that is to say, big, strong, famous, good, beloved of god, godlike, endowed with a warrior's skill, and greathearted. Every figure, because of the presence of a descriptive adjective, becomes more than a name. Thus the stretches of routine narrative that occur in epic—much more frequently in the *Iliad*— are often made animate, given personality by these epithets which, of course, no sophisticated auditor of epic poetry would be conscious of hearing, but which constitute a rhythm of heroic existence.

CATALOGUES

Passages traditionally termed catalogues are a feature of epic that is foreign to most modern literature. The term was coined in the days of Alexandrian scholarship in the second century b.c. It refers to a passage in which something is being enumerated or listed, correct in meter and poetic usage. Catalogues are common in most early epics throughout the world. The same things form the subjects of catalogues—ships, troops, a queen's suitors, those who have fallen in battle, places visited, and so on. A catalogue is first and foremost informational; one feels that if prose had been highly developed at the time of the composition of the *Iliad* and the *Odyssey* the material of catalogues would not be found in dactylic hexameters. Yet students of oral poetry in modern times have noticed the real enthusiasm that greets the beginning of a catalogue during a recitation and even modern literate poets have remarked on the virtues of cataloguelike passages in twentieth-century poetry. Poetry is a great help in remembering. Metered catalogues very likely supplied in illiterate times a handy means for transmitting a culture's necessary information. The catalogues we know from Greek epic, however, seem to be fulfilling form more than function. The poet has put them to structural or decorative uses, rather than informational ones. To see the catalogue form in Greek used to its fullest, one must go to Hesiod's *Theogony*, where the history of creation is related in a creative and synthetic philosophical fashion by means of a continuous list.

A catalogue was a tour de force requiring a more exact kind of memory because the passage is basically composed of proper names that will not fit so easily or so quickly into the dactylic hexametric line. Catalogues were considered to be a thing apart from standard narrative because they could be lifted from one context to another. There are several catalogues in the *Iliad* and *Odyssey.* The most famous is the so-called Catalogue of Ships in the second book of the *Iliad.* It is boring for us to read because most of the names have no meaning. Even when recognizable they mean little unless one knows the geographical reality for which they stand. Place names can be exciting, as they are in John Dos Passos' *U.S.A.* or more recently in Nabokov's *Lolita* in the passages describing Humbert Humbert's wild chasings across the United States. But we know the places mentioned; our familiarity brings the passages alive. The Homeric Catalogue of Ships must have had once a similar vitality. Among other things it represents imaginatively a real geographical trip, since the order of place names as they come in the passage corresponds to a logical circuit of much of the known Greek world. Later copyists, however, had either forgotten the geography or could not care, because the Catalogue of Ships is very frequently omitted from the manuscripts of the *Iliad.* In its origin it was surely meant to be as much a tour de force as a kind of introductory list of characters, because many figures in the Catalogue do not appear in the subsequent narrative, whereas several important figures are not mentioned in the Catalogue.

The structure of the Catalogue of Ships is essentially a listing of individual items of information—name of the hero (or heroes), his geographical origin, often an anecdote relating to him or his homeland, then the number of ships accompanying him to Troy. The same pattern appears in other demonstrable catalogues, such as the group of women who appear to Odysseus in the Underworld, or the description of the contingent of Myrmidons going into battle with Patroklos, that is, names, accompanying detail, usually biographical, and finally some notice of the relevance of the item to the dramatic moment. Elsewhere there are groups of names, such as the list of Nereids who come with Thetis to lament with Achilles the death of Patroklos. These names have none of the concomitant detail that the Catalogue of Ships displays. Students of oral epic in other cultures have noticed that catalogues can be treated in an accordionlike fashion, that is, reduced to lists of names or swelled to include considerable ancillary information. Beyond this, the singer seems at times to be playing with the form, making up names to create a list. In the *Odyssey* there is a list of names all of which come from nautical occupations. They seem to have been created and assembled as a play of words, rather than representing a carefully memorized traditional list.

Basically the Catalogue of Ships is objectively informative; proselike, it intrudes on the poetic narrative. The continual references to ships have occasioned the opinion that in fact this catalogue has been lifted bodily from an epic depicting the original congregation of the Achaian fleet at Aulis. The verbs of motion preclude that theory, however; one wonders in any case whether a poet would have allowed such a jarring incongruity when it wasn't necessary. More likely the word "ships" is jargon for ship's companies, units of men who lived, fought, and previously had sailed together, all in one ship.

The catalogue form, in Homer's hands, is elastic. He uses it elsewhere for narrative rather than informational purposes. For instance in the third book of the *Iliad* when Priam questions Helen about the Greek heroes assembled below the walls the formulaic question "Who is he, etc.?" together with its response is a common catalogue framework. Here however Homer does not try to complete the form. Helen's description of Agamemnon is formally cataloguelike, that of Odysseus is enlarged and made dramatic, then after a brief reference to Ajax and an anecdote on Idomeneus, neither elicited by a question from Priam, the form is dropped. Obviously Homer had something else in mind than a list, although the structure suited his purpose at the start.

We may perhaps see the catalogue form as a backbone on which is built the psychological drama of verbal exchanges between Agamemnon and his leading chiefs at the close of the fourth book of the *Iliad*. Essentially Agamemnon approaches each chieftain separately, names him formulaically with patronymic and epithet, and encourages him to battle. There is a response, equally formal, and Agamemnon moves on to the next leader. There is something about the essential isolation of each encounter, the manner of the repetition which may have a catalogue form as its source. Again at the beginning of the tenth book of the *Iliad* where the leaders of the Greek army are awakened serially and formally one senses the catalogue structure much dramatized and embellished.

The Catalogue always preserves the rhythm of separateness, of discrete elements juxtaposed, not conjoined. The rhythm tends to be formal, rigid, and static; it does not allow the organic connectives of running narrative that, for instance, the opening fifty lines of the *Iliad* reveal. There a connective thread in the idea of anger is expanded, shown to be dynamic, a begetter of more wrath, through the words "wrath" (line 1), "quarreling" (6), "quarrel" (8), "angered" (9), "was unhappy in his heart" (24), "don't make me angry" (32), and "angered" (44). Furthermore in these lines the relationships of Apollo, Chryses the priest, and Agamemnon are described statically, then as they create situations that react upon each other. For instance, Chryses is first described as "he who prays" (line 11), shown to be holding in his hand the staff of Apollo (14); shortly thereafter (37–42) he commences to pray to Apollo after Agamemnon has insulted him.

My examples of catalogues come mostly from the *Iliad*. The relative absence of catalogues in the *Odyssey* helps persuade some scholars that this epic was composed by someone other than the author of the *Iliad*. For the narrative style of the *Odyssey* is everywhere smoother, subtler, and more complex, whereas catalogues even when well integrated tend to be lumbering and mechanical, hence inimical to that style.

BATTLE NARRATIVE

The battle narratives in the *Iliad* seem to be what we might call catalogues in a state of transition. As examples at the beginning of Books Five (lines 37–83) and Six (5–65) are two battle passages that rather closely resemble the structure of the Catalogue of Ships. They are composed essentially of separate units of information: the names of the victor and the victim in each encounter, often an anecdote relating to either of them, then a realistic description of the fatal wounding. Very likely, originally catalogues in Mycenaean epic served the purpose of commemorating the noble dead of every major military engagement, as Irish catalogues of the thirteenth and fourteenth century do. These lists in meter giving name, biographical remarks, and a notice of the hero's valor in dying in battle in the course of time were absorbed into the saga tradition, lost their historicity, became a technique and a source of names and facts, and gradually were transformed into a fictional and formulaic element in the narrative. These battle narratives often seem dull to the modern reader. We haven't such a developed taste for the poetry of proper names. And, then, we have a psychological disinclination to attend closely to the details of physical mayhem (those who read books seem not to be the same people who enjoy televised brutality). One tends to skip over the battle scenes in the *Iliad*, which is a mistake. A considerable part of the poem's story is being missed. The battle narrative is not simply a recital of traditional saga names, nor the poet's bow in the direction of an insensitive, bloodthirsty, numerically superior part of his audience. The *Iliad* is just as much about war as it is about Achilles. These passages develop the important philosophical and psychological frame to the whole poem.

What personalizes the battle narrative are the small anecdotal descriptions of the men in combat. The major themes of these anecdotes are the status and wealth of the man, the circumstances of his birth, his place of origin, the circumstances of his marriage, and prophecies about him—in sum, all the enduring things of consequence in the human lot, save children, who are not often considered by the heroic mentalities of the *Iliad*. Only the very old (and Andromache) seem to have any concern for children, a reminder of the curious limbo of age into which the heroes have been cast. Their accomplishments and certain chronological considerations would put most of them in their middle or late thirties, when children would be a natural primary concern of a man. Yet so many of their points of view derive from that blushing golden moment when adolescence turns to manhood. Compare the mentalities in the *Odyssey;* they are definitely those of older men.

These miniature stories set into the battle narrative develop a kind of melancholic vision of the wastage of war that serves as counterpoint to the glory and vigor created in descriptions of the armor and of the act of killing. Some of these anecdotes are very similar to the pattern in the Catalogue of Ships:

> Then Aineias killed two of the best men among the Greeks, the sons of Diokles, Krethon and Orsilochos. Now their father lived in well-built Phērē, a very rich man, of a family sprung from the Alpheios River that flows in a wide stream through the land of Pylians. This man begat Orsilochos to be lord over many men.

And Orsilochos begat greathearted Diokles, from
whom came the twin boys Krethon and Orsilochos,
both of them well skilled in all manner of warfare. In
the prime of their young manhood they followed
along with Agamemnon in the black ships to Ilios
famous for its horses. And now the end of life which
is death covered them over. (*Iliad* 5.541 *ff*)

On other occasions the genealogy stays with the circumstances of birth and conception. The pastoral mood of creativity in nature contrasts sharply with the violent death of
the moment:

There Telamonion Ajax hit Anthemion's [literally
"blossomy"] son, the blooming young Simoeisios,
whom once upon a time his mother bore, when she
had come down from Mount Ida to the banks of the
Simoïs River, since she had followed after her parents
to look over the herds. That's why they called him
Simoeisios. But he never paid his dear parents back
for raising him; his life turned out to be very short for
him as he was struck down by the spear of greathearted Ajax. (*Iliad* 4.473 *ff*)

or:

[Euryalos] went after Aisēpos and Pēdasos whom
once upon a time a spring water nymph named Abar-
barea bore to blameless Boukolion [literally "cattle
herder"]. Boukolion was eldest son of the eminent
Laomedon, though his mother bore him a bastard. He
in turn while shepherding lay in love with the nymph
who conceived and bore two sons. And the son of
Mekisteus caused their strength and their glistening
limbs to give out and he stripped the armor from
their shoulders. (*Iliad* 6.21 *ff*)

Some anecdotes bring out the abnormality of war, something we, who equate ancient heroics with martial prowess,

should remember. The idea of another time and place, where a productive life is carried on, is in the story of the grand host who used to receive all passers-by, who now on the field of Troy has no one to help him. There is also the man who has married a beautiful bride of high station and great accomplishments whom he leaves as he dies on the field.

Many anecdotes concentrate on the sad inevitability of fate, for instance, the prophet who knew he was going to die if he came to Troy but despite this does come and dies or the prophet father who saw his sons' doom and vainly tries to prevent their coming. The same inexorable pattern is in the common story of the man who murdered a blood relative, flees to a foreign king, and enters his service to come to Troy only to die on the field. Most wearisome for the heart perhaps is the story of the young man who, caught before and ransomed to freedom, is caught again and killed.

Finally there is the chilling loneliness of death in a strange land: "and he himself collapsed prone . . . far away from fertile Larisa . . ." (*Iliad* 17.300 f).

This dark thread woven through the brilliant tapestry of heroic courage and grandeur on the field of battle makes these scenes a continual somber reminder of the other side to the celebration of death. Together with many of the similes, they function, although in reverse, after the fashion of the descriptions of Italian landscape found in the *Inferno*. Dante has brought light, life, and creativity into the black torment that is death. Here the relief is the reverse. The intrusion of darkness into the ritualized grandeur of the battle narrative has the same quality as the growing dawning in Achilles' mind of what it is to be mortal.

REPETITIONS

As we have noted earlier, approximately one third of the *Iliad* and *Odyssey* is made up of repeated lines, a high number. Before the process of oral poetry was well understood most scholars who were raised on the rhetorical principle of variety considered the two epics to be largely patchwork. In their theory a number of individually created episodes were loosely and unartistically joined together with appropriate lines taken from anywhere in the several episodes. The touchstone for determining the authenticity of any passage was its freedom from repeated lines. The theory is, of course, dubious since there is no way to determine which occurrences of any given line are the repeated ones. On the modern reader the *Iliad*, especially, can produce an impression of being stuck together, for the repetitions—particularly in the battle sequences—are frequent and often stark.

Repetition must be understood, however, as a natural and central ingredient in oral poetry. A poem heard is not a poem read. One can give closer attention while reading, if only because the reader alone determines the conditions of comprehension, particularly the speed of reading. We have said that roughly one half of the words uttered is lost in ordinary conversation, the lacunae being filled by intuition. In lengthy recitals of epic poetry with attendant fuss and movement in the crowd, there must naturally have been some loss of comprehension, although the formality of the occasion and the potential for amusement certainly induced more than normal attention in the audience. Repeated lines, formulae, all the mechanisms of repetition which are a boon to the poet in the act of creation are also aids to the audience in the process of apprehension. Modern critical notions of exactitude and originality derive from the reading of brief poems. We confront each word in our poetry. Oral epic is more like a novel, however, where the very abundance of words keeps the focus to a larger scale. One of the critical problems in literate epic from Virgil on is the uncontrollable instinct to make each word significant, because in literate epic the individual word is the building block, and because the tradition of lyric poetry impinges on the genre. Every word in oral epic just does not count, nor for that matter every line. Seeking significance, then, in a repeated line or two lines is futile.

Does perhaps the special nature of oral presentation preclude speaking sensibly of repetition? An utterance unlike the written phrase has no lasting future or past so that the oral poem does not exist in a certain sense beyond the one line being recited. The "winged words," as Homer calls them, are here and gone; impressions remain, but how long can the auditor's memory control the exact language? For the space of time in which one or two hundred more lines are recited, perhaps. Certainly not too much more. The repeated line, then, is as routine and mechanical as the repeated word. Nevertheless, routine repetition continues to impress the literate critic of the twentieth century. Much of the *Iliad* ought to be read lightly skimming, glass in hand. When the drama becomes stronger and the emotions grow more vividly engaged, one will naturally begin to pay closer attention. Narrative such as battle scenes is often akin to panorama. It needs to be viewed from far back, eyes asquint.

Aside from repeated lines, whole passages are sometimes repeated or very closely paralleled. These are generally the representations of common human situations which would naturally occur often in a lengthy narrative, for example, feasting, arrivals, departures, as well as the rising dawn, the coming of night, events which are realistically formulaic. Whether the repetition of these longer passages is nothing but mechanical is more difficult to say. The simile of the horse discussed in the first chapter is no routine comparison, yet its repetition does not yield any discernible significance. In so long a recital, one feels, the simile was too good not to be reused, especially when separated by some four or five thousand lines.

When in the *Iliad* Homer repeats the duel scene of Book Three so soon again in Book Seven we can assume that the poet accepts repetition as natural and does not feel compelled to play with it. First Menelaos and Paris, then Ajax and Hektor duel. Both duels are much alike, even to ending inconclusively. Our instincts for symmetry and variety which are the legacy from the high classical period of antiquity rebel at this. One of the duels ought to come along much later in the poem, say, amid the rather repetitive battle scenes that precede Patroklos' death. If one overlooks the repetition, or accepts it, the duels appear to function well where they are, showing that their positioning is planned. When Paris and Menelaos fight shortly after Helen has first appeared in the story, the duel lodges the action of the *Iliad* squarely in its saga context, which is the rape and recovery of Helen. The second duel formally engages two of the *Iliad's* major heroes. The description of their encounter is elaborate. The poet seems to be presenting in full here a specimen battle clash that will be briefly indicated many times over in the numerous engagements of men throughout the battle narratives. The second duel also establishes Hektor as warrior directly after Homer has sympathetically shown him as husband and father, knowingly going to his death in battle.

If the repeated scenes are to some extent mechanical, Homer seems not to be deprived from using their repetitious nature for effect where he chooses. But repetition so bores a modern reader that he almost invariably skips over the repetition, when often there are interesting if slight variations that are working in the context of the poem.

Four times in the *Iliad* heroes are described arming for battle. The parallelism in language is extremely close; in each episode the hero dons in order his greaves, breastplate, sword, shield (which must come before the helmet, because the shoulder straps would not go over the helmet plume—traditional formulaic language is surprisingly exact at times), helmet, and spear. The sparse mechanical quality of what is almost a list is somewhat relieved with descriptive detail, giving to some of the objects a material personality. In the case of Agamemnon considerable detail appears, to the effect that he becomes enhanced in heroic terms, enclosed in superb pieces of armor. This forms the prelude to his finest hour in battle. Since even Homer cannot creditably magnify Agamemnon's feats of arms, he achieves the necessary grandeur, the lonely splendor of eminence in a mosaic review of his equipment.

The same theme of arming for battle appears two other times in the *Iliad,* but with differences. When Athene goes into battle in the fifth book she, too, arms herself. The poet uses much the same language, keeping to a six-part description. Athene slips off her gown, puts on a chiton, takes up the aegis, puts on a helmet, mounts the chariot, and grasps a spear. Homer has taken the form partly in parody, partly in earnest, to show one of the martial figures of Olympos preparing to enter the battle like a heroic general. The retention of a typical form in this passage renders more grand the coming battle, for Athene enters the battle as a comprehensible military figure. On the other hand a touch of the ludicrous lurks in the somewhat inapposite use of the traditional form to describe the great virgin goddess.

The other instance is parody pure and simple, where the poet is intelligently manipulating the form. When Hera sets out to seduce Zeus in the fourteenth book she gets, as they say, "all gussied up," truly girding herself for the encounter. The description has almost no verbal parallels with the other passages, but the serriated quality is apparent and the rhythm is much the same. After washing and anointing herself, she dresses in an ambrosial gown, pins it together with a golden brooch, encircles her waist with a belt, puts on earrings, veils her face with a fresh veil, and puts sandals on her feet. The entire account marvelously and luxuriously drawn out is very funny counterpoint to the heroics of the typical arming scenes.

In the epics the ritualized communal event of eating is celebrated more than anything else save death. Eating generally has a sacred atmosphere because of the sacrifices which precede the event, supplying often the central ingredient of the feast, as well as libations of wine that ended the festivities. In the *Odyssey* there are two patterns for such descriptions. The more common, appearing six times, is as follows:

> A serving girl brought water for washing the hands in a beautiful golden pitcher which she poured into a silver basin, so they could wash. Then she pulled up a polished table beside them. And an honored housekeeper brought in and set before them bread, and any number of good things to eat, liberally dishing out from what she had with her.

Anyone who has ever served as acolyte will feel the ceremonial nature of the description. Repetition simply makes it high ritual, no doubt mirroring the baronial life at table. In any case, the ritual cleaning of hands, the arrangement of the furniture and the liberal serving of the food are the natural components of an idealized conception of a banquet. The setting, however, indicates the beginning of the feasting rather than the entire affair.

On three occasions the poet employs another description which appears each time similar, without an absolute line for line fidelity:

> The heralds poured out for them water upon their hands, while young men filled the bowls with drink up to the brim, and then served some to everyone, first pouring into the goblets a few drops for the libation. Now when they had made a libation and had drunk to their heart's content, then . . . [and we return to the narrative].

Unlike the other passage this episode reveals the final moments. In the passage just quoted the participants are only drinking and making libations, but this formula, as we shall see in a moment, can also describe the eating of food. We may say that depending upon the moment of the meal that concerned the poet, he had available two stock descriptions, one for beginning and one for ending a meal. He was, however, as we can see here, free to use the description for a drinking scene only.

Throughout the poem when he uses the passage first quoted he shows that he is continually aware of its several elements. In making imaginative use of the formulaic lines he shows also that the description, however repeated, is for him not at all mechanical. In the seventeenth book when the goatherd Melanthios comes in late for dinner, the others having already started, the poet says (the italicized part is repeated): "Then the workers set by him a piece of meat, *and an honored housekeeper brought in and set before him bread,* to eat" (*Odyssey* 17.258 ff).

The description is made over to fit the occasion. Melanthios comes in too late to wash his hands at table; he is not a guest or honored person (nor is there time) so no table is drawn over to him. The food is set down obviously in a businesslike manner here because usually in these passages there is a line—omitted here—which follows the italicized one above that stresses the liberality of the house. This passage occurs about one hundred and fifty lines beyond a description of Telemachos' first meal home after returning from Sparta but there naturally every element of the feast is included.

The very first meal in the *Odyssey* gets the most extended treatment. Telemachos and the disguised Athene sit down to eat. First the poet begins the passage with the serving girl bringing on the water for hand-washing. Then he extends the description: "And a carver lifted up and set by them a wooden platter of all kinds of meat, and next to them he set golden goblets, while a herald went about always ready to pour wine for them" (*Odyssey* 1.141 *ff*).

Now enter the suitors, and the poet brings in the other typical description, this time adding a number of lines that have to do with eating (the italicized lines are again the repeated ones):

> *Heralds poured out for them water upon their hands,* while female servants piled up bread in baskets. *Then the young men filled the bowls with drink up to the brim.* And they stretched out their hands to the food lying there awaiting them. *But when they had set aside their desire for food and drink* [a phrase equivalent in general signification to "now when they had made a libation and had drunk to their heart's content" but different, of course, verbally and metrically] the suitors began to think of other things, of singing and dancing. (1.146 *ff*)

The banquet has begun and ended in this scene for two sets of people. The typical language had been used and at times amplified. No other passage is so extended. Perhaps the poet of the *Odyssey* who clearly has in his control the technique of repetition wants to create an unusually full description for the first meal in order to set the peculiarly ritual mood of banqueting in the *Odyssey*, where material comfort and human relations, as they are realized through social convention, are important motifs, celebrated elaborately throughout in what sometimes reminds one of a novel of manners. Perhaps also the arrival of the suitors provides the clue for interpretation, that is, the quality of service, the elegance and richness of the house, set against the corrupt and boorish men who are feasting. In so doing they are wasting away Odysseus' substance, the very stuff that animates the entire description—bread, meat, silver and golden serving ware, polished tables, and wine.

SIMILES

The extended simile, that is, a comparison of some
length, is a hallmark of literary epic, found again and again
in Virgil or Tasso or Milton. It is a direct inheritance from
the Homeric epics. While extended similes are common
to literary epic, they are unusual in oral epics at least of
other cultures. Nowhere but in the *Iliad* and *Odyssey* are
they found in such number or so skillfully contrived. Oral
epic is an art form in which many of the techniques,
motifs, and attitudes are common from one culture to another regardless of the language or the nation in which the
epic appears. For this reason the Homeric simile is remarkable as a peculiar feature of the Greek oral epic tradition.

The simile may in fact be more remarkable as a demonstrably late feature in the Greek epic tradition. In fact
some scholars choose to believe that the "last Homer," so
to speak, he who composed the *Iliad* and *Odyssey* as we
know them, created the similes. The human world which
the similes sometimes describe displays customs and artifacts that anthropologists and archaeologists contend belong to a period toward the end of the epic tradition, rather
than to Mycenaean times. Many words used in similes occur in forms that linguists can date as late developments in
the Greek language. Furthermore, there are only eight
similes repeated in the whole of the two poems. Repetition
is, of course, often a criterion of an early date, since the
more common a phrase or motif is the more obviously it
seems to be worked into the very fabric of oral epic poetry.
On the other hand, the phraseology of the similes observes
all the other mechanics of oral formular poetry, for example, the traditional metrical positioning of words, commonplaces of meter, the repetition of theme, formulaic
phrase, etc. For this reason, and because they work so well
in the poetry, and perhaps, most important, because a

number of them seem to have developed out of one theme, they are probably the work of some time and many minds. If any synthesis can be made of this information we may say that the evidence suggests that similes were a little-used device which toward the end of the period of oral epic poetry in Greece became a far more important feature of the poetry.

There are other odd aspects. The *Iliad* is filled with similes, varying from nearly two hundred long ones to about thirty short ones. The *Odyssey* has only about forty long and fifteen short similes. The great majority of similes in the *Iliad* (about three-fourths of all) occur in battle narratives. Since the *Odyssey* has few battles and considerable dialogue in which similes are almost never found, the lesser number of similes there is reasonable. It is odd, however, that similes which are supposed to be a late development occur far more in the *Iliad* which is generally considered to be earlier, and in battle narrative which seems, at least to me, essentially more traditional, hence perhaps older.

The simplest, and—by now—shopworn, explanation for the heavy concentration of similes in the battle narrative is that these passages need something to relieve the tedium they engender. This is dubious. We find battle narratives dull, true. But did the original audiences? In what theory of literature can we accommodate the view that a poet spins out lengthy passages which he knows will bore his audiences? Arguing from the ancient poet's supposed obligation to tradition won't help either. There is too much obvious poetic rehandling of the material to let stand the belief that he felt any reverence for its absolute historicity. Battle narratives and similar passages fill the *Iliad* because the poet liked them and his audience did, too. It is very likely exactly the combination of descriptions of death, melancholy histories of the combatants, names, and geographical allusions *laced with the similes* that caused the pleasure. Similes do not appear in dialogue. So neither the first nor the sixth book of the *Iliad* has many, perhaps because they would clutter or be distracting. The focus is always on the action in epic, and in these books the action is redefined by the emotional, verbal reaction of the speakers. Where there is little speaking, as in battle narrative, similes supply the means to reconsider the action.

The extended simile often makes its point of comparison with the narrative action, then evolves organically, true to the dynamics of its own image. At the same time it leaves behind and does not return to any further parallel with the narrative. The comparison of Menelaos' wound with the staining of ivory which we discussed in the first chapter is of this sort. On the other hand, the simile comparing Paris to a horse, also discussed there, seems to adhere at every turn to points of similarity. The majority of similes, however, work like the former example.

Very likely the extended simile grew from simple little comparisons, like "he went along like the night," said of Apollo, or "she rose like a mist," said of Thetis. The development of the simile probably reflects the manner of the poet in creating the entire poem, that is, his beginning with an idea that is a whole, and creating by simply redefining what he has said. The style is one of evolution. In the following simile I have tried to translate as literally as possible to keep the word order. The poet states his thesis immediately (the joy of welcoming the moribund father back to life), then proceeds to reveal the dramatic potential behind the original statement:

> As when to his children appears their father's life
> as something joyfully to be welcomed back, when he
> is lying in sickness, suffering strong pains, wasting
> away for a long time, and a malevolent spirit was
> hanging onto him, but then the gods freed him from
> this evil, to the children's joy, so did the land and the
> trees strike Odysseus as something sweet to see again.
> (*Odyssey* 5.394 ff)

Although style encourages the poet to leave the original point of comparison, often the secondary elements of the simile reflect the elements of the plot as a whole. For instance, in the one just quoted the malevolent spirit can be equated with Poseidon who holds Odysseus back, and the gods who finally free the man of his sickness can be the consensus of the Olympian council that Odysseus should get home. The children's joy at having their father restored reflects the yearning of almost everyone at Ithaka.

Often closely spaced similes seem to reflect one another. In the first real battle scene of the *Iliad* in a short space (4.422–456) there are three similes. Each relates to a specific moment, yet all three are unified. In the first, as the armies are coming together, the Greeks are compared to resounding waves breaking on a beach. Homer is true to the fact that they are the invading army, beached on the shore and attacking the city. The Trojans are shortly thereafter compared to sheep waiting to be milked, bleating when they hear the sound of their lambs. The Trojans are throughout the *Iliad* portrayed as the defenders of their city and their families, to which the sheep crying for their lambs corresponds. Further, the sheep as victim is a common enough idea in the *Iliad*, fitting to the Trojans. Also the bleating seems to me to imply weakness set against the sound of crashing waves. The effect is much like the opening of the third book, where the sound of the Trojan approach is compared to the clamor of birds followed by Homer's chilling remark that the Achaians came on in silence. The poet of the *Iliad* always finds something ominously frivolous and unpredictable in the Trojan psyche for which Paris is the grand symbol.

The third simile moves the reader away from the immediate scene to a kind of poetic high, describing the battle as a clashing of storm-filled rivers, heard from afar by a shepherd. By bringing together the shepherd and the furious water, the poet has united the other similes, helping to give the simile world a real coherence and consistency. The known and partially visualized simile world becomes another dimension of the entire narrative scene.

In the fifth book of the *Iliad* when Diomedes takes the field he is compared at some length to a winter torrent that sweeps everything away in its path. As the battle progresses Diomedes triumphs, but he is finally stopped at the sight of Ares, the god of war, fighting at the side of Hektor. In his hesitation he is compared to a man who halts in dismay at the prospect of crossing a storm-swollen river. With this simile the poet implies that the thrust of battle, which is the energy of rushing water in both similes, has been taken from Diomedes. The comparison remains when, toward the end of the book, Ares leaves the battle likened to the black air of storm clouds, source, as we all know, of those sudden violent rains that produce rapid torrents.

Correspondences between the similes are often to be found. Nonetheless, there is certainly not the one-for-one ratio that appears in the literate poets. Nor is it likely that all the analogies were worked out consciously by Homer. Everything is suggestion, sprung from the subconscious or intuition in which enough ambiguity lies.

The world described in the similes is more homely than the heroic situation of the main story. Farm people and their occupations, the little people caught up in the necessary details of their existence form a world more like that which Hesiod describes in his *Works and Days.* Since Hesiod was not fictionalizing we take his description to be the world of the eighth and seventh centuries. Homeric similes therefore perhaps are the ground line that keeps our perspective. Although there are not enough similes to make this really so, one can almost see a saga world, a divine world, and a simile world, all three of them restatements of the human condition. Certainly Homer had no sense of such a schematization; nevertheless, it is there in part, contributing to the extraordinarily ecumenical vision of Homer. The other continuing theme of the similes is the world of nature. It, too, is not of the heroic world. Such similes treat mainly of animals, trees, rivers, or the ocean. There appears, especially in the battle sequences, one theme handled countless ways. It is the wild lion seeking his prey—usually domestic animals in the care of a shepherd. In all its variations this simile rehearses the archetypal confrontation of an invading army and a beleaguered city. Because the simile describes a situation from nature, it reiterates in the comparison the natural rhythm of death and survival that underlies the elaborate heroic war ritual. The development through similes of two worlds is akin to what Gerard Manley Hopkins saw in the imagery of Greek tragic choruses, which he called underthought and overthought. Overthought refers to the immediate surface meaning and underthought to the conception built up simply through imagery.

The significant aspect of Homeric similes is that they work through suggestion. Ordinary epic usage is direct. Scenes and attitudes are fully described. But the similes have an economy of language after the fashion of lyric poetry. More is demanded of the reader.

Consider the scene when King Alkinoos feasts Odysseus for the last time at Scheria, and the Ithakan waits for nightfall to be taken home. After several lines describing a lavish banquet scene Homer notices that Odysseus turns his head toward the setting sun, "As a man yearns for his supper for whom the whole day long the oxen have been drawing the plow . . ." (*Odyssey* 13.31 *f*).

Obviously the supper is Ithaka and the day's labor is ten years of wandering. Ironically, however, the Phaiacian surfeit of plenty produces hunger in a man who, by nature, moves on, lives off wits and a lean belly. The rest and recreation at Scheria, too, has only produced fatigue— the fatigue of impatience at delay, as well as the fatigue of manipulating a strange environment. The simile illuminates the complexity of Odysseus' personality.

The similes show a poet who is exercising close control

over his material. Such control, subtly extending into minutiae, somehow seems contrary to the manner of the practitioner of the formulae, the traditional theme, and the mechanical response. The relationship between the similes and the remainder of the narrative will always be enigmatic; but more than anywhere else in the two epics one senses in the similes the personal quality of poetic creation.

Chapter IV

THE *ILIAD*

Cattle and fine flocks may be had for the stealing,
tripods are easily come by, even horses' tawny manes.
But a man's soul is not to be snatched back again
nor captured when once it has fled the barrier of his
teeth.

Iliad 9.406–409

The *Iliad* sometimes seems to have developed like churned butter, bits and pieces sticking together until a perceptible amount, clearly butter and no longer cream, clings to the paddle. By simple accretion, new words and phrases came which explained or defined more fully what had gone before. In this sense over fifteen thousand lines become spontaneous and natural amplification and redefinition of the poem's initial word "wrath." This theory of composition does not necessarily require a poet with a strong sense of unity; certainly the *Iliad* does not have a tight plot. Its episodic quality has concerned scholars whose critical standards are derived from well constructed novels that do not admit such extraordinarily loose narrative. These scholars are at pains to account for improprieties like Achilles' absence from the second through the eighth book. Perhaps, actually, various episodes in the *Iliad* are random happenings and do not depend upon each other, while the intellectual mind animated by an instinct for order, insisting upon cause and effect moves the critic to seek patterns and connections in even the smallest places. The problem is somewhat analogous to the nineteenth-century art critic who understands and accepts the exact representation of trees in the background of Italian primitive paintings (scaled naturally for perspective) but who cannot accept the convention of the French Impressionists who turn these trees into blobs of color, shadow, and light. The latter technique is far more realistic because it brings out the truly blurred and synthetic view of distant objects which humans have. In the same way the sometimes unsubstantial linkage between events in Homer's narrative represents more honestly the generally inexplicable train of human affairs. Nonetheless each element of the story clearly has value for the poet; he has introduced everything with consideration, sometimes to tell a story, sometimes to comment upon that story, and even at times to offer alternatives. The story nevertheless always remains.

Currently the fashion in Homeric studies is to find evidence of symmetry. Many have long since observed that the events of Book One occur in reverse order in the twenty-fourth. If it is schematized, the symmetry seems still more real. For instance:

BOOK I

1. Apollo brings a plague and as a result the Greeks bury many dead.
2. Agamemnon and Achilles quarrel and Briseis is taken away.
3. Thetis and Achilles speak, and she then appeals to Zeus.
4. Odysseus goes to the island of Chrysa to take back Chryseis.

5. Thetis and Zeus speak and he agrees to her plea.
6. The gods quarrel.

BOOK XXIV

1. The gods quarrel.
2. Thetis and Zeus speak, and she goes to calm Achilles.
3. Thetis and Achilles speak, and she delivers a message from Zeus.
4. Priam goes to Achilles' camp to recover the body of Hektor.
5. Priam and Achilles settle their differences; Achilles returns the body of Hektor.
6. Lamentation of the women and the funeral of Hektor.

Evidences of reverse symmetry have been discovered throughout the poem. The parallelism is actually only very approximate. For instance, the scant lines in the first book (43–52) describing Apollo visiting the Greek forces with a plague and ending with the terse notice, "the place was thick with pyres of the dead, burning continuously," hardly correspond to the lamentation over the corpse of Hektor and the preparations for his funeral. Then again the scenes in Olympos in the two books differ greatly in quality and purpose. The first relates directly to the quarrel between Agamemnon and Achilles and the second is more a discussion. A similar problem in equation confronts anyone who attempts some mechanized schematization of the poem. The temptation, however, is very strong. First, because one does feel that some kind of ordering is going on that cannot be readily identified. Everyone who spends time with the *Iliad* will discover this. Second, because the oral theory with its attendant notions of a kind of mechanistic creation of poetry leads one to find further automatic creative devices. Finally, the story of the *Iliad* is hard to remember in detail; this inspires a desire to see the structure of the narrative.

The plot's looseness no doubt stems from the essentially ephemeral nature of oral poetry. The poet did add line to line. Beyond this, however, the story seems to show considerable organization that must have been the result of his having worked out a story line quite independently of creating the poem. Much of the story, of course, must have been traditional, which the poet simply took over, for it can be found elsewhere. Perhaps Homer acquired it in a simpler, more straightforward form, that is, the general and the hero quarrel, after which the hero retires until in "the nick of time" when almost all is lost he returns to the fight and dies gloriously—whereupon he is given a grand funeral. This plot with typical American modifications dominated C movies of the thirties. In our version the star fullback falls out with the coach, comes back to the game and wins, whereupon he and the girl fall in love at the school prom that evening. It is an important folk plot, but Homer has used it with sophistication. This plot turns on the psychological states of anger, rejection, fury, and acceptance; this psychodrama, as it were, is built upon the rhythm of the conventional plot although its elements are divided between the actions of Achilles and Patroklos.

Aristotle said that a story must have a beginning, a middle, and an end; the plot of the *Iliad* shows this. I should say that the books through the tenth are the beginning; from the eleventh through the seventeenth, the middle; and the last seven books, the end. Incidentally, originally there was no division into books. The poem was continuous, but capable of some kind of division by episode. Probably the Alexandrian scholars decided to divide the work into as many books as the Greek alphabet had characters (twenty-four) to identify them. The division attempts to follow the natural rhythm of the episodes. The beginning and end of a day are natural moments of pause and often book divisions occur there. There are, however, no *real* divisions. Occasionally episodes begin toward the end of one book and continue straight into the next. For example, when Achilles proceeds to arm himself at the end of the nineteenth book (349 *ff*) we have really the prelude to the battle in the twentieth book. One has to guard against the instinct to think in terms of chapters, intermissions, and the like, at these points. The action of the *Iliad* is absolutely continuous.

In the first part of the *Iliad* Homer establishes the lines of the plot by describing the quarrel between Agamemnon and Achilles (Book One). He also introduces hierarchy as a dominant motif in the story (Books One and Two). As is natural in a beginning, the characters are introduced (the catalogues of the second book, Agamemnon's review of his troops in the fourth book, and Books Three and Six). War is presented in its ritualized, formal aspect (in the duels of Books Three and Seven), as a major element that will affect the entire story (Books Seven and Eight) and as the context which delineates and illuminates the heroic personality of Diomedes (especially Books Five and Seven). Book Nine is a pivotal book in the story of Achilles. Highly dramatic and very unlike the preceding books, it is nevertheless motivated by them and dependent upon them. The crisis for the Greek forces in Book Eight forces Agamemnon to seek out Achilles. His subsequent rejection of Agamemnon's plea is in part measured against the valor which Diomedes has earlier displayed. The intensity of the ninth book is relaxed by the episode of the tenth, an adventure story involving Diomedes and Odysseus. Yet beyond that, the co-operation between the two is also a reflection upon Achilles' decision to remain in isolation.

The middle section is epic war. The battle for the wall built around the Greek fleet forms the action in which most of the major heroes get a chance to show their prowess. The narrative is unified by the actions of Patroklos, who goes to inquire after Machaon (Book Eleven),

gets waylaid, finally returns to Achilles to insist upon entering the fight, and is killed (Book Sixteen). The fight for
his body in the seventeenth book forms a natural pendent
to this. The ending of the *Iliad* commences with Achilles'
grief (Book Eighteen), proceeds to his mad rage (Book
Twenty-one) and ends in the peace of his exhaustion and
new understanding (Book Twenty-four). The last section
also has a series of resolutions: Achilles' acceptance of his
death, Agamemnon's public apology, a final review of the
major characters in the funeral games, and the return of
Hektor's body. These books are introduced by the description of Achilles' new shield that in itself is a summation, being an abstract and ideal picture of human existence. Several episodes, therefore, form the conclusion. The
structure of Greek tragedy shows the same disinclination
to move hastily to the end. The crisis generally occurs
somewhat after the middle of the play, and the remaining
events resolve this crisis. For instance, Oedipus discovers
his parentage some three hundred and thirty lines before
the ending of the roughly fifteen-hundred-line *Oedipus
Rex.* In Greek literature the aftermath is important.

The broad middle portion of this epic describes a long
and complicated battle around the wall which the Greeks
had erected to surround their ships. The central fact of
the *Iliad* is battle and war; Achilles functions within and
through it. Since he is so well conceived by the poet and
his dilemma is both so human and so personal, Achilles in
turn dominates the view of war. Formally, however, war is
the major event. Those who read the *Iliad* as a performance of glorious heroics, miss the sadness, the nostalgia,
and physical mayhem. In skipping the battle books they
are being sentimental. As Zeus becomes saddest when he
sees Sarpedon die in battle he becomes angriest in talking
to Ares, the god of war, his son by Hera. "Most hateful of
the gods are you to me, for you love discord, war and
battles" (*Iliad* 5.890 f). Still, while war is hateful to the
poet, the *Iliad* is no pacifist poem. Ares as son of the first

father and mother in the family of gods is completely legitimate and hence natural.

Since Horace first said it in the *Ars Poetica*, we have been accustomed to think that epic must begin *in medias res*, in the middle of things. The *Iliad* was his example. The formal beginning of the *Iliad* is probably the Catalogue of Ships and the Catalogue of Trojans at the close of Book Two. While not complete inventories of the major figures of the story, both catalogues in their formality and their listing of personnel are like playbills. Realistically this muster is inappropriate to the tenth year of the war, but Homer evidently wants a formal introduction so that he uses the catalogues. The prefatory mood continues in the third book where the scene turns to Troy and Priam and Helen are introduced, together with a bit of physical description of various Greek leaders. Several Greek leaders are further delineated in the fourth book when Agamemnon reviews his troops and Homer describes by means of their speeches their psychological relationship to Agamemnon. In the sixth book we get another view of Troy; this time the poet describes Hektor and Andromache. Form never dominates Homer's working, however. Most of the characters are introduced, as they should be, early on, but he provides insights at random moments. For instance, suddenly Menelaos appears as the totally second-rate person he is in an exchange between Agamemnon and Nestor in the tenth book. There is no strong reason for Homer's choosing this moment, yet it is another illustration of the *Iliad's* inherent realism. Such revelations do often come in unexpected times and places.

The action with which Homer begins the entire work is the quarrel between Agamemnon and Achilles. This quarrel over the girl, Briseis, is exceedingly serious. She is not just a concubine, with whom either one can sleep or even fall in love. True, Agamemnon can claim that he intended to bring back to Mycenae his concubine, Chryseis, because she is in every way the equal of Klytemnestra.

Achilles can maintain that he in fact loved Briseis. Both sentiments are the hyperbole of rhetoric in passion. The girls, like the rest of the plunder from captured towns, are valuable in so far as they confer status on the recipient. Briseis is called a *geras* (always translated in the good old days of quaintness "a meed of honor"). A *geras* is a special prize given to a major figure, apart from the general division of the spoils among all the army. The special prize defined the hero before the men of the army, as epaulets, tassels, swords single out the formally superior person in our own military. This means of definition was central to that society. The culture of the *Iliad* is called a shame culture; I suppose that it was peopled by David Riesman's "other directed" personalities. In such a culture a man's behavior is guided by the attitude of his peers, unlike the so-called guilt culture which depends upon internalized forces of approval and disapproval stemming from a conditioned superego. The mechanism extends beyond obviously moral behavior to the whole personality. So in the *Iliad* when Achilles suggests to Agamemnon, his acknowledged leader, that Agamemnon return Chryseis, he is asking that his overlord give up one of the distinguishing marks of his superiority. And Achilles makes this suggestion in assembly, one in fact that he himself called, before the entire army, those "other people" who confer status and identification.

The sensible thing is to return the girl. Apollo is decimating the Greek army because of the prayers of Chryseis' father. Theoretically in ten years Agamemnon has accumulated enough honors to let this one go by without losing his dignity. But Agamemnon is a weak person and the system in which he is top man is somewhat shaky (if we may judge by the criticism several times directed at it in the *Iliad*). He cannot tolerate her being taken from him without some substitute given. Simple greed is very much beside the point. Honor and glory and the mark of significance which they confer are all. So Agamemnon must take a concubine from one of the others. The quarrel which is about to start will be in deadly earnest since the essence of the heroic ego is being threatened. Anger sweeps the first book, pitting Agamemnon against Chryses, Apollo against the Greeks, Agamemnon against Kalchas, Achilles against Agamemnon, and finally, Agamemnon against Achilles. Human, quick, and dynamic, the anger shakes the foundations of the hierarchical order that has defined these men and their lives.

When Agamemnon demands another *geras*, Achilles' answer (*Iliad* 1.149 *ff*) is wild, strange, a rejection of heroic values. He questions Agamemnon's right to a greater share in the plunder since he always seems to lag behind when battle comes. Achilles thinks that his greater effort in war ought to be better recompensed. The fundamental impulse to heroic action—glory—is set aside and the heroic ideal collapses, as Achilles realistically talks of profit and fear as the motives of war. In this strong speech Achilles begins to reject the heroic world; why we cannot altogether say, except that he cannot endure serving a dishonorable man who in a sense threatens to emasculate him.

Agamemnon answers by cutting Achilles out of the social fabric. "Go," he says (173), "there are others who will honor me, especially Zeus," thereby reminding Achilles of the ultimate source of his power. A little later, he makes the truly devastating remark, "I won't give a thought to you." Homeric heroes, like movie stars, can endure anything but being ignored. The glory syndrome demands constant recognition, approbation, and, in fact, applause. Achilles is effaced, the more so because Agamemnon arbitrarily and haughtily then chooses to seize Achilles' concubine, Briseis, as recompense. The full force of his power is thus thrown to Achilles as a challenge, and Achilles is ready to kill Agamemnon. Common sense (in the form of Athene) saves Achilles from destroying any possible accommodation with the world in which he lives.

In her appearance lie the seeds that will grow to fruit by
the epic's end. Nothing she says to Achilles reveals high
abstract principles; she tells him that he will get three
times over the value of Briseis in gifts later on if he limits
his abuse of Agamemnon to words and puts the sword
away. There are no principles here, because the aristocratic
world of Homer depends upon right instinct not upon
articulated precepts. Common sense is fine wisdom; Odysseus whom Athene protects is the best example, a man who
bases realism in action upon acceptance. For Odysseus the
fact of our mortality dictates that we compromise and
accept. Agamemnon strains the heroic code too far when
he demands a new concubine as formal insignia of his
superiority at a time when no new prizes are available. By
determining to take one from some vassal he dangerously
forces a realistic appraisal of his worth. Stupidly having
gone that far he has no choice but to go all the way. Achilles, horrified and angry, is forced to look again at the
code. Although common sense kept him from killing
Agamemnon, suddenly it is not enough. He wants something more. When he talks to Agamemnon bluntly, dis-
regarding the heroic commitment, out of a strong personal
humanity, he goes past acceptance, past compromise. He
seems to be a superhero or an anti-hero.

Achilles begins to reveal the depth of his anger and passion when he talks to his mother, Thetis. We see still
more of this in the ninth book. In the first book Thetis
says only that he is fated to die young; in the ninth book
we learn that actually he has a choice. He may either live
out his life to old age ingloriously back in Phthia or die
young with glory on the battlefield before Troy. A terrible
choice this: life over glory, glory over life. The Homeric
hero's completest expression of self lies in glory. There is
a Greek word *aretē* often translated as "virtue" through
the tradition of the Latin *virtus* via the French *vertu*. In
essence *aretē* refers to that innate quality that defines any
object. So the *aretē* of a knife is its cutting surface, not the

carved handle. The *aretē* of a horse is its sure speed, not
the beauty of its mane or flaring nostrils. The *aretē* of a
heroic warrior is in the field of battle in the combination
of physical and mental qualities that cause him to
triumph. Therein lay the potential for Greek tragic
thought. The moments when the hero is grandest is when
he is exerting himself to the utmost, straining hardest
against the limitations to his strength and intellect. That
moment is the split second before death, the one invincible force against which we all must struggle hardest and
finally fail. The glory of a warrior, his fulfillment, his
aretē comes on the battlefield as he dies. Achilles knows
this; faced with the choice, without even choosing, he
knows he will die young gloriously at Troy. Because he
has choice, however, he cherishes life the more. If life is
to be sacrificed, then the glory must be truly great.

Especially for Achilles, therefore, the loss of his prize of
honor is terrible. As the *Iliad* develops we see he has little
time. Hence the urgency in his tone even in the first book;
hence the reason why he is completely willing to see the
Greeks suffer in his absence. He cannot think of anything
other than himself and his death.

When Agamemnon announces that he can do without
Achilles, the young man is set outside the group. His response is instinctive, to withdraw completely. Nothing
that is said will alter the resolve of either man, although
Nestor tries. The old man's speech is about hierarchy, the
need to rule and obey. This is the dominant theme of the
first two books and the theme is repeated by the catalogues in which the men of the two armies are arranged
categorically in a rhythmed, name-studded hierarchy. Homer emphasizes this facet of human existence by repeating
the motif. Not only in Nestor's speech and the catalogue
is hierarchy the preoccupation, but in the scene on Olympos and in the flight to the ships as well. Even later on in
the *Iliad* it is a refrain that returns, as, for example, when
Agamemnon reviews his troops in the fourth book.

Nestor presents the hierarchical philosophy in abstraction. "Yield to my persuasion," he says to them both, "for it is better to yield" (*Iliad* 1.274). This is a major theme, throughout the *Iliad*, the omnipresent alternation between stubbornness and yielding. Nestor continues by urging Agamemnon, however great he may be, to relinquish his claims on Briseis. He admonishes Achilles not to contend with a king, "since the sceptered king to whom Zeus has given glory does not ever hold equal honor." Although Achilles is physically powerful and son of a goddess, Nestor says Agamemnon is the greater, because he rules over more men. The vagueness reflects, as we have said, the fact that Homer inherited in his poetry the notion of kingship and vassalage that did not correspond to the facts of his time. But the ambiguity is turned to account. Agamemnon nowhere seems to have a clearly defined absolute power. The limitations which he may impose on Achilles remain in tension. Furthermore, the political system is enough abstracted and void of detail to slip easily into symbol for that vague, ill-seen, yet inexorable force in life against which man's free will always fights.

Nestor's arguments become dramatized in the second book, which portrays man in the mass, both in anarchy and under control. The second book has often troubled readers because it seems to depart so abruptly from the lines of the plot which the first book set down. We expect Zeus to fulfill his promise to Thetis, cause the Greeks to weaken, so as to make the absent Achilles more important. Ultimately, in the eighth book this design will be accomplished. Homer has a grander plan for his epic and adopts a more leisurely pace. Many things are at hand to be revealed. Achilles' private resentment is only one of them. In the second book the poet portrays the mass of men as a counterpart to the several individuals engaged in the action in the first book. Here are the two sides to war, as the opening lines of the *Iliad* promised, speaking of the specific wrath of Achilles and forecasting the numbers who were to die thereafter.

The plot turns so unexpectedly because Zeus sends Agamemnon a dream. The dream is certainly a crude way to change the direction of the plot. Cruder still is Agamemnon's strange determination to test the army's resolution to fight on at Troy. Totally implausible, awkwardly worked in, the maneuver nevertheless implies the importance which the poet attached to the ensuing scene. He seems determined to brave the difficulty of reversing his plot no matter how roughly the scene is brought in. The ensuing description of the soldiers in simile and in straight narrative is indeed worth the effort. The action of the second book is men convening, then rushing pell-mell, astray, wildly to the ships, then being reassembled in the most precise fashion. The flight to the ships underscores the pathetic weariness of the troops who have seen almost ten years on a foreign shore. The smell of rebellion echoes Achilles' mood earlier. More important, however, is the presence of Thersites and the behavior of Odysseus.

Agamemnon is testing the men, but in fact he is also being tested. And he fails. They flee to the ships at his suggestion, to be sure. Yet there is the feeling that his authority, unspoken and moral, and his purpose, exposed to them for ten years, is being gainsaid. This is reinforced by Athene's coming to Odysseus rather than Agamemnon to halt the flight. Agamemnon, the leader of men, is helpless. The situation verges on complete anarchy, as in the earlier scene when Achilles almost drew his sword on the lord of Mycenae. Sweet reason in the form of Athene appeared then, too. Odysseus, the most thoughtful and humane of Agamemnon's circle, proceeds to reinforce the system of command that has been so rudely upset. Homer gives samples of Odysseus' manner toward his peers and his inferiors. They demonstrate his extraordinary subtlety and understanding of human nature. The poet also intends to show further the many ramifications of the ordered world, to illuminate still more, and to remind us of, on the one hand, the isolation of Achilles and, on the other, his stubborn refusal to accept this system as the source of his existence.

Odysseus first takes from Agamemnon the staff which has been handed down in the House of Atreus, originally a gift from Zeus, and token of Agamemnon's hereditary majesty. Odysseus, too, becomes invested with majesty. To his peers he speaks gently, with a few veiled threats. To the common soldiery he is brusque, and belittling. "Let there be one king, one lord to whom Zeus gives the scepter and the judgments" (*Iliad* 2.204 f). All return to the place of assembly and grow quiet, except Thersites. This man, whom Homer describes as physically deformed and repellent, is the only man of low birth who speaks in the *Iliad*. But more extraordinary is that he is almost an analogue for Achilles in the scene of the quarrel. His arguments are the same; he is described as uncommon. Thersites is as uncommonly boorish as Achilles is uncommonly heroic. They find the same position, an attack on the system that endows Agamemnon with so many goods. As Achilles in his way was humiliated by being publicly ignored and stripped of his honor, Thersites is struck across the back and shoulders with the hereditary ruling staff. "He sat down, afraid, in pain, looking helpless, and he wiped away a tear" (*Iliad* 2.268 f). And his fellows, disturbed as they are, nonetheless laugh at him. This is not harsh tyranny. Thersites is made to find his place again, the rhythm of man's intercourse is steadied. Not so with Achilles, who withdraws from it.

The gathering of the gods on Olympos at the close of the first book seems to be a parody of the earthly quarrel. Zeus comes from having promised Thetis. All the gods rise at his approach; the Heavenly Hierarchy clearly exists as well. But Hera begins to quarrel with Zeus because he has made promises to Thetis on the sly. Zeus, who is one of Homer's best conceived figures, begins as husband, re-

plying to Hera's shrillness with words more of patience
than of testiness. But in a moment she goes too far. Still
unperturbed, Zeus tells her that what he wills, will be,
that she should sit down—all rather pleasantly done, then,
"lest all the gods who are on Olympos can't protect you as
I draw near, when I stretch out toward you my hands that
cannot be touched" (1.566 f). Naked power, coldly shown.
The poet says, "he spoke . . . and Hera was afraid. She sat
down in silence, and repressed her heart" (568 f). To
Zeus' Agamemnon and Hera's Achilles the god Hephaistos
plays Nestor. The old gentleman from Pylos is always long-
winded, always reminiscent, usually somewhat of a bore.
Because he is lovable he is laughable rather than odious.
Hephaistos is crippled and earnest which naturally produces unquenchable laughter among the eternal deities
gathered at Zeus' palace. Hephaistos plays the peacemaker,
reminding his mother of Zeus' power, and bustling about
pouring the wine. Unlike the terrestrial quarrel, this one
is resolved in food, wine, song, and laughter.

One is hard put to understand what Homer is about
when he introduces the gods in this fashion. The immediate response to the comparison is the realization that
quarrels don't matter on Olympos, because no god can
care that much, that nothing really matters for them.
They are gods who will live forever, therefore they need
not seek to define their existence. It can have no definition
because it is endless. The parallel between the two scenes
also dilutes the intensity, seriousness, and potential tragedy of Achilles' anguish. Homer must consciously wish to
do so; it happens again in the scene in which Achilles
fights with the river god and all the gods come to earth, in
a ludicrous parody of a battle. That episode is introduced
by a splendid exalted description of Achilles arming and
preparing himself, making the presence of these silly gods
all the more weird. While various apologists have insisted
that the gods are not being treated humorously, that, in
fact, the humor is only a by-product of modern-day

theologically sophisticated thinking looking at primitive religiosity, scenes such as these, or even the entry of the gods into battle in the fifth and seventh books cannot be patronized in that fashion. The poet of the *Iliad* is being seriously comic.

Homer strives to caricature heroism in these scenes, not so much to mock heroic behavior as to save it. Heroics are ideal, insubstantial, exalted almost to the point of the ridiculous. Belief in heroism characterizes intense young men; mature men of experience and vision accept the multiplicity of existence and reject heroism's rigid absolutism. The narrow heroic mind could not sustain a view of life as pervasive as the *Iliad.* Yet the heroic spirit animates the poem, and provides the central tension. Homer uses his divinities to relax the grandeur of the human behavior, so as to keep it from slipping itself into caricature. Man's limitations are exposed when gods who are little different from man in these scenes act out his vulnerability. Yet paradoxically, that Olympos should be so flawed gives man the greater stature.

In Homer's description of the war in these early books, Diomedes, especially, distinguishes himself in battle. The fifth book particularly could be called his *aristeia,* the Greek term for a hero's moment in battle when he is preeminent. Doubtless any epic poet knew a number of *aristeiai* of various major figures of the saga tradition. Homer, as a superior craftsman, has contrived to expand Diomedes' adventures in these books to stand for an ideal *aristeia.* Later in the battle for the wall he suggests, and no more, the *aristeiai* of several other heroes. In addition to his activities in this battle Diomedes takes a large and vocal part preceding and following the petition to Achilles in the ninth book, and in the night sortie that follows in the tenth. Enough of his personality is revealed to show that he is a paragon hero. These episodes establish Diomedes as an heroic alternative to Achilles. This is necessary. Achilles, who has withdrawn from the battle, is ac-

knowledged by all as the finest warrior on either side.
Nevertheless we do not see him that way but rather mood-
ily passing the time in his tent. When he deliberates in
the ninth book on his role in the war the image of Diomedes comes to mind. Diomedes' valor contrasted with
Achilles' inactivity accomplishes two things. We can see
how empty Achilles' situation is, changed from active participation on the field of battle to inactivity. Achilles' extraordinary personality becomes clearer when contrasted
with Diomedes' normal cast of mind.

The difference between the two is first implied when
Agamemnon in reviewing his troops rebukes Diomedes.
Diomedes and his friend, Sthenelos, are waiting, inactive,
presumably because, like Odysseus, at whom Agamemnon
has just been angry for equally erroneous reasons, he did
not hear the battle call, being far back. Agamemnon is
harsh and sarcastic, but Diomedes answers not a word.
When Sthenelos does, Diomedes restrains him, saying:

> Now, my friend, be quiet and listen to me. I'm not
> angry with Agamemnon, shepherd of the folk, who's
> trying to urge on the well-greaved Achaians. He gets
> the praise if the Achaians vanquish the Trojans and
> take sacred Ilion, but then again he gets the heartache
> if we are beaten. So come now, let's put our mind on
> the fighting. (*Iliad* 4.412 *ff*)

Diomedes' co-operative spirit is pointed up still more,
since Homer has had Odysseus, when rebuked immediately before, deliver a very spirited, stinging reply. One
expects this from a man whose first defense is words. Diomedes' quiet, on the other hand, characterizes him as loyal
to the principle of lordship, in contrast to his counterpart,
Achilles, who has not been.

Diomedes' reasonableness is blended with the requisite
warrior impetuousness. He is all over the battlefield
throughout this episode; his victims are numerous and important. Homer says that Diomedes put as much fear as

Achilles into the Trojans. He is favored by the gods. Athene gives him the magical power to see the various gods who are assisting their human favorites in the battle. She also fights with him like a loyal comrade against Ares. His prowess reaches new dimensions when he wounds Aphrodite. Still more grandly does he wound Ares with Athene pushing on the spear. Ares' cry causes all the fighters to shiver. Certainly no other hero finds such targets.

The power that sets Diomedes apart as superior does not prevent his acknowledging superiority. When Athene tells him not to fight with any of the gods save Aphrodite, he complies, even at first withdrawing his forces when he sees Ares take the field until Athene gives him permission to attack the war god. When Zeus sends bolts of lightning to stop him in his battle career, Diomedes wants urgently to continue the fight. Nestor tells him to give in to Zeus, but Diomedes typically fears being called a coward for quitting the fight. Three times the bolts of lightning come, before Diomedes finally yields.

He of all the heroes is marked by courtesy and gentleness. The encounter and dialogue between Diomedes and Glaukos is an archetypal portrait of courteous, gentle heroic behavior. The two exchange formal speeches showing their genealogy, and when they discover that their fathers had close ties, they agree to avoid one another and fight elsewhere on the battlefield. The pact is sealed by the exchange of their armor. When Nestor's horse is struck in battle, and the old man appears to be cut off, Diomedes hurries to the rescue. Significantly he calls for assistance to Odysseus who is in the vicinity, but the older, shrewder, more cynical Odysseus ignores him and rides on. Realistically, Odysseus, least of all, would be concerned to risk his life in saving Nestor, the garrulous, platitudinous bore and inconsequential fighter. Diomedes' concern stems very likely from Nestor's great age. As heroes often do, Diomedes thinks a good deal of his father, Tydeus. Many times in the *Iliad* the poet narrates the exploits of Diomedes' father, and he becomes more closely identified with his father than any other hero. The same relationship exists between Achilles and his father Peleus. The heroic desire upon the part of the sons to equal or surpass the valor of their fathers is softened in a clever way. For a hero to have an extraordinary father whom he might wish to emulate does not give him increased stature. Fathers are everywhere otiose but perhaps nowhere more than in heroic saga. For instance, Antilochos, always prey to Nestor's desire to give advice, is forever upstaged. The solution is a dead father, a divine (therefore absent) father, or a sick or enfeebled father. Tydeus is dead, Peleus is sickly (even his wife Thetis stays away, at home with her father, the Old Man of the Sea) and Laertes, Odysseus' father, is clearly senile, exiled to a country villa. The situation sets no limits on the heroic son's behavior. The memory of a great father enhances the son's glory; in turn it allows the greater poet, such as Homer, to remind his heroes of life's transitory nature.

Diomedes frames, so to speak, the dramatic episode of the embassy to Achilles in Book Nine. Agamemnon is so distraught when the book opens that he is willing to evacuate the Trojan beachhead and sail home. Diomedes curtly dismisses the idea, rather sarcastically suggesting that Agamemnon may go if he chooses, but that the others would stay on, steadfast of purpose. The previous long battle scene has demonstrated that the war belongs, in a sense, to Diomedes. Now his energy keeps it going. The same situation occurs at the close of Book Nine when the leaders are downcast to learn that Achilles has rejected Agamemnon's terms. Diomedes dismisses Achilles, and turns the mood to hope and courage.

As I have said, the detailed description of Diomedes as a first-rate warrior, a gentle man, and obedient soldier shows the hero par excellence. Homer uses Diomedes at the beginning and end of Book Nine to establish a contrast with Achilles. The latter becomes more clearly isolated from the elements that made him heroic. Unlike Diomedes, he has lost his purpose; the enthusiasm, din, and grandeur of the battle can scarcely be felt at his tent. Then, too, Achilles stands apart from the normalcy and goodness that mark Diomedes. By contrasting the two, the poet is not establishing Achilles as Diomedes' opposite. Before quarreling with Agamemnon and losing Briseis, Achilles, we may imagine, was very much like Diomedes. In the time that Homer shows us Diomedes in his prime, so that we may actually better understand Achilles' mind, Achilles has been alone in his tent re-examining the heroic point of view. He grows to want something more so that he is forced to reject the pleas he is offered in Book Nine. Achilles becomes too aware to exist any longer within the framework that Diomedes represents. But we would not understand this at all, if Homer had not first offered us Diomedes in the battle narrative.

The episode of the tenth book, commonly called "the Doloneia," stands somewhat outside the over-all narrative scheme of the *Iliad*. For that reason a great number of scholars believe it to be an interpolation, on the theory, I suppose, that interpolaters can always be recognized by the special delight they take in inserting illogical and awkward pieces into the narrative. Actually the episode is an important bridge from the highly emotional, thoughtful, and theatrical episode of Book Nine to the onset of a lengthy and rambling battle narrative. Furthermore it presents once again the major characters as a mid-point reminder of the story's personnel. Most important, it shows brains and brawn off on an exciting adventure. The adventure illustrates particularly their comradeship, and so reflects again the heroic and human ideal that Achilles has repeatedly denied in the preceding book. From the moment Diomedes talks of the importance of taking a companion, through his selecting Odysseus, to their clever infiltration of the Trojan camp, the memory of Achilles alone, withdrawn and rejected, stays with us.

The ninth book in which Odysseus, Phoinix, and Ajax go at Agamemnon's command to beseech Achilles to return to the war is much better organized than most of the books. It resembles the first book in this respect. One wonders if the poet were more actively and personally creating Achilles' story amid the details of the traditional saga that perhaps came to him almost automatically. On the other hand, the only really tight drama in the *Iliad* is that of Achilles. It would normally require considerably more attention in composition.

The simile describing Agamemnon's despair begins an entreaty that fails when Achilles chooses carefully, but passionately to step completely outside the context of the heroic world. Human passion in the form of anger moves him. The simile is repeated when Patroklos returns to Achilles' camp in despair over the Greek cause. Here begins an entreaty (that Patroklos be allowed to fight in Achilles' stead) that succeeds, an entreaty that brings on Patroklos' death, which produces a series of emotions that eventually brings Achilles back into the world he had left, symbolized by his compassion toward Priam and the heroic act of returning Hektor's corpse. There exists a kind of wheel or cycle where compassion plays against passion, and non-conformity wars with conformity. Heroic society becomes a symbol of living itself to which Achilles finally returns.

The three speakers chosen by Homer to face Achilles almost verge on allegorical figures. Odysseus—intelligence; Ajax—brawn with feeling; Phoinix—fatherly love and wisdom. Nestor should logically represent this last position, but Phoinix has special ties to Peleus and a special love for Achilles, so that the poet can have him operate more effectively in the scene than Nestor would. Neither Odysseus nor Ajax are really symbols because they have points of view that stem from the context of the entire *Iliad*. Yet the poet seems more than usually conscious of structure and symmetry in arranging the scene. The speeches repre-

sent the types of attitude that the situation logically demands. One finds similar care in arranging scenes in Greek
tragedy. The brevity of tragedy tends at times to inhibit
any real characterization so that still more the speakers
seem to be symbols. The dialogue of the *Oedipus Rex* is
similar to this scene in the *Iliad.* Oedipus as central figure
is like Achilles and he is subjected to three points of view:
Teiresias, who sees things *sub specie aeternitatis* and possesses all knowledge; Creon, who is not an engaged person,
therefore lacking in seriousness and essentially frivolous;
and Jocasta, whose intense concern makes her a sophist.
The structural similarity is curious because the *Iliad* far
antedates what we believe to be the period in which tragedy began. Actually there may well have been other scenes
of this sort in lost epics, so that the technique in the tragedy of several centuries later was perhaps a natural borrow-
ing from numerous examples. The typical scenes of conversation in the *Iliad* and *Odyssey* do not resemble this
scene, or tragedy either, because usually there are many
more speakers and no attempt is made to impress a sym-
metric form upon the conversation.

Odysseus speaks first, after he intercepts a nod from
Ajax to Phoinix. Although the old man should begin, Odysseus is confident of his own ability; he wants to keep emotion out, because if the argument is intelligent and emo-
tionless, Achilles' anger will lose its point. Formally, as
well, the offer of recompense should come first because it
establishes the hierarchical relationship of Achilles to the
group. While all of this is certainly so, Ajax is instinctively
right to want Phoinix, who most cares for Achilles, to begin. Odysseus displays a certain inhumanity compared to
the other two because instead of sympathizing with the
situation, he obviously plans only to manipulate it.

Odysseus' speech is polite, and in the beginning inten-
tionally cold and unemotional. He deals in practicalities,
recounting the ships destroyed, rather than the men killed.
He appeals to Achilles' vanity by remarking on Hektor's

new-found successes. From this sparking of Achilles' psyche, Odysseus turns to the human level. He talks of the human commitment from which there is no escape when he warns Achilles that if he does not help the beleaguered Achaians now there will come a time when he shall sorrow for that fact and find no remedy to his sorrow.

The emotional content of the speech increases as Odysseus turns to speak of Achilles' father, Peleus. Partly it is the poet's preparation for Phoinix; more important, the sacred source of heroic behavior is being advanced. Peleus, Odysseus reminds him, once said that Achilles will get his strength from Athene and Hera, but he himself must curb his spirit, because the desire to be understanding and sensible is more important. Peleus' remarks are an adaptation of the heroic ideal of a doer of deeds and a speaker of words; it is the union of action and intellect which in all its ramifications produces the complete hero. At this moment, as Odysseus says, Achilles has forgotten it or it has escaped him. The Greek notion of wrongdoing did not include the kind of active antagonistic knowing pursuit of evil as the Christian world understands it through the term "sin." To forget, to overlook, to misjudge better identifies their notion of error. Achilles' determination to search for alternative bases for action makes him willing to sacrifice his comrades and deny himself his normal function. He does this not out of willfulness, but because he is concerned with other things.

Odysseus continues by listing the gifts that Agamemnon will make in recompense. As Peleus' advice was the metaphysical foundation for the hero, the material wealth listed here is the external source of identity by which Achilles will be totally rehabilitated. Odysseus concludes by indicating still another important heroic comfort. If the gifts will not give Achilles a sense of glory, then he can find it in the animate reaction of the army he is defending.

Achilles' answer rises to a climax in the revelation of the prophecy of Thetis. He begins by disavowing rhetoric, preferring an unintellectual right response to a calculated intellectual response. "I must speak without consideration [i.e., spontaneously, from the deepest instinctive honesty]· I shall tell you what I am thinking and how that thing which is already a *fait accompli* will be" (9.309 f). A curious turn of phrase, yet full of meaning to this kind of mind. What has once been said or thought is already as though done. The relationship between thought, speech, and action is direct and uncomplicated. In this respect Homer places Achilles and Odysseus in total opposition, for the Ithakan is an intellectual, he can conceive of conceiving, hence he can organize thought, but also lie. The juxtaposition serves this scene, because Achilles' honesty has led him to withdraw from the battlefield and the same honesty moves him now toward cynicism. Paradoxically the cooler, wiser, more deceptive Odysseus sees with greater honesty. Tragedy in the fifth century found this paradox a source for considerable drama.

Achilles' ugly, sceptical denial of the entire heroic code begins to reveal that the uppermost problem in Achilles' mind is that of death ("The man who does much and the man who tried not at all, both must die" [9.320]). The futility that comes with death oppresses Achilles; he cannot find a meaning for his living self, until suddenly he lengthily and finally denies the war, rejects the scene at Troy, and announces that he will sail for home. He finds that he can define himself only through being alive. Glory, material things do not create him. The meaning of existence is existing. As he says, one can carry off and capture any number of herds or material objects, but there is no way to get back a man's soul once it has fled the body. Therefore life is all, no metaphysical superstructure or system makes it more meaningful. He will withdraw.

When at the very end Achilles tells Phoinix to stay, he wants, childlike, to win a moral victory by getting one of the other camp to come over to his side. Ironic and pathetic, because Phoinix comes only out of love. Phoinix'

speech that follows deals with wrath and dislocation and
yielding and compassion. His autobiography, to begin, is a
story of wrath, dislocation, and compassion; seducing his
father's concubine to save his mother's respect, being
cursed with impotence by the old man, fleeing the country,
and finding asylum at the court of Peleus, who cherished
him and made him whole again. The story that Phoinix
tells of Meleager is much the same. Killer of his uncle,
accursed and hated by his mother, he withdrew into his
rooms while his city was catastrophically besieged. He
yields not to his father's entreaties, a symbol of Phoinix,
nor to his friends, symbols of Odysseus and Ajax, but
finally to his wife, who is symbol of Patroklos, if not, in
fact, of Patroklos' death. For it is the latter event that
teaches Achilles what friendship meant to him and at the
same time brings him back to the battle.

Phoinix' speech is long, and often abstract, much more
like the poetry of Hesiod where ideas are being shaped in
epic language, but divorced from the drama of saga narrative. The special quality of the speech, the evidence that
Homer has gone outside his normal style to contrive what
he wants shows again that the entire episode is central
to his portrayal of Achilles. Indeed, it is, although coming
rather early on, the pivotal episode of the whole *Iliad*. A
particularly Hesiodic device is Phoinix' personification of
Prayers and Ruin; it is the high point of his speech as
well, carrying an intellectual and ethical motif that recurs
throughout the poem. He has just been asking Achilles to
control his strong spirit, to show pity, since even the gods,
who are far greater than mortals, can be moved by supplication. He then continues to describe the quality of
supplication:

> For Prayers are the daughters of great Zeus, drag-
> ging their feet, faces all screwed up with embarrass-
> ment and unable to look anyone in the eye. They keep
> trying to follow along after Ruin. Now Ruin is strong

and swift so that she far outstrips all of them, always
over the whole earth getting to men first to injure
them. And afterward along come the Prayers to heal
the hurt. (9.502 *ff*)

This is a brilliant description (considerably overtrans-
lated to bring out its full meaning) of the tiresome, continual struggle of compromise. The humility in yielding,
of accepting another's primacy at any one moment is in
the portrait of the Prayers. And the rhythmic alternation
of passion in Ruin, which in the context of this speech is
the ruinous collision of two men's wills, and compassion,
which is the Prayers, is the fundamental effort of living
with others.

When the old man finally ends he has made a speech so
morally effective in its abstract argument that Achilles
can only very weakly bid him not to confuse his heart with
weeping and sorrowing. In other respects the speech has
been so emotional, loving, and moving that at its end
Achilles stands in his wrath, totally isolated from his fellow
men. The progression, so far, has been from the quite cool,
unemotional speech of Odysseus, to the much warmer, yet
still intellectual discourse of Phoinix. Now Ajax speaks,
completely from the heart. He clearly does not understand
what Achilles wants when he argues that men will even
accept recompense for the death of a blood relation. But
Ajax is never a thinking man; he is most effective talking
of Achilles' inhumanity. The close of Ajax's speech brings
out all the love that fighting men have for one another, an
appeal so emotional and honest that it cannot be met.
Achilles' reply again is lame.

Achilles is given the opportunity in this book to return
to the world in which he functions successfully, to which
he has strong human obligations and which has made him
the hero that he is. Beyond this he is shown the inexorable
necessity of yielding in one way or another in this life. In
each of his answers Achilles refuses. He withdraws from

the world that has created him, because he can no longer find identity in it. In denying the system, he denies at the same time the world and his fellow men. His heart is hard, love and compassion seem locked out, and Achilles grows to seem in this episode very much in the wrong.

But for Homer nothing is ever black or white. Achilles has long since begun to yield subconsciously. After Odysseus' speech he vows violently to return directly to Phthia; after Phoinix' speech he says that on the morrow he will decide whether to go or not. Finally, after Ajax' speech, he bids them tell Agamemnon that he will not return to the fight until Hektor has attacked his own ships. He has now accepted hot hate and the sweetness of revenge as the emotions that will give him dimension. They are successful until Patroklos dies.

The quarrel between Agamemnon and Achilles has two results. First, it causes a major dislocation in the Greek forces, a disunity that brings about a major setback for the Greeks. The poet has given that turn of events greater depth by making it seem to be the work of Zeus at the behest of Thetis. Achilles' refusal to co-operate in battle, however, makes it militarily realistic. The other result of the quarrel is the inner workings of the soul of the angered, isolated Achilles. What he finally drives himself to do in the ninth book shows that as a hero, as a young man, as a human being he has in every way defied the natural order of things. When Achilles opposes the very rhythm of existence he is a puny opponent for a great cosmic force. He is a kind of Thersites battling, shouting, arguing against his betters. As Thersites is struck by a harsh blow from Odysseus and made to understand his place, so Achilles will inevitably suffer the effects of the natural order reasserting itself in the face of his disavowal. Achilles will be hurt. The narrative from Book Eleven through Book Seventeen brings us the consequences of the quarrel as they arise separately and as they come together. The Greeks are driven back; Patroklos is finally killed.

Achilles' comparison of Patroklos to a clinging child at the beginning of the sixteenth book marks him as doomed when once he proceeds to arm himself in Achilles' equipment. He is the lesser man. In assuming the armor he symbolically dares deeds that he is not able to accomplish. Much earlier Nestor had told Patroklos that while Achilles was nobler and stronger, Patroklos' strength lay in advising his friend, because he was the older. Now counsel fails Patroklos, because he is not thinking; he acts out of pity for the retreating and exhausted Greeks. Achilles, unthinking too, yields to the entreaty because of his affection and love for Patroklos, emotions which the comparison mentioned above also implies. These emotions which obscure the potential danger are simply outward manifestations of the episode's fatal quality. The situation seems ready for crisis when Achilles can say so strangely: "But we will let these things [his quarrel with Agamemnon] be as having happened earlier. Somehow it was not meant that I was to go on being angry forever in my heart . . ." (16.60*f*).

Patroklos' doom is reinforced by the fairy tale motif of the fatal injunction: as Cinderella must return before midnight, so Patroklos must now proceed to the very walls of Troy. The poet diminishes the supernatural quality by introducing the realities of Achilles' potential jealousy should Patroklos gain the walls and thereby too much glory. Yet the injunction together with the wearing of Achilles' armor sends Patroklos out enchanted, and so, doomed. Homer has well contrived the grandeur of Patroklos' scene, although in several ways it is formally a rehearsal of Hektor's death. The universe sorrows when Patroklos kills Sarpedon and Zeus sheds tears of blood for his son. Moments before Zeus considers saving Sarpedon from his death. Hera argues with him and suddenly the world is motionless as the natural rhythm of the universe (fate) is stayed in anticipation of chance (Zeus' will).

The poet continually shows his affection for Patroklos: he calls out to him when he begins fighting wildly and fiercely in general combat for the last time. He calls out to him again when Patroklos has gone too far. The sun has begun to set, a cosmic darkness surrounds, the hero has rushed forth three times—the magical enchanted three attempts of fairy tales—and tries a fourth. And a god strikes him down.

Again the poet calls out to him as Patroklos speaks his dying words, in a speech that is marvelously clear-eyed. Patroklos sees suddenly and accurately all that has happened. "Baleful fate and the son of Leto killed me, of men it was Euphorbos. But you were only the third who struck me down," he says to Hektor (16.849 f). When he prophesies Hektor's death, Hektor's optimism seems foolish, juxtaposed to all that Patroklos has said. Hektor is fooled here as Achilles is never fooled when his own death is prophesied. But then, Achilles has prior knowledge.

The ninth book showed one side of Patroklos' personality—namely his devotion and loyalty to Achilles. In that episode he never spoke; he seemed Achilles' alter ego. The poet has contrived in describing Patroklos' death to make him suddenly an importantly sympathetic figure. His initial concern for the dying Greeks, the emotional warmth in the portrayal of his relationship to Achilles, the enchanted and doomed manner in which he rides forth to this battle have given him a sympathetic and melancholic stature. The poet achieves the greatest empathetic response in the audience by continually calling out to Patroklos; he becomes an unknowing victim whom we wish to recall. Suddenly, therefore, he becomes important and necessary to the audience. The poet has achieved for us the revelation that will take place in Achilles' heart when he learns of Patroklos' death.

When Thetis and the Nereids come to mourn the dead Patroklos in the eighteenth book, their lamentation is out of all proportion. As I remarked in the first chapter, Homer very likely took many elements from a description of the death of Achilles in another epic. The source is irrelevant.

Thetis laments her son; she holds his head in her hands. As Homer says later: "The women cried over [the body of Patroklos], they cried for Patroklos as an excuse; in reality each lamented her own misfortune" (*Iliad* 19.301 *f*).

So here Thetis begins a dirge for Achilles. His death, long since anticipated, becomes a kind of fact, although it occurs beyond the scope of the *Iliad's* story. Patroklos' death, however, motivates Achilles to return to battle, and ultimately to his death. Thetis, therefore, can mourn him as a doomed man, and his actions can henceforth be seen as those of a doomed, or indeed, dead man. Achilles is now free; the problem (of whether to live unimportantly or to die gloriously) he faced in the ninth book is resolved. He has found death and is no longer paralyzed into inactivity. He had masked the desolation he experienced when he withdrew from the army, the emptiness filled by his anger and hot resentment of Agamemnon. But the loss of Patroklos reveals a more profound emptiness. The hate has also lost its meaning. His love for Patroklos in sum shaped his life. Now he is gone, and Achilles will die; his life will have had no meaning. He despairs and suffers anguish now as ferociously as he once waged war or once hated Agamemnon. The distinguishing mark of Achilles throughout is his superabundant vitality. As Agamemnon said of him at the start of the quarrel: "This man wishes to be superior to all other men" (*Iliad* 1.287).

In Achilles this is no simple political desire. He wants all things, to be all things, to surpass all men, to break through the limitations of natural man, so as to realize himself. He grieves deeply for Patroklos and for the emptiness that once again appears in his life, as it appeared before when the glitter of a hero's triumph was taken from him by an unfeeling overlord. From this moment on until Priam comes to him he will fill the vacuum that he suffers with monstrous rage coming from resentment of the universe. He will be filled with cosmic fury and madness.

Achilles pours forth this rage upon the Trojans and

upon the natural world itself as he fights the river. Homer
has contrived a surrealistic *aristeia* that commences normally in the high style, when Athene stirs Achilles to arm
for battle. No detail of a hero's entry into battle is
omitted: the divine attendant, the assembling host, the
glittering armor, the martial glance of the warrior, all in a
description set off with apposite similes. The passage
builds to a crescendo as he mounts his chariot and calls
out to his horses, ordering them to bring him safely back
to camp. Then strangely enough the edge of this golden
panoply is lifted to see the melancholic reality behind, as
his horse, Xanthos, answers him—a hint of the surreal to
come—to say that they cannot ward off his fated death.
Achilles' reply to the horse is simple. The very oddness of
a colloquy with a horse isolates the moment from the preceding description of glory. Achilles, the man, not the hero,
speaks and he says in a few words what Hektor had said to
Andromache at their last meeting.

> "Xanthos, why are you prophesying my death?
> You really needn't. I know full well even myself that
> my doom is to die here, far from my father and
> mother. Nevertheless I will not stop fighting until
> I have given the Trojans their fill of war." (19.420 *ff*)

Like Hektor, he knows that death will shortly nullify his
actions. Yet life, while it is there, is to be lived in terms of
these actions. Achilles is lonely here, as Hektor was not.
When he said good-by to Andromache he was husband,
father, son, defender of a city and of civilized life. To
Hektor's valor there was considerable substance. The
death of Patroklos has taken this substance from Achilles.
Achilles has accepted again the form of his life but he has
not found its substance.

The entire battle narrative far transcends reality to de-
pict a wild, feverish, disordered Achilles who is lusting to
fill the vacuum. He kills Trojans insatiably. One does not
sense his engaging a series of Trojan heroes separately, but

rather plunging and skewering numbers on his spear. The
glut of battle is in the choking river. Nightmare begins as
the river accosts Achilles himself. Stranger still, throughout
all of this the gods come down to war in typical Homeric
battle fashion. From the first Homer insists that all the
gods are present, even to every nymph. The battle then is
truly cosmic. God, man, and all of nature are engaged.
The gods assemble in mock catalogue style and descend to
the earthly fray. Throughout the fight their style of battling is wildly ridiculous. Even when the standard formulae
are employed the effect is far different. When Ares is
knocked down by Athene, he falls in the typical fashion
of the vanquished, only far greater, but then Athene
laughs.

I am not sure what Homer means by the laugh, whether
he mocks the ritual of battle. Has he mounted his gods in
this episode to be a kind of carnival mirror of humanity
that distorts and makes grotesque man's action? Or is the
commentary, rather, on god? Achilles fights throughout
this episode in anguish. His frenzy stems from desperation,
but also from a valiant and courageous desire to force sense
into his life. Over against this harrowed but determined
man, Homer has set a group of ridiculous gods who act as
humans. Yet, it is absurd, because, though gods, they cannot affect divine events. They are impotent, because again
they have no way of measuring or testing their lives or
their living. It is the dilemma of immortality.

Homer lays bare Achilles' mood in the lengthy description of his encounter with Lykaon. The boy, son of Priam,
previously captured by Achilles and ransomed, returned to
Troy only twelve days earlier, pleads for his life. Homer
describes him in every way as young, fresh, and innocent,
contrasting sharply with Achilles' slightly mocking tone
that comes out dull and tired. The boy speaks of his
family, he speaks in genealogies. To this Achilles says:

But, my friend, you die too; now why carry on so?

Patroklos also died, and he was a far better man than
you. Can't you see how tall and handsome I am? I am
the son of a good father, and a goddess mother gave
me birth. But just the same, you know, death and
powerful fate are waiting for me. (21.106 *ff*)

In this episode there had been a markedly large number
of genealogies. Aineias delivers his at great length and
Achilles also gives one toward the end. Shorter genealogical histories occur, as, for instance, when Lykaon talks of
his parentage. The world of order, of connection, of human
care and human bonds can be seen in these histories of
families, friends and relations. The fighting in this episode
more than ever seems antithetical to this human fabric,
and Achilles' response to Lykaon grows out of the poet's
use of a genealogical motif. Patroklos' death has nullified
human relations for Achilles. Again the dying Patroklos is
symbol of death, itself, and Achilles seems to be fighting
still against its inexorable finality. The speech to Lykaon
shows that underlying all this is Achilles' sense of isolation.

Between Thetis' stylized keening and the exalted hys-
terics of the battle that I have just described, the poet introduces two scenes that return us to the normal rhythm
of human existence. One is an abstraction of normal human existence—the description of Achilles' new shield. The
other is a dramatization of this normalcy—the formal reconciliation of Agamemnon and Achilles.

The poetic description of material objects of art is one
of the ancient world's favorite literary ornaments. It is
called *ekphrasis*. What Homer has done here, however, is
to idealize such a description, moving beyond any real
shield to make a statement about existence. He manages
to include most of the basic antitheses in the human situation: the permanent and the fleeting, the beautiful and
the ugly, the serene and the excited, the ideal and the real,
war and peace, the finite world and infinite heaven. He
begins with the rim, depicting Ocean that stands next to

the universe, then moves down to the specifics of two cities, one at peace, one at war. In the former there is a scene of marriage, symbol of union and conciliation, celebrated in music and dancing. There is also depicted the reconciliation of a quarrel through judgment and good speaking. In the other a slaughter by ambush takes place. Hate, Confusion, and Death are the leaders, the very antithesis of the civilized arts—music, dancing, oratory—through which in the first city order and continuity exist. Order continues to be celebrated in the scene of the plowing by rows where the plowsman receives wine, a symbol of fertility, as his reward. Workers are depicted working in unison, in rhythm, a king watching over them. Each to his appointed task, hierarchy prevails. The reward is again fertile harvest. The poet shows grapes ripe for the plucking, young people present, and again singing. Order, fertility, the arts of civilization are praised again. Then occurs a refrain of the ambush on a natural level; lions attack the herds and the sheep. The lion image recalls the common battle similes. We are briefly reminded of the *Iliad's* war to which shortly we shall return. The description then closes with dancing; creative joy is the final element of the description.

Amid the carnage of the battlefield Homer has often offered a vision of another world in the brief biographies of the fallen, through the similes, and now here in what is a summation of their meaning. The description gives us respite from the violent emotion of the preceding, at the same time providing a focus or context in which to place the succeeding war scenes. Achilles' mayhem is made more insane set against this shield. More important, the shield represents what the city of Troy contains. When Hektor dies shortly hereafter, his death is prelude to the death of Troy. Troy's end is a constant melancholy theme in the *Iliad,* now intensified. The glorious return of Achilles and, later, his heightened understanding is balanced against the sorrow of the dying civilization of Troy.

The scene of reconciliation between Agamemnon and

Achilles formally closes the quarrel. We are again back at the point where the *Iliad* began except that Achilles is no longer the same man. His personality is the same, great-spirited, impetuous, impatient with his humanness and the external restrictions of this world. He has changed, how-ever, because he has experienced new things, and he has acted upon that experience. Agamemnon makes the amends, offering an account of his behavior that lays re-sponsibility upon Zeus, Destiny, and the Erinyes. He speaks long about the supernatural force of Delusion. Vain and insecure, he will as a great leader not admit his error before the army assembly so simply as he did before his intimates earlier. Rather he develops an elaborate philo-sophical account of the powers of Delusion. Delusion is that force in the universe which seduces or leads on an otherwise sensible man into a course of action which will have undesirable consequences. Delusion wars against com-mon sense and innate moral instincts. Delusion finds an opening when man is more than usually secure and he has relaxed the stays and props to his will. Delusion makes him stumble. One of the fundamental strengths of the *Iliad* is the poet's confusion—deliberate or innocent—over the relative importance of fate and chance in human existence. Human activity is therefore neither enslaved obedience to destiny's rule nor random caprice. Zeus, the ruler of men and gods and arbiter of the universe, is in some way subject to fate, so man can act and yet must expect some control over his actions. The *Iliad* seems to extend the fundamental premise that moral error is externally in-duced. Man is led astray, except perhaps specifically in the case of Paris, whom Hektor implies knew exactly what transgressions he was making. Error is an aspect of evil, whose workings in this world are described by Achilles at the close of the *Iliad*. There are two jars, he says, one filled with evil, one with good. Zeus takes from the jar of evil sometimes mixing in the good and scatters at random. That is man's lot, much evil, less good, arbitrarily received.

A bleak account, but the natural background to Achilles' career throughout the *Iliad.* The search for meaning in existence must take place in the here and now if the supernatural realm can offer so little. Agamemnon's speech in the nineteenth book and Achilles' in the twenty-fourth help to correct any subconscious Christian impulses to see Achilles' behavior in the ninth book as a sin that is punished by Patroklos' death in the sixteenth. Rather, Achilles better resembles King Lear who, godlike, lets the hierarchical world loose and suffers the consequences.

The wise Odysseus makes the conciliation complete in all aspects. He forces Achilles in this scene to accept human attitudes and values. The great hero, demoniacally moved by a frenzy of anguish, is now possessed by a compulsive need to play out his life in fighting. Once he has accepted this objective he proceeds single-mindedly, again inhumanly. Achilles must formally accept gifts from Agamemnon before the entire army. In this way he acknowledges and accepts the framework men have created to make society exist. Specifically he re-enters the heroic world, the ambience of prizes, honor, and glory that gives him his identity. Furthermore, Achilles must eat and allow the army to eat before he returns to the fight. He argues that food is nothing to him, only blood, slaughter, and the groaning of men. The same single-mindedness moves him to say earlier that gifts meant nothing to him, set against the fact of his death.

Odysseus' speech in answer is the classic statement on survival. The character of Odysseus as he appears in the *Odyssey* comes through strongly here. "There is no way the Achaians can mourn Patroklos with their belly," he says (19.225). The dead are dead and life is all. Odysseus tries to show Achilles the way to consecrate life, but Achilles is not ready to yield yet. Achilles' anger against Agamemnon and the Greeks, turned to anger against dying without having been anything in life, is ultimately a refusal to be human. Here Achilles' denial of bodily needs is another side of that refusal. The hero who is god-marked, god-loved must meet stronger demands. As Paris once says of his god-given beauty that has caused such ruin: "The glorious gifts of the gods are not to be thrown away, you know, whatever gifts they may happen to give, although no one willingly would ever take them" (*Iliad* 3.65 *f*).

Man must die, man is frail, but the god-marked hero bears the necessity to escape the limits, for he has the energies that make the limitations all but impossible. This is the urgency that drives Achilles when he upsets the human scheme by isolating himself in a monumental rage. He attempts in this fashion to escape submission, reason, and compassion—all symbols of man's humanity. Patroklos' death forces sorrow and love upon him. But he will war with the world once more in the grotesque and fabulous battle soon to take place. And when he has done with what is almost orgy, he will fight with Hektor, hero confronting hero, in a duel scene that sums up all that is heroic, all that is grand, all that is tragic in war.

The *Iliad* centers upon the fortunes of the Achaian forces, and upon Achilles, yet the poet never forgets the Trojans. He has contrived some of his best scenes with the Trojans. Because they show women, children, and old men, they are memorable and appealing scenes. These are the constituents of human existence that care for that existence and wish to perpetuate it, especially, of course, the women. Insofar as the fighting can be understood as some kind of elemental symbol of existence itself, then the Greeks are totally sympathetic. The motives for the fighting *qua* fighting, however, are so perilously removed that the war almost verges on nonsense or the meaningless. The rape of Helen does not always hold up as satisfactory cause for such a war. The Trojans, on the contrary, are fighting for a way of life, a past, a future, every kind of security as well as for their very lives. They are surrounded and doomed, and they command considerable sympathy.

Homer shows them in their city only in the third, sixth, twenty-second, and twenty-fourth books. In brief sketches he manages to portray them so that they are never forgotten.

The poet keeps in view the two different worlds of Troy. The one is Helen and Paris; the other is Hektor, Andromache, Hecuba, and Priam. Our first portrait of Troy is the former, in the third book. We have discussed Helen elsewhere. In short, she is so beautiful as to make the fathers of the city, who have lost numerous sons in these ten years, accept the war as a reasonable consequence of her stolen beauty. She is conscious of her blame in this war; she hates herself for it. Paris she has grown to find weak and uninteresting. Yet she is the victim of Aphrodite. The goddess of love has in a sense created her and if she were to desert her, she could destroy her as well. As a beautiful adulteress, Helen already faces the hostility of everyone except Hektor and Priam. So it is at the end of the third book, filled with self-contempt and contempt for Paris, she nevertheless goes to make love with him. This is the peculiar solitary confinement for those who find their meaning in sexual intercourse. Paris is the male version of Helen. Obviously both handsome and sexually astute, he only, of all the heroes, at times appears to be amused or frivolous on the field of battle, and this is indicative of his basically sexual nature, a nature that strives to create rather than destroy. Like Helen he is a victim. In the lines quoted earlier he tells Hektor that those whom the gods have favored cannot cast off their gifts. Paris uses them instead and the poet has given us a sense of this in the magnificent simile of the horse at the end of Book Six, which is the heroism of Paris.

Paris and Helen help to create the feeling that Troy is doomed, a motif in the saga not otherwise overmuch exploited in the *Iliad.* The Trojan King Laomedon cheated out of their pay the gods who helped build Troy's walls. The princely Trojan boy Ganymede was so beautiful that

Zeus, lusting after him, snatched him up to Olympos to
have as his cupbearer; Paris incurred the enmity of Hera
and Athene by awarding the judgment of beauty to
Aphrodite. These are all facets of Troy's past. They are
expressed in the situation of Paris and Helen. Frivolity,
irresponsibility, enchantment, destiny—these are the components of their story. They are the cancer in Troy's side.
Yet, hardest of all, they cannot be truly hated; they are
too beautiful.

The sixth book develops the other view of Troy as counterpart to the feeling of weakness and inherent doom that
the third book suggested. Homer rather awkwardly moves
Hektor from the field of battle to Troy in order to achieve
this scene. Homer has the priest Helenos send Hektor to
Troy on an errand any minor figure might have done. The
interval of time that it takes him is filled with the formal
and static meeting of Glaukos and Diomedes. Even
here, however, one feels that Homer's instinct was right,
because there is a steady progression of feeling that offers
a commentary on the events. The sixth book moves from
the longish description of Agamemnon killing Adrestos,
who had pleaded to have his life spared, through the meeting of Glaukos and Diomedes to the farewell scene between Hektor and Andromache. The movement is from
war's impersonal killing to reconciliation to compassion.

The elements of the scene at Troy in the sixth book are
from civilization: mother, wife, son; the hospitality in offering a glass of wine; the procession to a shrine; affectionate laughter; a tearful baby. Hektor's wife, Andromache, is
characterized here briefly. She appears only two other
times in the *Iliad*, to lament her dead husband in the
twenty-second and the twenty-fourth books. Each speech is
severely functional. Here she describes herself as bereft
of parents, destitute of family by the fortunes of war, totally dependent upon her husband. In the other speeches
she projects the grim life of her orphaned boy Astyanax
and her own widowhood. Andromache has no personality

in the *Iliad,* nor do any of the other women. There are no
subtle characteristics that mark them as feminine, except
perhaps for Helen. Andromache gives stock speeches,
she is alternately typical wife, typical mother, typical
widow. Hers is the lamentation for the destruction and
desolation that war brings to a family. The entire fabric
is shattered, mother-child, father-child, husband-wife,
brother-sister. None of her speeches springs from the particular dynamics of the dramatic moment. They are idealized and abstracted, delivered, one senses, almost as rhetorical set pieces. Yet they, like the description of Achilles'
shield, highlight the context of the war in a most important
way. Unlike the shield description, they are passionate, an
emotional plea for human life.

Hektor is described in these Trojan scenes through his
relationship to the women, again a mark of his civilized
nature. The poet achieves the delineation in two ways.
In the sixth book a conception of Hektor comes out
through the workings of the story. At the end of the *Iliad*
when the same three women, Andromache, Hecuba, and
Helen cry over his body, the lamentation consists of three
formal memorials to him. The man whom these two
scenes create is consistent. Here in the sixth book he won't
take the wine his mother offers him because it would be
impious for him to take wine with bloody hands. Furthermore it would weaken him when he must return to the
battle. He declines to stay and talk with Helen because he
must hasten back to the battle, and he wants to see his
family. He is ever courteous, thoughtful, and kind, as
Helen remarks at the very last of the *Iliad,* but as first
described by Paris, he is hard and single-minded. The in-
terview between Andromache and Hektor is kept from being maudlin by subtle touches. Andromache shows a
woman's typical determination to direct her husband on
matters she does not understand. He replies to her truly
pathetic and lonely speech in an exceedingly *thoughtful*
fashion. The scene ends with their mature humor at their

infant son's fright. The moment is perhaps the single most moving in the *Iliad* because it alone shows two people involved in a loving relationship with each other.

This is Hektor's farewell to Andromache, Homer never shows them meeting again. Hektor knows he is doomed. He can only meet death, not agonize over it as Achilles will do. Hektor is earnest, sincere, and honest, qualities which he displays again in the twenty-second book when he is so marvelously introspective as he awaits the onrush of Achilles. Whereas Achilles is the object of universal admiration, it is respect that Hektor receives from Helen, Andromache, Paris, and especially Zeus. He has no illusions; his world is going and he will go with it, acting as the code demands. As he says to Andromache in the beginning of his reply to her, "I would feel shame if I were to avoid battle" (6.441 *ff*). Virgil seems to have tried to model Aeneas to a large extent upon Hektor, that is, civilization's defender. Although Aeneas seems at times as world-weary, he is not, however, so humane. On the other hand, in comparison with Achilles, Hektor seems the lesser figure, first because the story centers on Achilles' situation, but, then, because Hektor somewhat stolidly accepts what fate or life has to offer, whereas Achilles continually reacts to it. The heroic encounter with life is deep in Achilles, far transcending the field of battle. There lies eternal glory. When Achilles kills Hektor in the twenty-second book the sorrow we feel is not mixed with any sense of miscarriage.

It is fated that Achilles kill Hektor and that Troy thereby fall. The clumsiness that a notion of overriding destiny brings to the story is lightened by the sense that Troy in her weakness and folly has willed destruction upon herself. The poet reminds us of Paris and Helen enough to keep that motif alive. More specifically, Hektor has chosen to disregard good advice when he decides to stay outside the walls (which, typically, he later on realizes). During the episode of the battle for the Achaian wall the poet several times introduces Hektor's comrade Poulydamas, who offers sound strategic advice that Hektor immediately follows. Then fatally, when Poulydamas urges retreat in the face of the now rampaging Achilles, Hektor rejects this. All too humanly, Hektor is tired and desperate after ten years of war. As he says, he is tired of being cornered, and the gold (time) is running out. Hektor can claim that the war god is impartial so that he, Hektor, will stand to fight Achilles. Is this perhaps another way of saying that death is neutral and therefore nothing? In the face of death, then, Hektor will fight for the glory of winning. There is no other way to define his living, and going behind the walls as Poulydamas suggests would deny this essential neutrality: that life is in the living of it, not the fleeing of it. On a simple narrative level, of course, as Homer reminds us, Hektor is being foolish.

The twenty-second book has no spatial reality; it is surrealistic: there is no true distance between the onrushing Achilles, Hektor waiting at the gate, Priam and Hecuba on the wall, and our participation in these events. Furthermore, when the two heroes race around the walls the narrator lets us look on from a distance and brings us in close in a breathless way. Like a Greek vase painting where each element is given equal spatial expression, the episode has little sense of perspective. Achilles charging, Priam calling, Hektor waiting, the two men running, the city's turrets crowded with spectators, the Achaian army watching—all are immediately present in the scene. The poet has formally organized the episode. He begins with Priam and Hecuba entreating their son—the first in a long speech, the second briefly. He reverses the proportions at the end with Hecuba's short lamentation preceding Andromache's lengthy one. The episode opens and closes with speeches of bereavement, the two worst kinds to a Greek mind: the aged father bereft of children and the orphaned son. As in certain other episodes involving Achilles we find here much more stylization.

Achilles comes on as the dog star, feverish, glittering,

unavoidable, evil. He comes from a great distance, swooping down, it seems—in truth, Hektor's doom. Hektor is compared to a snake in his hole waiting for a passing man. The basic sense of the comparisons continues in the next two similes, Achilles, airborne as a falcon, Hektor a fawn flushed from his hiding place. From the start the contest is shown to be tragically and ironically unequal. After the fashion of every heroic duel, Hektor formally awaits the attack. His parents call from the wall, yet still he waits. Then Homer suddenly shows again why he is called "the divine poet." He breaks through the careful, formal mode of exposition with a soliloquy by Hektor that reveals the human being. Shame, sorrow, fear, and finally simple courage command his thoughts in succession (22.99 ff):
"I'm too ashamed to go in now. What a fool I was. Well, let the issue be decided one way or the other." Then, almost in delirium, "Why don't I put down my spear and go up to him and tell him he can take Helen, everything, back." And in the end, wistfully, "There's no way I can flirt with him now, playing peekaboo from a rock or tree. Better to start the fight." In paraphrase, these are the thoughts that cross his mind. The last, an image from the days of peacetime, like several other moments in this episode, presents the gentle, civilized Hektor, as well as sharply contrasting the present moment of war with peace.

The speeches of Priam and Hecuba just before this are typical parental entreaties. Hecuba bares her breast and Priam refers to his genitals. But Priam's speech goes beyond to enumerate the sons he has lost, to describe the evils yet to be visited upon Troy. Even his environment will turn against him when the house dogs will despoil his corpse. The speech is a summation of Troy's fall that paces Hektor's own defeat. The poet has made the death of Hektor a personal tragedy, but he also sees it as humanity's catastrophe as well.

The poetry describing the chase about the wall is tightly organized. Twice there are similes (22.139 ff, 189 ff), each followed by a description of the action they symbolize. Each time thereafter the poet reveals Olympos where Zeus the most impartial of gods sorrows for Hektor. And each time his inclination to protect the Trojan is checked, first by Athene, then most awfully by the scales of fate, after Hektor has circled the walls three times and begins the magical fourth turn. The simile of the man haunted with a nightmare of an insecure flight shows the delirium in which Hektor moves. Twice visions of peacetime are conjured up. Homer describes in simile a racing contest on the occasion of a great man's funeral games. Another time as Hektor runs past two springs, Homer evokes the years when Trojan women washed the clothes there, "in the time of peace, before the sons of the Achaians came" (22.156). Hektor, the defender of city and civilization, runs past reminiscences of that civilization.

Nowhere in the *Iliad* does Homer sentimentalize his story. The theme is war, which in turn means killing. Homer accepts this always as the natural rhythm of his narrative. Death, being inevitable is neither good nor bad. Life, on the contrary, is a blessing; leaving it is sad. Which is to say, life is always to be preferred. They who would like to believe that Homer glorifies death are sentimental. Over and over he contrasts the wastage and the sorrow of war with the beauty and humanity of peace. He simply accepts war as natural. Nowhere is this better demonstrated than during the extremely emotional description of Hektor's mad, sad flight to his death. Objectively, almost proselike, and, I am sure, without irony, Homer sings:

> There they ran, one fleeing, and one in pursuit. A noble man fled in front, but a far greater man pursued him, swiftly, since they were not contesting for a piece of hide, nor for a sacrificial animal, which are prizes for men who are swift of foot; no, they ran for the soul of Hektor, the tamer of horses. (22.157 *ff*)

Andromache's speech that concludes this episode might equally have been sentimentalized. As she begins, it is immediately one of the saddest moments in literature, but it is saved from bathos and the maudlin by her clear-eyed sensibility throughout. Her descriptions of dependency and orphanage keep the audience at one remove, exactly as Athenian tragedy does. The Greek genius for verbalizing and externalizing psychic pain is nowhere better captured than here. As so frequently in the *Iliad*, the final note is one of waste.

> But in the halls lie clothing, you know, delicate and fair, made by women's hands. But I shall burn these, all of them, you know, in the burning fire, since they won't be any use to you, because you won't lie in them, but they were to be an honor from the Trojan men and women. (22.510 *ff*)

The Greeks had a completely different understanding of conclusion than our own. The twenty-second book moved through the most intense dramatic crisis, to which any aftermath is difficult. Something so ritualized and formal as Patroklos' funeral and the attendant celebration is particularly hard for us to comprehend after the emotion and high drama of Hektor's death. Nonetheless several ends are served. For one, the death of Patroklos is now accommodated into the human scheme of things. The funeral removes him formally and socially as well as offering his spirit the necessary *rites de passage*. The funeral games that follow serve to present, as in a theatrical finale, the major Achaian figures of the narrative. At the same time the poet shows Achilles completely at home once again in the heroic world he had abandoned in the first book. He moves among his fellow Greeks sure of his stature and function. But Homer does not leave us with the funeral games. Formally they correspond to the catalogues at the close of the second book. As the poet began his poem by moving immediately into the drama before the Catalogue, so he closes it now by offering another close glimpse of some of the participants after the games. This bow to structural symmetry at the same time allows him to offer another kind of aftermath, that is, the final purgation of the soul of Achilles. Having first imposed this psychological drama upon what must have been a tried and true heroic narrative he now manages to resolve each of the issues earlier raised and still remain true to an underlying scheme.

Though Achilles now moves among his peers, he is in fact still detached. His relentless wrath of the earlier books is now given over to relentless sorrow and fury. As Apollo says, it is equally bad. Even the gods, who have no dimension to their existence, who cannot die, know how to pity, can empathize with man's mortality. But Achilles cannot yet accept humanity. He is still striving for absolutes, some absolute emotional position that will create at least the sense of immortality. To be compromised is to be finite. The antithesis to that for which he strives is yielding, and pity, yet through the alchemy of Priam's presence, he is brought to pity. When Thetis tells him to return Hektor's body, he answers abruptly: "So be it; whoever brings ransom, let him take the body" (24.139).

The scene that ensues is presided over by Hermes, the god charged with the leading of the souls of the dead into the underworld. Ostensibly waiting for Hektor, he is ready for old Priam and Achilles as well. The mood of this final episode is subdued, yet again the two main participants are strong men throughout their grief. Priam bitterly attacks the inadequacy of his living sons and fights with his tough old queen, Hecuba. Achilles orders Hektor's body to be prepared out of sight of the old man so that he won't be put in the position of killing him, should Priam grow violent. The power of life animates both these great men, although they are overcome with sorrow.

The death of Hektor has dashed Priam's world to pieces. As the poet of the *Iliad* has so many times insisted, in a meaningless world, we make meaning in the action of our living. The old king, who has lost his future and his past in the destruction of his family, approaches the brooding Achilles. "Coming close to Achilles, with his hands he grasped Achilles' knees and kissed his hands, the terrible hands, the man-slaying hands which had killed for him his many sons" (24.477 ff).

This final gesture of conciliation leads Achilles to think of his father's life and of his own, of the accommodation that mortal man must make, given the random and arbitrary shower of evil or good mixed with evil that an indifferent Zeus disposes. In the context of such irrational evil Priam has performed for Achilles the sane and healing act. Ironically the old man is then too overcome with his grief to continue—ironically, because the moment parallels Achilles' despair when Patroklos has died. The young man tells the old Trojan king the story of Niobe who went on to eat after the cruel heaven sent death to her children. Achilles is now ready to accept the dimensions of human existence that Odysseus outlined for him after his reconciliation with Agamemnon. The elements of the story that Homer had announced in his opening phrases have now all been developed. Propriety, a sense of the completeness of things, causes the poet yet to attend to Hektor. The Trojans lament all that he was as a person, his body they commit to the ceremonial flames. As Homer says simply, ending this long and complex story, truly without beginning or end, or even with limited ramifications, "Thus they buried horse-taming Hektor."

Chapter V

THE ODYSSEY

You stubborn man, full of so many plans, deceits,
not even in your own land have you any intention
of stopping your cheating, your lying words,
which you know you love from the bottom of your heart.
                    Athene to Odysseus, *Odyssey* 13.293–295

The *Odyssey* is quite a different work from the *Iliad*.
The difference does not lie, however, in the mechanics of
the lines. The impression is that two poets created these
poems, both using a common style. The remarkable thing
is that these two poems can be so personal and so different,
and yet the poetic language so similar. Clearly the oral
poetic technique was formidable, as it took hold of the
poet. The opening invocation to the Muse is real, for the
Muse (the epic formulary style) does possess the poet.

Structurally the *Odyssey* divides into three parts. The
first four books constitute one section, commonly called
the Telemachia, which describe Telemachos' conflict with
his mother's suitors, his general impotence, and his travels.
The second section, Odysseus' adventures before returning
to Ithaka, goes from the fifth into the twelfth book. From
the thirteenth until the end he is back at Ithaka winning
his house and holdings away from the suitors. The structure of the story in the *Odyssey* is considerably more complex than that in the *Iliad*. The action of the latter is

more or less continuous. Apart from the sense of pause that the arrival of night and attendant sleep give to narrative, action in the *Iliad* proceeds almost without any sense of interruption. The poet of the *Odyssey*, on the other hand, has set his narrative within three distinct frames, which strike one's consciousness. For example, the *Odyssey* opens with a council of the gods discussing the hero's fate. It is arranged that Athene will prod Telemachos at Ithaka and Hermes will speak to Kalypso on the island of Ogygia. Athene accomplishes her task in the first book; its consequences occupy the next three. Then, logically, we move to see what Hermes is doing. Homer in the fifth book again introduces a council of the gods virtually repeating their earlier ideas, so returning us to the point in time when Athene set off for Ithaka. Simultaneous action in widely separated places is made to happen sequentially—the epic technique knows no other way—but the reappearance of the Olympic council establishes the fifth book as the beginning of something different. The demarcation which this second formal introduction creates is furthered by the way in which the fourth book is concluded. After describing the preparations for a second feast at Menelaos' palace at Sparta, the poet, abruptly, in a manner unique to either poem, begins a description of the suitors at Ithaka. His manner is awkward, for the suitors' plot against Telemachos could more easily have been planned as the boy sails out of Ithaka at the end of the second book. The poet, however, wishes to return to the opening ideas of the narrative in Book One, namely, the roistering suitors and the grieving Penelope. Instead of sparing himself an awkward transition in the fourth book, he clearly wants this episode to terminate the description of Telemachos' coming of age.

In a less bold manner he has created a transition between the travel adventures and the homecoming in the early part of the thirteenth book. Odysseus is transported from Scheria, the very much fairy tale island of the Phaia-

cians, to Ithaka on a Phaiacian boat, in which he rides fast
asleep. Hermes going to Ogygia was the introduction to
fabulous adventures as this boat ride is their conclusion.
The never-never land of Scheria does not impinge upon
the reality that Ithaka represents because the sleeping hero
does not consciously pass from the one to the other. The
poet makes the sense of separation more complete by including the story of the transformation of the boat and
crew into rock as it approaches home again. Upon seeing
this, King Alkinoos says that they shall never again trans-
port strangers. In other words, the fairy tale Phaiacians
will not appear in the normal world again. The third section of the *Odyssey* is now returned to the familiar context
of human action.

The subject matter of the *Odyssey* is also unlike the
Iliad. The latter is saga on the large scale, interspersed by
dramatic moments that are considerably more intimate.
Nevertheless, many of these moments too are almost objectively formal and enlarged as, for instance, the arrival
and lamentation of Thetis at the death of Patroklos. The
foreground in the *Iliad* is again in keeping with the saga
world, almost invariably on a broad scale. Gods look down
from on high, the Trojans look from the battlements, the
Greeks gaze across the battlefield, men are marshaled in
vast numbers. Elements in the *Iliad* that seem to be unlike
saga are few. The sophisticated humorous presentation of
the divine world, the strange, almost hallucinatory behavior of the river fighting Achilles, these seem to be the
poet's very personal adaptation of his material, but still
material that was originally part of saga. The origins of
the *Odyssey,* on the contrary, seem far more diverse.
While there is a strong saga element, definite fairy tale
motifs appear in the poem, and parts, as well, seem un-
traditional, personally created, that which we would call
fiction.

When the heroes who fought at Troy are described in
the *Odyssey* we are clearly back in the saga world. The de-

scription of Achilles' funeral, for example, in the twenty-fourth book was very likely a commonplace of high heroic epic. But the most conspicuous theme from saga is that of Return. Nestor and Menelaos between them describe the homecoming of several of the major figures from the *Iliad*. Clearly episodes relating the return of a hero were as common as the *aristeiai* describing their triumphs in battle. The story of homecoming had a name: *nostos*. The several *nostoi* are a leitmotiv throughout the *Odyssey* which is over-all a *nostos*, being the return of Odysseus. There is a hint in the *Odyssey* that epics of *nostoi* were currently fashionable. In describing the homecoming of Agamemnon the poet lingers over details that ordinarily an epic poet takes for granted. Indeed, the occasional remark on newness and originality suggest that the particular *nostos* of Odysseus, as our poet conceived it, was perhaps not merely fashionable, but almost novel.

While the theme of homecoming and the particular developments of that theme were very likely traditional, the domestic drama in the palace at Ithaka, as well as the scenes of human involvement at Sparta, Scheria, Ogygia and elsewhere, strike me as being the poet's own invention. Any adequate assessment of originality is, of course, doomed to failure since there is no way to secure sufficient criteria for testing. To what degree anything in either epic is the product of memory cannot be established reliably. The basic elements of the epic language and style everywhere are formulaic and traditional. Beyond this, larger elements seem to have come whole to the poet out of the tradition. One feels that the Catalogue of Ships was memorized verbatim. Battle narrative seems sometimes to be created out of memorized bits of several lines. Episodes such as the funeral games or the farewell between Hektor and Andromache seem more formulaic and objective than, say the Phaiacian games or the conversation between Menelaos and Helen at Sparta. Menelaos' account of his struggle with Proteus seems more a traditional story piece than Telemachos' encounter with Nestor. And so on, and so on . . . mere impressions, nothing more. The poet possesses the technique with which he can create as he chooses. It is hard if not impossible to determine where he follows and where he is not following the tradition. He seems to be creating what looks traditional in the great, climactic battle between Odysseus, Telemachos, and the suitors. For me the passage illustrates the differences between the rehearsal of previous poetry and the development of something new. Modeled rather closely on the battle narrative of the *Iliad,* still the passage is clearly something the poet is making up as he goes along. He has a problem in that few of the suitors have been distinguished with names, and Odysseus, in turn, has only a few men helping him. The poet is therefore short of names, the staple of battle narrative. Instead of names in almost listlike fashion that characterize battle narrative, the poet shows the suitors missing their very few human targets and hitting objects in the room; similarly he calls Odysseus' helpers sometimes by their names, sometimes by their occupations, as, for instance, "the swineherd" or the "herdsman." In short he has created the sense of names, the sense of a series of identified people out of the minimum which he had at hand in the plot. The form of the battle narrative remains and many of the familiar formulae appear, but the scene is personal in a way that saga is not.

The fairy tale element is represented by witches such as Circe, fairy tale people such as the Phaiacians, giants like the Cyclops. In addition structural devices within the poem recall the fairy tale world, such as the return in the nick of time, the playing for time (in Penelope's making the shroud, just like the storyteller in A *Thousand and One Nights*), or the recognition scenes. Odysseus' adventure stories are more obviously fabulous, but fairy tale motives have been introduced throughout the poem.

An epic hero is rather out of place in this context, yet, as has often been discussed, Odysseus is no typical hero.

In the *Iliad* he is consistently portrayed as the most intelligent of the heroes. He is given to philosophic, abstract
language—as when he calms the troops, or pleads with
Achilles. He shows a far more developed awareness of the
human lot throughout the *Iliad*. It verges on cynicism, and
for this reason perhaps he seems to be less like the other
heroes. And perhaps less liked. Agamemnon fairly snaps at
him when he is reviewing the troops, and Achilles assumes
that he will lie or employ some sort of deceit when they
meet in the ninth book. As a thinking man Odysseus very
likely has trouble tolerating formalized heroic behavior.

The *Odyssey* shows Odysseus to be given to lying.
Hardly a straightforward person, he is cunning and always
suspicious. The Homeric heroic mind does not generally
hold these to be virtues. Yet in a world of want and disaster
a developed sense of the hostility of one's environment is
undoubtedly laudable. In any case these characteristics
can be handled as the narrator chooses. Generally they
seem to be talents that Odysseus luckily possesses rather
than perverse tendencies that he ought to suppress. In a
person less heroic and far younger similar traits would suggest mischievousness. Perhaps, in fact, Odysseus is derived
from some such character. Many literatures possess a figure
known technically as the Wily Lad, who continually cheats,
lies, steals, makes fun of his elders, tricks them, and generally is a light-hearted nuisance. Tyl Eulenspiegel is such
a figure. The young god Loki in the *Eddas* is another. Sly
baby Hermes tricking pompous stuffy Apollo in the *Hymn
to Hermes* reveals the Greek version of the same folk type.
Odysseus is definitely a heroic man, and a serious human
being. Yet he has moments in which he appreciates the
ridiculous, when he satirizes his fellow men, when he is
deceitful, that bring to mind this folk figure. Since there
are so many elements of folk poetry in the *Odyssey* there
is nothing strange in believing that Odysseus' special non-
heroic aura in this poem comes from the poet's adaptation
of the personality traits of a Wily Lad. When at times

Odysseus seems to be, or considers himself, a runt, or a victim, a source for this, similar in part to the Wily Lad, is very likely the underdog hero of fairy tales, such as Cinderella. Odysseus, as a fusion of the ambitions and attitudes of both the heroic saga world and the fairy tale world is a formidably complex human being. The poet very naturally is then led to questions of his hero's identity and to hymning his unique humanity.

The poet of the *Odyssey* immediately establishes an ethical and theological basis for his story different from the *Iliad*, one that underlines human will. Since a speech of Zeus introduces this almost in the first lines of the *Odyssey*, and in relatively abstract language, one is tempted to infer that the poet is answering Achilles' speech about the random and irrational distribution of evil. Achilles' speech comes toward the very end of the *Iliad*, as a kind of summation of the process of cause and effect that has governed the action. In essence he says that man is affected from without, and receives good or evil arbitrarily. Zeus says quite the reverse in the *Odyssey*: "I must say, it's really something the way men blame the gods. For they claim that evil comes from us whereas in fact they through their own stupidity and wrongdoing suffer miseries beyond measure" (1.32 *ff*).

Zeus proceeds to offer the example of Aigisthos, who was warned by the gods neither to seduce Klytemnestra nor kill Agamemnon. Yet Aigisthos disregarded their instructions and was himself killed by Orestes.

The emphasis on human responsibility, established so early in the story, changes the main conception of the narrative. Events seem not to be fated as they were in the *Iliad*. (For example, "I know in my heart . . . the day will come when Troy shall perish.") The gods do not enter the human scene to affect the action. Man becomes far more master of his own affairs and suffers more in proportion to his own mishandling of them. The ancients considered the *Iliad* to be far more tragic than the *Odyssey*, and per-

haps for this very reason. The metaphysical dimension is
not so often present in the *Odyssey*. The focus is upon
man, symbolized by the first line: "Sing in me, O Muse,
the *man*, the man of many turns. . . ."

The epithet *polytropos* that I have translated here "of
many turns" has more meaning than a simple phrase can
indicate. It implies someone who can agilely change his
course when cornered, or who has the imagination to proceed in new directions, that is, a man of several personalities. Consistent with the emphasis upon man, this epithet
indicates the concentration on delineating character that
dominates the poet's handling of the narrative. This in
turn springs from the complexity of the story's hero.

Another distinguishing mark of the *Odyssey* is that the
story is created by the repetition of a very limited number
of themes. The theme of arrival and reception, for instance, is often repeated: Athene at Ithaka, Telemachos at
Pylos and Sparta, Hermes at Ogygia, Odysseus at Scheria,
Odysseus (as beggar) several times over at Ithaka—to name
a few of the more important instances. The theme of wandering occurs again and again in stories throughout the
poem. A type woman in a number of manifestations appears throughout. In this manner the poet has much simplified and clarified his narrative; he has also enriched it
by making comparisons and reminiscences easier. The unity
of the *Odyssey* is more conspicuous than that of the *Iliad*,
where the action is far more various.

In creating the Telemachia (the episode of the first four
books in the *Odyssey*) the poet has managed a sophisticated narration. While focusing on Telemachos as the hero
of this small adventure, the poet frames it with a picture
of the suitors so as to join it immediately to the greater
issue of Odysseus' winning his home. The view of the suitors coupled with Telemachos' quest and travels allows contrary ideas of human conduct to be set forth, which in turn
illuminate the hero. For Odysseus, the most fully realized
and complex of all heroes, consistently displays virtuosity

in his own behavior. The poet here has far more interesting narrative techniques than the poet of the *Iliad.* Before Odysseus appears in the story he has been described by a number of people. Through this means we get not only factual material, characterizing material, but also emotional responses to the hero. The poet indulges his taste for the view within a view when he describes Menelaos telling of Proteus revealing the whereabouts of Odysseus. This technique foreshadows the poet's description of Odysseus' description of himself and his adventures. The Proteus story in turn brings the attention back to Odysseus, helping to bridge the Telemachia to the travel stories. Furthermore, all the major Return stories have been narrated in the Telemachia, so that the saga background, especially the saga connection between the *Odyssey* story and the Trojan War, has been established. At the same time Odysseus' essentially heroic nature has been emphasized before we meet him in the fairy tale world.

The Telemachia develops a number of themes that continue throughout the entire poem. The dilemma of Telemachos is one of them. Athene first comes upon him moping, dreaming of his father, powerless among the suitors. This impotent yearning is reflected in Telemachos' halting variation of a young hero's common proud declaration of his parentage. Athene has just identified Telemachos as Odysseus' son by their striking physical similarity, and Telemachos replies: "My mother says I am his son, but, of course, I wouldn't know. For no one really knows his own parentage" (1.215*f*).

One of the questions in the plot is whether Telemachos will mature, will finally be able to gain some mastery over the threatening affairs of his household. Furthermore, the quotation shows, can he ever come to know his father in any real sense? Unless he grows more secure and aware of the heroic world, which his father represents, he will not. So the additional question becomes Telemachos' quest for his own identity. Through understanding his heroic parentage, he will achieve heroic stature himself. The issue calls for a delicate resolution. As I have remarked, heroes generally have impotent fathers. Were their fathers also of heroic temper then that and the added fact of seniority would cancel out the younger men's primacy. Likewise, heroes cannot have heroic sons because a similar collision in supremacy would ensue. Homer very gently brings Telemachos to manhood when it is desirable, but keeps him more adolescent in Odysseus' company. For instance, in the sixteenth book, when Odysseus and Telemachos begin to discuss strategy against the suitors, Telemachos just cannot believe that he and his father have the strength or means to prevail against so many men. The boy still does not know the heroic temper or might; the poet at that moment keeps him the lesser figure. Moments later, however, the young man offers some sage and penetrating objections to Odysseus' plan of discovering the loyalties of the farm hands. For a moment he is his father's equal. The delineation is never strained, as in the case of Aeneas' son Ascanius, whom Virgil cannot resist using as an important symbol for son. Often a very young boy in the story and at other times a budding hero, Ascanius seems like Orphan Annie, perversely young and old at the same time.

The story of Telemachos perhaps comes from a common folk story of the son in search of his lost father whom he ultimately kills as they duel in meeting, unknown to one another, at his land's border. The later Greek epic *Telegonia* is a ridiculous version of this motif in which Odysseus' son by Circe, Telegonos, does in fact kill Odysseus when he sets out to find his father. The poet has much altered the story for the *Odyssey;* a major alteration is Telemachos growing up. This is unusual in Greek literature. Heroes do not change. Neoptolemos, the young man in Sophocles' *Philoctetes,* is another conspicuous example. Perhaps Telemachos in part served as model. Perhaps the original story of the son in search of his father was transformed and then modeled after the Orestes story. Certainly

Homer is unusually fascinated with the details of Orestes'
avenging the death of Agamemnon. Telemachos is very important to Homer, so much so that it seems he created the
Kalypso episode to keep Odysseus out of Ithaka long
enough for Telemachos to reach his later adolescence.

Early on in the story Telemachos starts to become more
commanding. Shortly after Athene's departure in the first
book, when Telemachos has been given some encouragement, Penelope appears to complain of the bard's singing
a melancholy song of Troy. Telemachos answers her rather
sharply, suggesting that she return to her room and con-
cluding: "Go to your room. . . . Speech shall be the concern of the men, of all of them, but mostly my concern.
For I have the authority in this house" (1.356 *ff*).

The ancient literary critic Aristarchos declared that these
lines, which occur elsewhere in both the *Iliad* and the *Odyssey*, were interpolated here, probably because the sharp-
ness of tone is contrary to the usage between son and
mother. And Penelope is taken aback. "Amazed," says the
poet, "she went back to her room." To my mind they definitely belong here and are consistent with the charmingly
tentative behavior of Telemachos before the suitors
throughout the opening scenes, now overly brusque, and
now ready to cry. Telemachos in the second book prefig-
ures his father, and presages his own future maturity. He
is the commanding figure who will bring order into the
chaos. The second book is in microcosm part of the story
of the last twelve books, where Odysseus in disguise tests
the suitors, forcing them or tempting them to commit
themselves to injustice, much as Telemachos invites a conflict here. Slowly the young man changes until in the fifteenth book he is confronted by a fugitive, Theoklymenos,
who asks for protection and a passage in flight. When
Telemachos becomes his protector he assumes all the powers, responsibilities, and privileges of true heroic manhood.
The episode occurs as Telemachos is about to sail back to
Ithaka. He will soon be meeting his father. With this story

Homer has indicated that Telemachos is in all ways ready. Since Theoklymenos is brought in importantly here, and ostensibly for no reason, he is perhaps Homer's means of showing what Telemachos has learned from Nestor at Pylos and Menelaos at Sparta.

The scene at Pylos begins and ends with a sacrifice, at Sparta with a party. Both scenes emphasize a knowledge of ritual detail. The descriptions of Nestor's sacrifices are some of the most involved in either epic. Both scenes also emphasize the importance of a knowledge of social behavior. Correct social behavior here and elsewhere is usually in terms of hospitality, which is logical in a work involving so many comings and goings, and in a civilization that gave to strangers sacred rights and immunities. Immediately upon Telemachos' arrival at Pylos, the young boy shows his confusion as to the proprieties of arrival. Not only young, Telemachos is a country rube. The poet consistently describes Ithaka as out of the way, relatively poor and unimportant. When, for instance, Menelaos tells Telemachos how he had hoped to settle Odysseus as king in one of his cities, he shows the insignificance of Odysseus' Ithakan principality. Telemachos, then, in voyaging to the mainland has much more to learn than simply the fate of his father. The boy's ignorance and his gradual education into the ways of men parallel the travels of his father, who much of the time is a human being among fantastics and marvels. He, too, is a student in these situations, although actively curious in a way that his son is not.

Athene's answer to Telemachos' nervous questions contains the creed, the initial reason for self-respect, of an aristocrat, or any man. "Telemachos, part of the time you will think up something yourself, part of the time a god will help you. For I don't think you were born and reared without the gods being interested in you" (3.26 *ff*).

Odysseus' self-assured and courageous manner throughout the poem stems from the same attitude. He trusts in

himself and in destiny or god because he has the security
of a favorite. Slowly Telemachos comes to acquire the
same. In the manner of theater, the poet dramatizes in the
speeches the subtleties of social convention. No sooner has
Telemachos arrived than he meets Nestor's youngest boy,
Peisistratos, who becomes, like Orestes, another model for
the Ithakan. Peisistratos is a paragon of the young gentleman. As he passes the wine to Athene, his speech is a
model of propriety. He bids Athene pour a libation, then
pass on the goblet to Telemachos "since I believe that he,
too, prays to the immortals. All men need gods. But he is
younger, the same age as myself. Wherefore I shall offer the
golden cup to you first" (3.47 ff).

Although the poet tells us that Athene rejoiced in the
intelligence of this just young boy, one does sense a touch
of the prig, a mind that is a trifle prescriptive. Again in
Sparta Peisistratos speaks on the subject of manners, describing Telemachos' timidity and gaucherie in the new
society that he is encountering. He is equally subtle and
discreet in trying to stem the weeping of his dinner companions. Again, he is excessively platitudinous, so that
while a good example for Telemachos in some things he is
not in everything. The examples of young manhood which
are held up to Telemachos are to learn from, not to imi-
tate. Odysseus' son could never really behave as either Peisistratos or Orestes does. The poet stresses a kind of restraint in Peisistratos that would be unsuitable to the more
impetuous, temperamental Telemachos. Peisistratos is, in
short, his father's son. Nestor is in all ways the same as he
was in the *Iliad*; especially, he is garrulous and not to the
point. When Telemachos asks him specifically for news of
Odysseus, the old man ignores the question and sets out to
review the entire subject of the returning heroes. The poet
mocks this mentality in a way never done in the *Iliad*. For
when Telemachos on his way back from Sparta approaches
Pylos where his ship is beached, he asks Peisistratos to drop
him off at the beach, rather than bringing him back to the

palace "otherwise the old man won't let me go, being so anxious to entertain me in his house. But I've got to get going in a hurry" (*Odyssey* 15.200–201).

The poet's humorous approach to character, always present, is never stronger. The dull, lonely old man who feeds on polite young men, and the youth who will go one step short of rudeness in desperation at being bored again, become characters in a comedy of manners. But Nestor is a sympathetic figure. He is the first person of consequence whom Telemachos meets. The old man shows an old-fashioned piety, gentility and serenity, grounded in the worship of god and confidence in his ways. Nestor's attention to the detail of worship reveals a man who knows how to do things, who understands the ways of the world and the universe. He does things tidily, with precision and sureness. The poet has used far more concrete details than is either customary, or really necessary. The impression is one of routine, order, and knowledge. All this is lacking at Ithaka, except at the swineherd's hut. In the fourteenth book the poet describes Eumaios in a way that makes him a counterpart to Nestor. The orderliness of the farm buildings, their complexity, the symmetry of the animals, produce the same sensations. Furthermore, he is first described as cutting himself a pair of sandals. Technique and tidiness are the motifs. If perhaps these seem insignificant set beside the more profound problems and ideas of the *Iliad*, one would do well to reflect on the mood of catastrophe that lurks behind the narrative of much of the *Odyssey*. Perhaps no better example is to be had than Eumaios' description of his infancy and subsequent kidnaping. From king's son to houseslave to abandoned swineherd is his experience. The utter insecurity of this and other biographies in the *Odyssey* draw attention to the haphazard quality of existence, to its irrationality and ruthless changeability. The particular quality emphasized over and over again is the mutation of experience. Those who are wise build a bulwark against this in order, precision, and technical skill.

Otherwise the personality, one's identity, will be lost in the contrary shifts of events.

Nestor has offered Telemachos a glimpse of normalcy. Sparta offers another view. The life of Menelaos and Helen is still grander, more foreign to Telemachos' experience. He arrives at the end of an elaborate wedding party; he sees a palace filled with wealth that he associates with gods. The attention he receives is as elegant as the material possessions surounding him. Menelaos, however, is not overwhelmed by the luxury of his life. He is quick to reprimand his servant who delays admitting the young man. He remembers what it is to be a wanderer, for whom the essentials of existence become sharply defined. When Telemachos in whispers remarks to Peisistratos on the splendors of the palace, Menelaos overhears him. From Telemachos' simple country boy observation, Menelaos makes an important reflection: "Dear children, no man at all could try to rival Zeus. For his house and possessions, you know, are immortal" (4.78 f).

This is the only fundamental distinction in the Greek mind between god and man. Various gods may err in a variety of ways, but their lives go on forever. No matter how man may avoid failure, he still must die. The characters of the *Odyssey* accept death as that which gives proportion to life, which does, indeed, define man, vis-à-vis god. The ease in which Menelaos and Helen live is not only physical, it is emotional, too, because they have accepted themselves. Nor does this produce spiritual torpor. They still know how to grieve, for they break down unrestrainedly crying over the lost Odysseus. Basically, however, their mood is comfortable. Acceptance, toleration, and the relaxation that comes from having endured much are the characteristic psychological states of homecoming. They are returned. The bitterness, tension, and, of course, as well, the high heroics have been left behind at Troy. Homer manages to describe almost all the emotions of return before he finishes the *Odyssey*. Eurykleia's joy at seeing Telemachos back from Sparta is as nothing to the kisses that Eumaios lavishes on the boy. Profoundest is the scene when Telemachos and Odysseus, first reunited, break down the walls of sorrow long pent up. Homer compares it to the crying of birds who have lost their young. Quite apposite, because here the father and son, newly found, are crying literally for the years and relationship forever lost.

The after-dinner conversation between Helen and Menelaos accomplishes several things. A major function of the saga of Return is to tie up loose ends of the Trojan story. Certainly great curiosity must have attached to the reunion of Helen and Menelaos. In this scene Homer most subtly paints the generalities of a reunited couple with the underlying resentments and anxieties of this particular husband and wife. He manages to convey these through anecdotes which tell about Odysseus at Troy. These anecdotes show still more of the hero's personality, as the earlier remarks of Athene and Nestor had done. Furthermore the particular subtle suggestions and implications of this conversation are another example for Telemachos of the manner in which human beings engage one another. Odysseus' capacity for deceit (laudable here), his readiness to enter into any disguise (an unheroic trait inspiring mixed feelings of awe and repugnance), his endurance, are brought out in these two anecdotes. Quite humorously they tell us much more interesting facts about the speakers. Helen's tale is of Odysseus' appearance in disguise in Troy as a beggar. Helen alone identified him, but kept silent and aided him, for, as she says, she had already repented of following Paris to Troy and was anxious to return to Sparta and to her husband. She obviously intends to prove her loyalties and sympathies with this story as the earlier rhetorical remark she made in derogation (4.145 "dog-faced me") did.

Menelaos begins by complimenting Helen's storytelling skill, ignoring the last six lines of her speech that opened up for discussion her role in the war. It is, however, to this that he addresses himself throughout his anec-

dote. He describes an incident at the time when the Trojans had brought the Wooden Horse into the city. Helen
comes to mimic (with her witch's skill) the wives of the
Greeks within, so that the men wll speak out and reveal
themselves. This event, which occurred after the one Helen
described, naturally denies the sentiments she had advanced for herself. Menelaos does not leave it at that. He
is sarcastic: "Some god must have bade you do it," and
then a little vicious: "Godlike Deiphobos followed along
with you." (Deiphobos was the husband whom Helen took
after Paris was killed, at the time she maintains she was
pining for Menelaos.) This subtle, tense interplay shows
in perfect clarity the weakness of Menelaos, the isolation
and helplessness of Helen, their animosity and the recon-
ciliatory attempts which they quietly employ to ease it.
Exchanges of this delicacy are not unusual in the *Odyssey.*
The two longest involve Odysseus' relationship with Nausikaa and finally his reunion with Penelope. Both are marked
by innuendo and the bold significance of things left unsaid. Odysseus is truly master of human dealings through
speech. The Telemachia concludes with a slight revelation
of the growing familiarity of Telemachos with the ways of
the world. At Sparta he shyly allows Peisistratos to speak
for him until the moment following this awkward exchange
between Helen and Menelaos. The conversation cannot
very well continue; the king and queen fall silent, and
Telemachos changes the subject. Telemachos has learned
enough, from Nestor's son, to enter the conversation and
cover the impasse which the royal couple had created. Not
only does he speak, but he motivates the action. The following day he grows still freer in turning down Menelaos'
gift of horses. Menelaos is delighted with his boldness, and
responds to it with affection. Telemachos, we feel, has begun to achieve his majority.

A second theme of importance that appears in the
Telemachia is the overshadowing power of women. Even in
small moments this becomes clear as in the poet's descrip-

tion of the aged nurse, Eurykleia whom old Laertes, Odysseus' father, honored like a wife, but never took to bed because he feared his wife's anger. Apart from Odysseus and his son, who is in effect a pale counterpart of his father, the poem centers on women. They are not only powerful enough to dominate the narrative, but they provide the leitmotiv as well. For instance, it is typical that in the underworld Odysseus should see not only the customary figures, but also the famous heroines of the saga tradition. Then, too, the patron saint, so to speak, of the family is the female goddess, Athene, who is always at hand. She, however, never seems truly feminine except in the very intimate scene in the thirteenth book, where she talks to Odysseus in a way that borders on the sexual. The human ladies are consistently feminine, unlike the ladies of the *Iliad*. What is more, they are almost always threatening. In this respect the *Odyssey* shows the same fear of women (as the source of all evil) that operates in Genesis and in Hesiod's account of Pandora's box. Even Penelope from the first bears a striking resemblance to Circe, the acknowledged witch of the *Odyssey*. The suitors, waiting for her to finish the shroud with which she is deceiving them, are in their riotous debauchery really no different from the pigs transformed from men whom Circe has charmed. There is something sinister about the shroud itself. It is perhaps an unconscious symbol of the way Penelope ultimately deliberately leads the suitors to their doom. Penelope seems often threatening the fortunes of her own family. The poet emphasizes this by indirectly comparing her to Klytemnestra, who killed her husband, Agamemnon, upon his return from Troy, with the help of her lover, Aigisthos. Homer frequently presents Telemachos' situation as somehow analogous to that of Agamemnon's son, Orestes, who avenged his father's death by killing the guilty adulterers. Orestes is a model of loyalty to father and to house. Telemachos has suitors, not one lover to contend with; and his mother remains loyal to his father as

Klytemnestra did not remain loyal to Agamemnon. Klytemnestra's fall from virtue seems, however, sometimes a
warning to Telemachos that he may expect the same of his
own mother. Women are capricious, and a man may never
know their minds. In Nestor's terse description of the onset
of Klytemnestra's affair, it is inexplicable and yet inevitable. Aigisthos began to beguile Klytemnestra, but at first
she resisted such a monstrous deed. And she was sup-
ported by a poet whom Agamemnon had left behind to
watch over her. Then Aigisthos removed the poet and took
her, as Homer says, "he wanting to," "she wanting to." Penelope could inexplicably change as Klytemnestra did, so
that each time the Orestes story is mentioned as encouragement to Telemachos an element of uncertainty and
suspense are also brought to the narrative. The unspoken
insecurity over the stability of Penelope's feelings is made
vivid in the underworld when Agamemnon describes in
gory detail the grim and heartless murderess his wife
showed herself to be. Again and again he warns Odysseus,
harping on female caprice and treachery.

In a poem in which intelligence and awareness play so
great a part the women are always coolly wise. Helen is an
example of a pattern that informs all the women. To be
sure she is characterized much as she appeared in the
Iliad, but the poet chooses a special emphasis. Menelaos
is again, here as in the *Iliad,* neither overly bright nor
overly perceptive. When Telemachos, still unidentified, begins to cry after Menelaos has been discussing Odysseus,
the king does not know what to do, whether to let the
young man mention his father or question him further.
For contrast, Helen sweeps into the room, proceeds to remark on the physical similarity between Telemachos and
Odysseus, and so identifies him. Her intellectual superiority to her husband is then reinforced in Menelaos' slow
acknowledgment of her observation. Her commanding presence has already been established in the elaborate, detailed
description of her entrance. The description has qualities

associated with other women in the *Odyssey*, monumental, ornate, and variegated.

The immediate parallel to this scene is the reception of Odysseus at the palace of King Alkinoos. He is told to approach Queen Aretē as suppliant, the implication being that she tends to control the domestic affairs of the palace. The subsequent reactions of the royal couple would bear that out. Athene offers a genealogy of Queen Aretē and an account of her position in Scheria that indicate her uncommonly important place. The words of Athene both serve to magnify and also act as formal introduction in the same way as the description of the entering Helen. When Odysseus has made his petition, he sits in the dust of the hearth, until one of the elders reminds Alkinoos of the hospitality due a stranger. Like Menelaos, Alkinoos is not too quick. Like Helen, Queen Aretē quickly notices something familiar in the stranger, in this case some palace clothing which Nausikaa had loaned him.

Helen, of course, is an extraordinary woman—the daughter of Zeus, immortal, and a sorceress, a witch, which she reveals as she puts a magical potion of forgetfulness into the wine. Students of religion like to call Helen a "faded goddess," that is, a figure who was once worshiped as divine before slipping into saga as a quasi-human being. But a trace of the supernatural remains. Homer felt both her divinity and her femininity strongly enough to make Athene fly away after the visit to Nestor. Rightly so. A disguised Athene could never endure or be endured in Helen's palace. As queens, legitimate wives and mothers, Helen and Aretē are analogous to Penelope, whose superiority in wits to the suitors is never in doubt. Only to her husband, Odysseus, does she yield, but only after deceiving him. Odysseus is uncommon if for no other reason than he is portrayed as a woman's equal in intelligence, almost possessing what males today like to call a woman's "cunning mind." Odysseus' adventures are in part sexual, culminating in his reunion with Penelope. The poet has so created his women, however, that the sexuality becomes more than mere sensuality; the eternal dialogue between the sexes is maintained on the sexual level and Odysseus responds to the challenge.

One of the more interesting subtleties of the poem is whether Penelope penetrates from the start her husband's disguise. That she does has been argued very skillfully. Once heard, the argument seems irresistible. Through Books Eighteen and Nineteen the change in Penelope from general helplessness and hopelessness to resolution and finally to the determination to have the issue decided on the following day is inexplicable unless she knows that Odysseus is at hand. Furthermore, Penelope as an analogue to the astute and perceptive Helen and Aretē certainly has the wits to catch the hints that are offered her. Great suspenseful strides take place in the story suddenly. The skill of the author elsewhere in motivating the action is not likely to have deserted him here. Penelope subtly helps Odysseus destroy the suitors, thereby proving once again woman's intelligence and sinister strength. The climax, however, comes when she lies about the bed. Odysseus' marriage bed, which he built with his own hands from a live olive tree still rooted in the earth, is like their sexual knowledge of each other, personal and immutable. Penelope, true match of her husband, warily insists upon this last test of his identity. She bids Eurykleia prepare a different bed for them. For this instant Odysseus is undone. She conquers him with deceit, his own weapon. She makes him lose control of the situation, makes him doubt his identity and where he is. Finally she forces him to identify himself involuntarily. Intellectually he is completely unmanned, and the victory is hers. Yet in his submission to her he nonetheless achieves his mastery. Their reunion is the archetypal dialogue between the sexes.

As a corollary to the power of women, men are seen as their victims. The suitors, as I have just suggested, are in some sense victims of Penelope. They are given moderately sympathetic portraits early on to reinforce this notion. In the assembly of the second book Antinoos puts forth a not completely unreasonable case for the suitors. Essentially the suitors seem to be in their rights, wooing the queen. Their remaining at the palace seems underneath to be some determination to use up the wealth that they cannot otherwise possess. The subterfuge of the shroud is vaguely presented. The logic of most of the second book is kept conveniently vague so as to allow our sympathies to fall to both parties in the conflict. The episode as a whole shows a group of young men who have more or less sullied their legitimate claim to seek Penelope in marriage by their outrageous behavior in her house. They have furthermore angered Zeus and ignored his plain warnings to them. They are acting out the folly of Aigisthos which was Zeus's example at the very first.

In their stupidity the suitors are also gluttonous and sensual, and prefigure the behavior of Odysseus' crew, who are destroyed through their lack of self-control when they ravenously eat the cattle of the Sun God. While it is the god who actually destroys them, throughout the adventure stories Odysseus has caused their misery. The crew is in this sense his victims. Later when Odysseus has returned to Ithaka the suitors in turn become his victims. Several times he is aided by Penelope who dazzles them into irresistible yearning. But it is Odysseus who provokes them into betraying themselves ethically when he appears at the palace as a beggar. Antinoos reappears in this scene as the major antagonist. Athene suggests to Odysseus that he go among the suitors begging, "so that he could learn which of them were just and which were lawless" (17.363). Just as in Greek tragic thinking the force of Atē (Delusion or Temptation) provokes men to evil action, so does Odysseus move through this scene. Antinoos recklessly tries to cast him out, deny him and injure him. The poet again achieves that mysterious blend of sympathy and antipathy for these doomed young men. Antinoos is symbol for all of them; in

so despising the beggar he moves dangerously close to of-
fending unwritten law. What he does is, in any case, in-
human, lacking in grace and civility. He dramatizes the
suitors' lack of manners, which from the very first book of
the *Odyssey* characterizes them. Their gaucherie, crudity,
and brute insensitivity stand in sharp contradiction to the
ways of the world at the courts of Nestor and Menelaos.

Another important theme introduced in the Telemachia
is the search for truth. The voyage of Telemachos to the
mainland to seek out his father's whereabouts is symbolic
of it. Many of his father's voyages are impelled by a similar
curiosity. The pursuit of truth is, however, highlighted by
the continual mood of mystery that hangs over the story
of the *Odyssey*. The tale is filled with uncertainty, largely
due to the uncommon amount of falsehood practiced by
the characters.

When Athene first appears to Telemachos she lies to him
about herself; Penelope lies to the suitors about the shroud;
Telemachos lies to his mother about his trip; and Odysseus
lies constantly, culminating in the cruel deceit he practices
on his broken father, Laertes, at the close of the epic.
Here is falsehood to no purpose at all. Such, however, is
Odysseus' instinct that neither truth nor clarity springs to
his lips first. The poet is properly sympathetic to this. He
can even use it humorously as when Odysseus, lying to
Eumaios, is not believed. In mock horror Odysseus echoes
the remark of Achilles of the *Iliad* "Hateful to me as the
gates of Hell is he who lies" (14.156).

As a man of many turns no one can lay a hand on him.
When he is asked to identify himself by his host after having been received hospitably, he generally contrives a fake
identity, which he will often offer in a lengthy and embellished form. The primitive attitude behind this is that a
man who knows your name has power over you. The clearest manifestation of this in the *Odyssey* is the Polyphemos
episode. Odysseus tells the Cyclops his name is Nobody,
thereby rendering Polyphemos' call for help futile ("No-

body is doing me in" 9.408), but once Odysseus truly
identifies himself, Polyphemos can pray to Poseidon to
ruin Odysseus, which the god almost does. Odysseus is, in
fact, the human counterpart of Proteus, whom Menelaos
describes meeting in the fourth book. The magical old sea
creature can be forced to tell the truth only after one has
held onto him, literally "pinned him down" as we would
say, while he transforms himself into every conceivable being or thing, trying to escape. Whether or not the poet
consciously saw Proteus as an image for Odysseus, the parallel exists. Appearance and reality is a theme throughout
the poem, conceived as a problem in knowing, but equally
important as a means to evasion. Far more often than in
the *Iliad*, the poet in introducing speeches comments on
the wisdom, the awareness, the deceitfulness, or the cynicism of the speaker. Much of the *Odyssey* turns on Odysseus coming to know and to be known. For most of the
characters, in fact, recognition and identification are the
most important actions.

For Odysseus his home island of Ithaka promises finally
his recognition. Characteristically the poet can present this
hero in the midst of his wanderings telling Polyphemos
that he is called Nobody. From this point he moves back to
the discovery of self and acknowledgment by his familiar
world. He awakes on Ithaka to an island transformed into
the unrecognizable; he meets Athene in disguise. He is
never more frustratingly alienated, especially in the cruelly
surrealistic moment when the disguised Athene announces
that the completely unfamiliar landscape is in fact Ithaka.
In this crisis he maintains his integrity by keeping secret
and hidden his true identity. That is, he lies to Athene,
which is the magic charm that swiftly opens the door to
complete understanding. Three momentous revelations are
contained in this instant of time. First, the goddess reveals
herself to him not by sign or omen, not as a bird, but in the
true and recognizable lineaments of an anthropomorphized
divine being. Odysseus achieves an intimate and direct un-

ion with the supernatural force that in hidden ways has
followed his life until now. Second, Athene proceeds to offer Odysseus an explanation of himself which has made
him her favorite. From the divine lips, these words give the
substance of the man stripped of superfluity:

> It would take someone quite cunning and deceitful
> who could surpass you in trickery. . . . Stubborn,
> clever, never tired of falsehood, . . . you are of all
> mortals best at planning and speaking. . . . I cannot
> ever desert you when you suffer because you are so
> smooth, so intelligent, so sensible. (13.291 *ff*)

In this encounter Odysseus has been initiated into the
nature of things, including his own identity. As the goddess
finishes speaking, she dispels the mists of unreality and
Ithaka, his land, stands as the third revelation. Odysseus'
personal homecoming is now realized. The identification
of Odysseus, the individual man, has begun. What is still
to come is his return to house and home. Throughout the
suspenseful events of mounting an attack upon the suitors,
in the midst of cunning, bold, and skillful actions, Odysseus gradually becomes integrated into the emotional and
personal landscape of Ithaka by a series of recognition
scenes. First, Telemachos recognizes him, then his ancient
dying dog, then the nurse Eurykleia, and finally Penelope.
These revelations are all of a different order: Telemachos
must, of course, be prompted into recognizing a man whom
he actually never knew, whereas there are a number of subtle points to indicate that Penelope is aware early of his
true identity. Argos, the dog, like all true faithful beasts
whose psychic depth compensates them for their being
dumb, instantly recognizes his master, absent these seventeen years. Eurykleia knows when she sees the scar on Odysseus' thigh.

Eurykleia's discovery prompts the poet into a digression
on the origin of this scar. As preamble to that incident we
learn the sources of Odysseus' name. His grandfather, Au-

tolykos, the poet says, excelled all men in thievery and in making false witness, skills given to him by the god, Hermes, whose devoted worshiper this Autolykos was. When the old man is asked to name the child he replies: "I come here as a man who has been angry with many, both men and women, over the fruitful earth. Let his name then be Anger" (19.407 ff).

The etymology for the name Odysseus is likely the poet's fancy. There is a definite resemblance to the not too common epic verb *odussomai*, which seems always to mean "angered at." Many critics would prefer that it mean the "object of anger" in view of the hostility that Odysseus has encountered in the course of the story. The latter seems somehow more appropriate, but the evidence does not support it. Then again, Odysseus may mean simply Anger, thereby both the object of anger and the source of it. In any case, he who is angry invites anger, and he who is the object of anger has usually bestowed it, so that the name is meaningful either way. The poet has linked the name to the scar as though it were an external symbol of the psychic blemish which is the state of anger or which the object of anger may acquire. The lines are enigmatic, hinting at the stranger side, the unheroic side of Odysseus' nature. The covert, dishonest, always slightly hostile behavior of the hero is perhaps a natural manifestation of wrath. The peevishness, the maliciousness, however merry, of the Wily Lad, are perhaps prompted by a fundamental existential anger. The passage certainly does not deserve undue attention, although as part of a moment of revelation it has strong relevance. Still, Autolykos was only one grandfather. The strange distemper which he brought to Odysseus' bloodlines was diluted by heroic blood of ancestors descended from Zeus. The *Odyssey* as a poem is itself just such an amalgam—in sum actually a distillation—of ingredients originally foreign to each other. The electricity with which they charge the narrative is reproduced in Odysseus, who represents a similar blend of disparate elements. The warring within his psyche, the paradigm of Western man's peculiar eternal dissatisfaction and disenchantment, makes this story not only continually relevant and popular, but the natural vehicle for the Christian myth recast, of course, in theologically suitable dress.

Four times while at Ithaka Odysseus gives a fictitious account of himself. They are interesting as insights into how he identifies himself. These stories are obviously fictitious, yet they call into question the entire description of adventures which Odysseus narrated at King Alkinoos' court. Many have noted, for instance, that the events of the later tales parallel each other, and furthermore are lodged firmly in the historical reality of the Trojan saga world, whereas much of the travel stories is humanly impossible (although this does not seem to me an altogether valid distinction, since nowhere in the adventure narrative are we made to feel implausibility about the events). On the other hand, from the very first the poet brings in doubt about the verisimilitude of the whole, by making Odysseus' intentions suspicious.

"Now then do not be devious in your answers to what I am about to ask you. It is far better for you to speak out," says Alkinoos (8.548 f) when finally after some thousand suspenseful lines Odysseus' uncontrollable grief at Demodokos' song has given the king an opening for the question which Odysseus has been so studiously avoiding. The long-felt suspense of Odysseus' hosts is echoed in the longest introduction to such a question from host to guest ever. Everything is poised for a great recital. Odysseus' initial reply emphasizes the majesty and artistry of what he will say. He talks of bards, and the pleasure which they bring people. This is the greatest joy at banquets. Slowly, rhetorically, by question, by advertisement, he builds to the revelation of his name. The prelude is so artfully contrived, so obviously and consciously so, that Odysseus seems actually to be supplanting Demodokos. The banquet is finished; we are in Alkinoos' *megaron.* Demodokos finishes, another entertainer begins. Odysseus' propensity for lying raises suspicions. Even Alkinoos seems subconsciously suspicious later on when he compliments Odysseus' skill ("You have told it all out in sequence, with skill, just like a bard" [11.368].) and remarks how unlike the world's many liars and cheats Odysseus is. Here one cannot know Homer's intent or even attempt to divine it. The poet in so many ways raises doubts of Odysseus' veracity that perhaps the travel tales too are but another in a series of deceptions. Here the dupes are not only the Phaiacians, but the readers as well.

In another sense none of these autobiographical narratives is false, because Odysseus in creating a fictional image of himself is actually at the same time playing with the ingredients of his own personality. At Ithaka he identifies himself falsely to Athene, Eumaios, Antinoos (and the suitors in general), and Penelope. In each of his false autobiographies he uses the same context, namely that he is of a princely family on the island of Crete. He insists on his aristocratic background, either because it is true of the real Odysseus, or because there is an aristocratic cast to his features that he cannot truly hide (Menelaos once says to Telemachos and Peisistratos, "The race of your fathers is not lost in you. You are of the race of god-nourished kings, the sceptered ones, since the lower orders could not have produced ones such as you" [4.62 ff]), or more likely he chooses to emphasize the calamitous fact of his reversal from the heights to the depths. Odysseus is always a family man in these stories, true to the peculiarly strong homing instinct in this hero. He is a victim often; in one story someone of greater importance tries to force him to serve under him, and elsewhere his half brothers try to do him out of an inheritance. He is an outcast as the bastard but best-loved child of a ruler surrounded by jealous legitimate brothers. He is a misfit when he cannot serve another because he is too talented, or when he, penniless, acquires a rich wife on his own merits. He is the runt as the younger brother of Idomeneus, and aware that he is not so competent or heroic. He is unheroic when he kills one man by night in a sneak attack, or when he sees that a battle is being lost, throws away his shield and turns suppliant before the conquering general. The psychological facts of these stories coincide so well with the character traits which both the *Iliad* and *Odyssey* give Odysseus that it seems clear that the hero is finally paradoxically creating truth out of fiction. The poet emphasizes that Odysseus is conscious of himself in almost every one of these stories. Certain elements of the stories are veiled allusions to events of the travels. For instance, going to Dodona to consult the oracle of Zeus is the underworld journey to Teiresias, the reconnoitering crew in Egypt who are attacked is the war with the Lastrygonians, and the mutiny of the crew is analogous to his real crew's attempts to thwart his plans. I have elsewhere remarked that the poet of the *Odyssey* is considerably more conscious of himself and his technique than the poet of the *Iliad*. Although perhaps an overly sophisticated notion, one sometimes has the impression that the poet, in using the themes of reality and unreality, is trying to bring out the paradox that fiction is often more truthful than reality, or that unreality can be a means to truth. If this is true of the story, then it is more likely from the poet's subconscious, although the *Odyssey* seems so surprisingly subtle that one is tempted to concede him almost anything.

The travel adventures seem to be largely traditional fairy tale material, but the poet has rearranged them considerably to suit his own ends, and to display his virtuosity, if not that of Odysseus (more than once the Phaiacians applaud Odysseus' skill). First, Homer seems to have created a travel adventure in the episode with Kalypso. Then he has taken another, the voyage to Scheria, to use as a context for all the others. The long recitation by Odysseus shows signs of having been transformed by the poet from a probably traditional tale in the third person into a highly personal account in the first person. This sort of variation marks the poet of the *Odyssey*; the whole of the Telemachia was conceived in the same fashion. Apart from stylistics, the change to the first person allows the travel adventures to become another of the series of answers to the question, "Who are you?" that occurs so often in the narrative. The adventure stories are part of Odysseus' own sense of identity, yet in turn they pose questions about appearance and reality that the story of Menelaos' encounter with Proteus symbolizes. When Alkinoos praises Odysseus for his story, he tells him that the Phaiacians would scarcely consider him one of the common liars and cheats that peddle their tall tales about. Deception being what it is in the *Odyssey*, the remark immediately arouses suspicions of veracity and intent, as does elsewhere the praise of Odysseus' style in storytelling.

To this the Kalypso story is prelude. Kalypso means "concealer"; mechanically she does just this for the poet, concealing Odysseus while Telemachos has a chance to grow. Kalypso herself seems to be nothing more than a rather quick and pallid imitation of Circe, simply a plot device ready to hand. There is nothing distinctive in Homer's description of her and her island. The goddess is simply a warm woman. Perhaps the one unusual feature is the naturalistic description of her cave and its surroundings. Elsewhere Homer, like almost all Greeks, seeks out the man-made or things scaled to humans for description. Kalypso's vines, plants, and other natural wonders are all described. The implication is that she, being only a version of Circe, did not exist strongly enough in the poet's mind to have a humanized ambience. Whatever the reason, the naturalistic description points up the loneliness of Odysseus' life set against the rich man-made clutter of Menelaos' court.

The Kalypso episode is our introduction to the hero, objectified as his own account of his travels could scarcely be. His conversation with Kalypso creates an impression of him that lasts for the rest of the story. Shortly before, when Kalypso protests Zeus' command to Hermes, she shows herself to be a warm, agreeable creature who loves Odysseus. This portrait of Kalypso more sharply defines the facets of Odysseus' personality as they are revealed in his reaction to her announcement that she will not only let him go but help him, too. Her conversation with Hermes shows her to be a generous woman. Yet Odysseus' first reaction is instinctive mistrust of the woman with whom he has been sleeping for seven years. He next realizes that going by raft, as Kalypso had directed, will not be easy. His quick mind is in contrast with the normal epic mentality that accepts without question the management of divine or semidivine beings. Later in the episode the detailed description of building the raft shows the craftsmanship, the technical skills, which this man of many turns possesses. Finally his sense of the malignity of gods is enough to cause him to force her to swear that she intends no harm. A man who is alert, suspicious, aggressive and quick to understand all the ramifications of the moment—this is the image that emerges from Odysseus' first speech. Kalypso's reaction is the same as Menelaos' when Telemachos spoke up aggressively and assertively in rejecting the horses. She smiles and strokes Odysseus' hand. She becomes the vanquished woman. Directly after swearing in the most awful and solemn fashion (as deities should), she cozily talks of her compassion, they wander home, and she herself proceeds to serve him his food, although there are maids who perform the same task for her.

When, after they eat, Kalypso begins to speak, the motives for her attention become clearer. She will make one last attempt to keep him there. She forecasts tremendous suffering for him, she offers him immortality, she offers once more herself as certainly sexually superior to his wife Penelope.

When Odysseus answers, the poet calls him "the man of many ideas and plans"; "quick-thinking," we would

say. His cleverness comes from wanting to be polite and
tactful, not out of fear, for she has sworn an oath not to
hurt him. True enough, Penelope cannot compare, he says,
yet I must go home, and I have suffered too much now
to care about the misery ahead. In essence he has rejected
immortality for home, the greater value lies in humanness
even with or perhaps because of its temporal limitations.
In that direction lies both homecoming and suffering. The
Return is in a way a reinstatement, a rediscovery of self.
Strange environments and the disorientation that they
cause do, it is true, make for self-examination. Expatriates
are forever finding the self. Odysseus, himself, according
to later tradition, could not endure to remain in Ithaka,
but set out himself on additional voyages. Still, wandering
precludes complete integration into an environment, the
absolute realization of self, that the Greeks especially insisted upon. The emphasis which they placed in later
days upon the *polis*, the city, derives from notions of man's
inseparable connection with place. Suffering, in turn, is
the process whereby a man learns his uniqueness, which is
the other side of environmental integration. Suffering
integrates one internally, because one can only suffer alone
(using "suffer" in the sense both of experiencing pain and
enduring it). God, who is not only immortal, but also
finally onmipresent and invincible, can never know limita-
tion of any sort. He cannot therefore create life in the
living of it, establish boundaries to a psyche, and define
the way. Eternity, ubiquity, and insensibility are not only
hard to grasp, they are stultifying in their implications.
Odysseus' most profound manifestation of his essential
heroism is a rejection of Kalypso's offer, despite what we
learn about the grayness of afterlife in the Underworld in
the eleventh book. Odysseus' boldness here is contrasted
with the fate Proteus prophesied to Menelaos. After death
he is to join Helen in the Islands of the Blessed for all
time. This gentle, undemanding pretty couple belongs
there, although one would rather have Helen going

through eternity with Paris, than with so solemn and dull
a man as Menelaos.

Odysseus rejects immortality *after* he has visited the
Underworld. There he is told by the prophet, Teiresias,
that death will come gently to him. Old age will be the
cause, but not the accursed senility and ugliness which
the Greeks so feared. Teiresias specifies that it will be a
"shining" old age. Shortly after Odysseus meets Achilles,
Agamemnon, and Ajax. In contrast to Odysseus' clear-eyed
and even-tempered attitude, the three saga heroes are bit-
ter, resentful, and desolate. Ajax, silently hostile, will pass
all eternity nursing his grievance against the Greeks who
deprived him of the prize of Achilles' arms, which so diminished his honor that he killed himself. Agamemnon,
still the great man, pompous, does not comprehend the
tide of complex passions that brought him down ("But
the most pitiable cry I heard was that of Priam's daughter,
Kassandra, whom that deceitful Klytemnestra slew as she
clung to me" [11.421 *ff*]). His obtuseness in the *Iliad*
when he praised the virtues of Chryseis and announced
that he would take her back to Mycenae did not leave
him when he decided to bring Kassandra back to Klytemnestra's palace. Agamemnon has discovered that the gross,
ugly manner of his death has somehow cancelled out his
life. Betrayal is his theme. As Klytemnestra has betrayed
him, so life has betrayed him. Every other man is as likely
to be its dupe. In the twenty-fourth book Agamemnon
calls Achilles "lucky" both because his death was glorious
and because the subsequent funeral conjured up all the
heroic dimensions of his life. In essence then Achilles received, finally, what was due him in the *Iliad*. In the
existential world of the *Iliad* Achilles at least was complete
and fulfilled as a hero. Yet in the *Odyssey* when Achilles
says that he would willingly be a serf to have life back
again, he seems to contradict the man who chose to die
young gloriously on the field of battle, rather than live
out an inglorious life to old age. Here as elsewhere the two

poems and their philosophies do not correspond. Death for
Homer is the loss of all vital physical powers, a shadowy
impotence that replaces vigor, action, personality, and sun-
shine. Still there is no assurance that had Achilles the
chance to live again he would have chosen the course of
inglorious old age. That, too, would have been impotence.
His bleak, terse comment reveals more than anything else
a horrible loathing at being dead. The values supporting
the choice that Achilles made in the *Iliad* seem to put
Odysseus' destined placid end somewhere in unheroic
limbo. But the poet of the *Odyssey* has the focus elsewhere. Odysseus' daring throughout the poem reveals
neither contempt for life nor fear of death. The poet sings
of life and the winning of it (the reason why the ancients
saw this epic as comic rather than tragic), whereas the
Iliad is the story of death.

Odysseus' refusal of immortality, still, is in many ways
a paradox. Homer has shown us what life means to Odysseus in the contrast he draws between the adventuresome
hero and his craven crew. The chasm is vast that separates
the noble from the ignoble lust for life. Odysseus is concerned with living, whereas the crew is concerned with
survival. At each dangerous turn of the journey Odysseus
seeks to learn the new while the crew looks for escape.
Everywhere they seek food, he seeks information. Ironically, the crew's efficient concern for survival brings about
their own death. Confronted with hunger and surrounded
by the Sun God's tabu cattle, they cannot look beyond
the physical act of immediate survival to spare the sacred
beasts. Thus they perish, whereas Odysseus, the much enduring, the much exploring, the gambling man, survives
through a sophisticated prudence. The paradox seems important to the poet because he mentions the episode in
the opening lines of the epic.

The mentality behind Odysseus' actions is found in the
reply that Paris gives to Hektor in the third book of the
Iliad when he is reproached for his constant sexuality.

"The gifts of the gods are not to be thrown away," he says. In one sense Paris is saying that once the human condition is set, it should be exploited to the full. For Odysseus this exploitation becomes the search for the new and the strange wherever he is in this earth or in whatever of his life. This striving after consciousness, so particularly Western, provides the underlying energy of the *Odyssey* and much of Greek culture. Carved at Delphi was the famous inscription "Know thyself," echoed in Socrates' equally famous remark in the *Apology,* "the unexamined life is not livable for men."

Here is the background for Odysseus' refusal of the gift of immortality. Immortality betrays the fairy tale mentality and the hero, wandering in the land of marvels, rejects it as alien. Immortality—eternal stagnation—must finally be beyond the ken of one who lives completely in this world. Immortality is for the survival-minded, not the venturesome. Eurylochos persuades the crew to eat the cattle of the Sun God with this argument.

> All deaths are hateful to us wretched mortals, but most pitiable is to die of starvation and meet your doom that way. . . . If (the Sun God) is angry because of his straight-horned cattle and wants to kill us, and the other gods follow along with him, I should rather die drinking down at one fell swoop the ocean wave, than to die slowly on this desert island. (12.341 *ff*)

Yet the survival-minded fear death; the crew is afraid of the experience of dying as Odysseus is not. Not a little of his objection to immortality is that the experience of living makes sense only in the dying. No curious man would give this up. Beyond this Odysseus understands man's essential weakness and insignificance. The weakness and insignificance make living, being alive, the central good. Therefore to live fully, to experience all life's ramifications is to participate in the good. It is to experience

joyousness. Immortality by removing frailty and transitori-
ness also denies to life its supreme value. Odysseus' advice
to the suitors says just this:

> Of all the things that breathe and crawl on this
> earth, nothing does earth produce of less consequence
> than man. For as long as the gods give him manliness
> [moral integrity, virtue—the word *aretē* means many
> things] and his knees work, he thinks that he won't
> suffer evil in the future. But when, as will happen,
> the blessed gods make things wretched, these too he
> must bear with an enduring spirit though he be suf-
> fering. For man's mind and disposition is no more or
> less than the father of men and gods causes it to be
> each day. . . . Wherefore let no man ever ignore the
> unwritten laws of this universe, but keep in dignity
> and silence whatever gifts the gods may happen to
> give. (18.131 *ff*)

Odysseus sets out on his raft from Kalypso's island and
Poseidon blows up a frightening storm. The episode is in
a sense Odysseus' *aristeia*, the Homeric word for that moment in battle when a hero achieves his finest form. The
heroism of his suffering, his self-control and wit, continue
throughout the turmoil of majestic winds and waves.

Odysseus is praised for his endurance. In microcosm the
experience Odysseus endures when violently tossed about
in the storm after leaving Ogygia is man's life experience
as the poet often shows it. The mood reflects very likely
the unsettled period of migration following the collapse
of the Mycenaean Empire. In daily and incessant turmoil
and shift, endurance becomes the most important mental
attitude. Eumaios also endures, but his position is bleaker.
He has no illusions of his master returning, yet he does
not despair. He chooses rather to endure and to suffer.
Odysseus' endurance is sparked by the thought of homecoming, hence his mental and physical pace is livelier,

which perhaps explains why he survived when his crew perished.

As the storm buffets Odysseus, the poet has increased the resemblance to an *aristeia* on a thematic level by including a great number of similes throughout the episode. Constantly Odysseus remains the thinking man. Ino's gift of the magic veil is not accepted in the blind frenzy of self-preservation. Odysseus thinks, and chooses how he will use it. As a free man he operates on top of the world of magic. At the point of being driven to death on surf-battered reefs he can think logically and completely. His prayer to the river asks the customary sanctuary and protection offered to the wanderer and stranger. The human as an alien in the natural world, having confronted the enemy in the storm, knows the rhythm of the universe. Odysseus prays not simply as a religious man but also in the spirit of Archilochos, the Greek poet of a slightly later date, who says: "Rejoice not in your blessings nor grieve at your misfortunes, overmuch. Learn the rhythm that holds man."

Even at the very end, when finally thrown up on the shore after days of battering, privation, and total desolation, Odysseus can reason with himself over where he should hide himself for the night. The speech begins slightly emotional and breathless, but immediately the intellect takes over, alternatives are weighed, and a choice is made. The moment caps the entire book, a book that more quickly and incisively sets forth a character than anywhere else in Greek epic.

The poet proceeds to dramatize the implications of the personality whom he has just created by means of the travel stories that Odysseus tells to the Phaiacians. Actually his experience at Alkinoos' court is similar to any number of these stories. Scheria, the Phaiacians' island home, is just as fabulous and magical as the various stations in the travel stories. Homer reminds us that the Phaiacians had once been neighbors to the Cyclops and that now in Scheria they were "far from mankind who must work to exist." In setting them out of geographical reality the poet has set them outside of all reality. Nevertheless, Odysseus' experience among the Phaiacians is not only far more detailed than the travel stories, its emphasis is different. The travel stories are unified by the themes of temptation, curiosity, and bold escape. Temptation and curiosity are on Scheria, to be sure, but they are of another order. Odysseus comes as a stranger to the Phaiacian manner of life and he learns to handle himself among these people. But unlike the travel stories where intellectual curiosity motivates him to learn, here he learns of necessity, for Alkinoos' court holds for him a peril and a temptation in Nausikaa.

The constantly recurring note of the sixth and seventh books is marriage. The preceding scene on Kalypso's island turned very much on the husband-wife relationship of Kalypso and Odysseus. The dangers in that situation are all potentially real at Scheria. For Odysseus the trap, the enchantment or temptation is twofold: how to avoid with tact (remain himself, yet deal with these people) the marital ambitions of Nausikaa and her family; how to avoid the real temptation of a marriage with Nausikaa. The heroic triumph of Odysseus over the wild elements of nature is now repeated in his intelligent good behavior in society, the triumphant manipulation of his fellow men. Good behavior, a trite paltry phrase, is actually one of the few truly necessary bases of human existence. In a traditional, totally ritualized society the pattern of behavior is made for one. The travel stories of the *Odyssey* portray people who are part way or completely outside a ritual. Odysseus' attempts to establish relationships with them is his special kind of heroism. The emphasis in these books upon marriage, sexual relations, and the human body as well as other sensual motives mirror Odysseus' sexuality—perhaps the major feature of this heroism, although, in the *Odyssey*, much muted and overshadowed by intelligence. It remains true, however, that his most significant encounters are with women, and that the resolution of any conflict is generally sexual intercourse. The *Odyssey* stands certainly as man's archetypal confrontation of woman.

In his relationship with Nausikaa, Odysseus shows equal portions of sensibility, grace, and intelligence, so that the episode is as subtle and complicated as his reunion with Penelope. The Nausikaa episode has a frame beginning with Homer's comparing the young Phaiacian princess to Artemis, virginal, chaste, and robust. Odysseus repeats the idea in his initial speech to the girl ("If you are a goddess . . . I myself would compare you to Artemis" [6.150 *ff*]). The frame closes with the story of Aphrodite and Hephaistos where exactly the opposite qualities are presented, that is, indulgent sensuality, foolish adultery, and public scandal. Not long after the song Nausikaa says farewell to Odysseus. In the entire episode Nausikaa is almost a protagonist. She tries to seduce Odysseus, politely enough, to be sure, and she rejects him at the end. Her sensibility to the possibility of marriage and later to its impossibility makes her one of the cleverest, most sensitive girls in literature. She is testimony to the poet's conscious elevation of intelligence, sensitivity, and verbal skill over all other human attributes.

Athene picks up the theme of marriage when she appears to Nausikaa in a dream. The dream itself, as we moderns know, is Nausikaa's subconscious wish in any case. Athene talks of the need of clean clothes, for the time of Nausikaa's wedding must be near at hand ("You won't remain a maiden very long" [6.33]). Nausikaa upon awakening alludes to her bachelor brothers' need for fresh clothes, because, as the poet says, she is too shy to speak of her own possible marriage. Only here does the poet introduce that sort of stage direction. Once having established the conflicts between desire, propriety, and maidenly shyness, he unfolds a superb scene of human beings reacting to one another. When Odysseus steps forth from his hiding place he supplicates Nausikaa in alternating allusions to her physical comeliness and to her marriageable state. The speech is intensified by Odysseus' naked predicament, which the poet amplifies by noticing his concern to cover his manliness, his decision not to embrace Nausikaa's knees, as any ordinary suppliant would, and his determination to wash himself, although young girls customarily wash men in the *Odyssey*. These contradictions to normal behavior show his sensuality and that he is conscious of it. He is in the midst of lovely young girls, virginal and naïve, as he knows. His defenses are down and he wants to avoid trouble.

Nausikaa's response is flavored with the idea of marriage. She even mentions it openly to her maidens ("would that such a man were called my husband" [6.244]). When she apologizes to Odysseus for not wanting to walk with him through the city, she demonstrates her cool prudence, her middle-class good sense, as well as a conception of public good behavior that contrasts with Aphrodite's spectacle later on. Nonetheless, the whole speech is a none-too-subtle hint that Nausikaa would like to marry Odysseus. She has presented her case indirectly and at an early stage—as befits a girl in a position of power who desires a defenseless male.

Everywhere the episode is marked by taste and intelligent subtleties. The Phaiacians are obviously the most civilized people in either epic. As Alkinoos says:

> We are not great boxers or wrestlers, but we can run swiftly on foot, and are the best when it comes to ships. For us the banquet, the lyre, dancing, changes of clothes, warm baths, and couches are always the nicest things. (8.246 ff)

The Phaiacians possess all the ingredients for enjoying human existence. Their *politeness* shows how they cherish human beings.

Notice how Alkinoos asks by indirection if Odysseus is

perhaps a god, in a subtle attempt to get Odysseus to reveal who he is before the ritual moment for asking identities has arrived after the dinner. In turn Aretē quickly notices that Odysseus is wearing palace clothes and uses it as an opening to his identity. ("Who are you? I thought you came from overseas. How did you get those clothes?" [7.238 f]) Odysseus, stalling, answers her several questions in reverse. As soon as he has finished describing where he got the clothes, Alkinoos cuts in, thereby freeing him from further identifying himself which by now it is clear Odysseus does not care to do. Notice how nicely Odysseus lies for Nausikaa when her parents object to her not having had the manners to lead Odysseus up to the palace. ("I didn't want to [go with her] out of fear and shame" [7.305].) Alkinoos puts his case for Odysseus marrying Nausikaa very cleverly, if suddenly. After rather abstractedly offering the marriage, he speaks longer about the means of transporting Odysseus home. As persons of sensibility know, if one has a shocking or daring proposition to make, he had best offer at greater length an alternative, far less drastic course of action, so his prey will not feel desperately cornered and react desperately. Odysseus effectively says no to the idea of marrying Nausikaa by saying nothing. Alkinoos understands this, and quietly assumes that Odysseus has a wife and children elsewhere, to whom he alludes in a later speech ("When you are dining in your halls with your wife and children, you will remember our manliness" [8.242 ff]). The farewell between Nausikaa and Odysseus vibrates with all the things left unsaid. She gives him a chance to mention why he is leaving when she says, "you owe to me first your life," but the brevity of her speech eliminates any real need to answer anything. Odysseus, the perfect gentleman, says no more than Nausikaa. He does not mention his family as he had to Kalypso with whom he had been sleeping. He subtly alludes instead to the moment of their meeting when he says that he will pray to her as to a god, echoing

his comparison of her to Artemis in his initial speech of
supplication. He thus returns them to their nicest moment, when everything was fresh and possible for them.

Temptation of the subtlest sort has been met and
mastered by everyone concerned. The travel stories that
intervene and fill the time at Scheria show Odysseus repeatedly tempted by his intellectual curiosity and the crew
by their greed. The temptation of the crew runs as a
counter theme, a kind of sensual curiosity, usually manifesting itself in gluttony. The crew is a variation of the
eternally banqueting suitors on the island of Ithaka. As a
foil to Odysseus they betray an utter lack of prudence, a
dismal ignorance of the limitations to human existence.
They and the suitors are the world's stupidity and folly.
The Kikones have time to raise help to attack the band,
the crew having refused to leave, even after acquiring an
abundance of plunder, because there was too much wine
and meat still left for the eating. The crew got lost among
the Lotus Eaters because they too insisted on eating the
lotus.

The disaster of the Cyclops' cave, on the other hand, is
Odysseus' doing. For no practical reason, since they are
all well fed and relaxed, he determines to investigate the
surroundings. The size of the cave indicates that a giant
inhabits it. Encouraged in his curiosity, Odysseus prepares
a ritual response to hospitality, a gift of wine. Such is his
intelligence (or is it luck?) that he supplies the very gift
that will disarm his host. When the cave appears to be
empty the men want only to gather food and be off. Odysseus, on the contrary, is curious to see the owner. He appears quite nonchalant about any potential danger. The
nightmare that follows is certainly Odysseus' fault, as the
crew is quick to remember later on (10.437).

The visit with Aeolos contrasts Odysseus, who enjoys
talking to the god of the winds, with the crew who, after
departing, greedily and imprudently open the sack of
winds hunting for gold. The poet, however, does not con-

ceal the risks and sometimes the inhumanity in the cold
drive of Odysseus' curiosity. Members of the crew are sent
unwillingly among the Lastrygonians to reconnoiter, only
to satisfy their lord's curiosity. An attack is provoked; all
are destroyed except Odysseus and the crew of his own
ship. Odysseus is quick to plan an escape for his ship.
His common sense saves him; the others are gone. These
episodes reveal another facet of the hero's personality.
Here the poet seems to be using materials from stories of
a Wily Lad, an amoral (magical) trickster whom I described before. Odysseus here is carried away by temptation, willing to sacrifice everything to explore the unknown.
He grows ruthless, pitiless, and relentless, almost mania-
cally daring, as a Wily Lad is always inclined to be.

He cheers on his crew in the only language they understand, "Come now while there's food and drink on the
swift ship, let us think of food . . ." (10.176*f*). But when
he sights smoke on Circe's island, he is determined to
investigate. Again he is obdurate before their tears ("But
nothing came of their crying," he can coldly, or perhaps
even cheerfully, say to Alkinoos [10.202]). Again those
sent ahead are ruined through eating. Again he is im-
placable; he will follow after them to Circe's house. For,
he explains, "strong necessity lies upon me." What duty
does he feel? Serving his men, or satisfying his curiosity?
While the former is more logical, the latter more nearly
agrees with his previous disregard of the crew. The poet is
properly ambiguous. But this is again only a facet of a very
complex personality. Brutality and callousness do mark his
relations with the crew who, one must admit, never appear to be a very sympathetic lot. Nonetheless, Homer
portrays them as considerably victimized. They are also
in this way analogues to the suitors who more than once
appear to be victims. Perhaps the determination that
makes Odysseus cold, hard, and insensible to his crew must
be associated with the period of wandering. When Eumaios describes his lost master in the fourteenth book,

he pictures Odysseus as a superlatively good man—full of love and affection for his people. Perhaps these qualities are only drawn out in familiar surroundings. The problem is not simply behavioral, however. Odysseus, as the poet presents him, is a deep and strange man.

The temptation which Circe offers Odysseus is more than the chance to learn the ways of a witch. She is also a woman; once again the overtones of a sexual battle between male and female appear. The episode is important, because Circe, the witch par excellence, seems in many ways the basic type for all women in the *Odyssey*. Their coolness, high intelligence, their dangerousness, their manner of yielding are all exemplified best in this strange creature who turns to swine men who eat her food. The role of woman as feeder from a mother's breasts to a wife's cooking is suspect, for it caters to necessity that can turn man to animal, losing in his need the self-consciousness and freedom of will that set humankind apart in the animal kingdom. Woman's sexual attractions do the same thing, more devastatingly.

Fear of woman as a sexual object is also present in the enchanting aura of the goddess Circe. Hermes advises Odysseus to rush at Circe with a sword, when he is tapped by a wand. This seems to be an archetypal duel of the sexes played out in phallic symbols, one an enchanting, magical wand, the other a virile sword that can cut and thrust in the world of reality. As if to make it more obvious, Hermes promises that the drawn sword will prompt Circe to invite Odysseus into her bed. The contrast is between the obvious male appendage, his sexual symbol and weapon, and the hidden female power of sexuality. Odysseus is further advised by Hermes that he sleep with Circe to obtain his ends, but that he control the situation, in other words, go not as seduced but seducer. She must swear not to harm him once he is naked. The conversation between the two prospective lovers later is a masterpiece of mistrust and suspicion which they both take for granted.

It has been suggested that this attitude, which one encounters frequently in the *Odyssey,* reflects a growing consciousness of the basic difference between men and
women. Such a revelation perhaps created a sense of
alienation between the sexes. Each would develop an inherent need and determination to dominate the other sex,
so as to incorporate the difference. The hostility may also
reflect, however, the invading Indo-European male-
oriented people's confusion and resentment at finding an
indigenous population oriented to the female. Homeric
epic reveals women who are free, active, and powerful. In
the historical period the culture almost everywhere in the
Greek world was male centered, male dominated. Male
homosexuality became often in theory if not in practice
the most desirable and complete human relationship. An
extraordinary change has clearly taken place from the society which Homer reveals and that of several hundred
years later. The pressures and effects of the beginning of
this change are perhaps already in the *Odyssey.* The artist
in Homer, however, saves him from the tendentious. Both
sexes have virtues, however much woman may seem to
threaten man. It is to Penelope that Odysseus continually
longs to return. Circe, too, in her way is so attractive that
Odysseus remains for a year. It is obviously a good year.
Therein lies her and every woman's final enchantment.
They alone can provide whatever good for which man
lives. Man's dilemma is in humbling himself to accept his
need.

All the travel stories that I have been discussing are in
some way mere rehearsal for Odysseus' adventures in
Ithaka. Again temptation, curiosity, and bold escape are
the sources for the hero's action. Ithaka provides the final
solution to Odysseus' curiosity by offering a number of
recognition scenes in which he becomes fully reoriented
into the world he had left behind twenty years before.
His rediscovery of Ithaka culminates in his reunion with
the source for all his homing instincts, the faithful Penel-

ope. Almost all scenes now have to do with planning a clever and bold escape from the throng of young men who hold his family and possessions in thrall. The odds are no more with Odysseus now than when he found himself shut in Polyphemos' cave. The same wit saves him here as saved him there.

For the hero, homecoming provides the final and greatest exercise in resisting temptation. Heroic self-control is needed to maintain a beggar's disguise that must be psychological and spiritual as well as physical. Helen's account of Odysseus' disguised entry into Troy drew attention to his stoic capacity to lacerate himself, to achieve complete realism in his disguise. In his relations with the suitors Odysseus finds another laceration in accepting humbly their gross arrogance. The agony of submission is compounded by the necessity to maintain silence, to feign emotional distance before those he loves. To have come so far, to have waited so long, and still to endure deprivation is temptation indeed. Throughout these scenes as a counter mood runs the hero's exhilaration at practicing so great a deceit. All the components of Odysseus' extraordinary personality come together in the vengeance he exacts upon the suitors.

Masking inward joy with outward cool; humble in his understanding of the powers which hold man; arrogant in his assumption of his own worth; sociable and personable toward every kind of person, though never sympathetic, always private, sensual, and fastidious, cruel and cunning, serious and dignified; Odysseus is the most exciting and profound character that Graeco-Roman paganism ever conceived.

The poet's evident interest in appearance and reality, truth and falsehood that marks almost every episode of the story perhaps stems from historical circumstances. Perhaps the *Odyssey* is testimony to a change in the meaning of poetry. Oral saga poetry holds a considerably more important position in a culture than one may first realize.

The identity of an illiterate culture depends completely on the poetry. Not only does the poetry articulate the culture as it is, but more important, what it was, thereby giving the culture stability and continuity. Oral saga poetry for such a culture is its history and school as well as its art.

The subject matter of saga is realistic—as opposed, for instance, to fairy tale. Saga generally bears the inherent assumption that the events of which it is made are true. Modern oral poets often observe that they repeat *exactly* what they have learned from the previous generation of poets. Thus they believe in the purity of the oral tradition. In addition, Homer's symbolic dependence upon the Muse shows some sort of belief that the poet himself does not control the transmission. Because a culture uses saga as history and the means to affirm its identity, the culture too must insist upon saga as being fact. Therefore, for its practitioners as well as its auditors oral saga poetry was very likely a true record of real events. One senses this attitude especially in the *Iliad.* Although the poet has demonstrably organized his material, embellished it and invested it with further meanings, it remains easy to believe that he was unconscious of this. He has a way of offering his story rather than imposing it that reflects the unconscious assurance of the man who speaks the truth.

When, however, Hesiod remarks in his *Theogony* that the Muses know how to tell lies masked as truth he seems deliberately to be insisting upon the fictional nature of the saga poetry of Homer. Hesiod perhaps reflects a growing awareness among the oral poets that in fact they were manipulating the materials in their poetic tradition to the extent that epic poetry was not actually a true record. They were then able to begin to define reality, to explore it. For they were in effect re-creating what seemed to be a true account, out of materials handed down, supposedly descriptive of real events, but reshaped consciously by themselves. Therefore reality lay inherent in the story materials, but reality could also be created by the poets. Thus it is that Odysseus can play with the elements of saga in creating fictional autobiographies for Eumaios and the others in Ithaka. In this reorganization of the traditional realities, false to the true Odysseus, the hero is in point of fact shaping a true description of his personality. This is the tantalizing paradox that animates the entire poem.

Chapter VI

THE *AENEID*

Sunt lacrimae rerum
Virgil *Aeneid* 1.462

The Homeric epics held first place in the Greek civilization as long as it existed. They were in a sense the only epics and Homer was the "divine poet" with no rival. Throughout most of the Christian era, however, men of letters have accorded this honor to the Roman poet, Virgil, who composed a roughly ten-thousand-line epic in Latin, the *Aeneid*, in the last century of paganism. Partly this is due to the survival and supremacy of Latin in the centuries following the eclipse of the ancient world. But more than that Virgil created a poem that seems to bring together so many facets of the Graeco-Roman world that the *Aeneid* stands as a complete monument to those two ancient civilizations. As the gap widened between that ancient period and the succeeding generations of men looking back to capture its essence, the *Aeneid* grew in stature until it became almost the universal pagan poem. Virgil, I should imagine, would have been surprised to know how thoroughly he overshadowed his predecessors. Certainly the *Aeneid* is testimony to the extraordinary influence which the *Iliad* and *Odyssey* exerted on later poets. Virgil would have seen himself as part of a tradition, as someone handing on in his own image the inheritance of earlier centuries. Yet the *Aeneid* truly is much more than a poem. While the *Iliad* and *Odyssey* are portraits of people in action, the *Aeneid* is a vision of the world.

We know of no real successors to the *Iliad* and *Odyssey* in the ancient Greek world, partly, we may assume, because the introduction and spread of the alphabet fostered the psychology of literacy, partly, we may like to believe, because the supreme achievement of these two epics left nothing for later bards to say. Our particular notion of classical antiquity encourages the second interpretation. We often forget that so much of what has been preserved to us comes from the conscious selection of a human sensibility rather than the freak hand of Fate. A succession of scholars, schoolmasters, and editors for centuries chose the best. These best, anthologized as it were, stand like moments of light in the darkness of our relative ignorance so that one easily develops an image of genre after genre in some truly organic fashion growing, flowering, and dying.

Apart from the Homeric epic we happen to know there existed several other epics which were gathered together at a much later time into something called the Epic Cycle, which has survived only in small fragments today. They seem, by and large, to have been an attempt to tie up all the loose ends of the Trojan saga into an historical perspective. As the ancient commentators to the *Iliad* remark, Homer manages to include if not centrally, then by allusion, almost every event connected with the entire history of the Trojan War from the apple of discord to the final destruction of the city and the return of the Greek heroes. The poems of the Epic Cycle single out a number of these events for the lengthier dramatic narrative treatment that typifies the *Iliad* and *Odyssey*. We know little about them, their true dates, whether the poetic style is truly oral, and, if so, how they were written down. One can see, however, that the central preoccupation of their authors was detail, logically enough, since the point of these poems

seems to be the tidying up of the saga, the drawing together of the flotsam and jetsam of the tradition. The final
outcome of this impulse to tidiness was the creation of
absurdly logical plots. The *Telegonia,* for instance, attributed to Eugammon (sixth century B.C.) described the arrival at Ithaka of Telegonos, a son of Odysseus by Circe,
who upon killing his father, marries Penelope, leaving
Telemachos with nothing to do but to marry Circe. It is,
I suppose, a slightly more genteel variation on the theme
of Oedipus.

Literacy brought to poetry economy as an aesthetic
principle. The word and the mythological image formed
the stuff of lyric poetry and fifth-century tragedy. Much
more like epic is the history of the Persian wars written in
prose by Herodotos in the latter half of the fifth century.
Anecdotal, garrulous, catholic, Herodotos created a vision
of man individually and in mass set in a cosmos of profound dimension, acting grandly and humanly in constant
dialogue with god. But this history was not, of course,
really epic, any more than Proust's *Remembrance of
Things Past* is the legitimate successor to Milton or Dante.

Nonetheless a few epics were being written which we
mostly know only by name. Some described the founding
of cities and their early history, others the achievement of
newly arisen dynastic houses of tyrants. The language of
the few fragments we possess shows a clear similarity to
Homeric epic usage, although the particularly formulaic
quality is diminished. These epics were evidently not overwhelming critical successes at the time of their composition. The succeeding centuries had turned to tragic drama
and to prose for their enlightenment. Epic became a
curiosity piece.

The age of learning and scholarship in the third and
second centuries before Christ, largely at Alexandria in
Egypt (hence the "Alexandrian age") commenced to define the various genres that had come into being quite
spontaneously in the earlier, more creative periods of

Greek civilization. Writers of heroic epic for the first time became self-conscious as a result of the minute textual and structural analysis being made on the *Iliad* and *Odyssey* by a host of scholars. Epic usage came to be an important determinative in solving textual problems in the Homeric corpus. Along with epic usage notions of epic propriety, a far more subjective criterion, came to be employed in judging the validity of the texts. It was to this principle that the scholars looked when casting out the description of Aphrodite drawing up a chair for Helen or Telemachos speaking sharply to his mother. Some of the scholars in the early Alexandrian period also wrote epics, so that a well-developed intellectualized notion of the heroic epic as an art form grew up. For many this endeavor encouraged an insistence upon an adherence to the structure and plot motifs of the *Iliad* or *Odyssey*, or both if possible, as an aesthetic principle of epic.

The result in one form is the preciosity of Apollonios Rhodios' *Argonautika*. In his choice of language Apollonios sets out to reflect Homer most intimately by never *exactly* imitating the older poet's usage; in his plot he introduces as many motifs found in the older epics as is logically possible. All is done by indirection so that the reader must participate through his own learning. While there is much that is stiflingly self-conscious and pedantic, the work as a whole manages to convey a unified, if bleak, epic action. Apollonios' problem lies in trying to create the quality of heroic poetry without being able to successfully create a hero. For parts of the poem he has made this dilemma work for him, but as a whole the work is flawed because of it. The poem thus reflects the conditions of the time in which Apollonios wrote.

The Argonauts' world is that of the anti-hero, and very likely Apollonios Rhodios consciously understood his hero, Jason, in these very modern terms. He seems to be consciously setting off Jason's vacuity and impotence by means of the surrounding high epic structure. The older epic hero, an Achilles or Odysseus, who achieved meaning for himself through his own action in a hostile world, the hero of simplicity and directness when individuality still mattered, and uncommon exalted behavior was common to superior men, could not have functioned in the cosmopolitan, overpopulated world of Alexandria, where the complexity of human existence, the emergence of psychological motivation, and the acceptance of, even dependence upon fate made men's sense of self a shaky thing.

Certainly Apollonios Rhodios contrives to undercut every one of Jason's earlier entrances into the story. As, for instance, in the first book when he arrives to set sail in the *Argo* his crew of heroes seem already to be assembled. Good dramatic sense dictates that the central figure be last to arrive so as to be able to hold center stage, and this applies to narrative poetry as well. In this poem, however, Jason has no sooner arrived than two more heroes come on, and we are told that everyone marveled when they saw them. Just before this when Jason sets forth from his palace he is compared in simile to Apollo. A cry goes forth from the crowd, he is swept on. Yet in this triumph Apollonios Rhodios directs our attention to the wistful melancholia of an old priestess who was too feeble to push through to touch the departing hero's hand. The feeling of bold, potent exhilaration which is the aura of the hero markedly evaporates.

The *Argonautika* is an epic in search of a hero. This seems to have characterized all epics of the period. Evidently it was not possible to use successfully the stories of Dionysos or Herakles, demigods and civilization builders. Epics did exist about one or the other of these heroes combining a traditional yearning after the memory of the youthful and extraordinary emperor Alexander, who brought Hellenism to the East, and this very learned age's interest in geography, ethnography, and history. These heroes were, however, too remote, the factual material too disparate. Instead of epic there was a pastiche of encyclopedia notes in meter hung loosely on a featureless demi-god.

Rome's emergence as a Mediterranean power and her subsequent conquest of Greece slowly caught up the Roman people into the intellectual and creative ferment that was taking place in the Hellenistic world. As the Latin poet Horace said toward the end of the pagan era, "Captive Greece made untamed Rome her captive and brought the arts to rural Latium." The Romans began to try their hand at all the various literary genres that had flowered spontaneously in Greece and had been so carefully classified by the Alexandrian mind. Rather than finding inspiration in the classical age of Greece for guidance Rome looked first to the Alexandrian period of decadence and scholarship which had established rules and principles for literature. Much that was created was mere slavish and stultified copying. After a time the Romans grew more confident of their own skill and the strength of their own cultural ambience. Still, whenever they chose to compose grand literature they always cast a glance at their Greek models.

This was the inheritance of Virgil whose *Aeneid* came to be a model for almost all epics thereafter. The *Aeneid*, it sometimes seems, can have little meaning for anyone ignorant of the *Iliad* and the *Odyssey* because it is so obviously dependent upon them at every turn, in the best Alexandrian tradition. Yet students of later European epic need look back no further than the *Aeneid* because Virgil has created a poem that in another sense is completely original and independent. Virgil truly ends one tradition and begins another. He stood in the company of one who was intent upon doing the same in the political life of Rome—Caesar Augustus.

The battle of Actium in 31 B.C. between the young Octavian Caesar and Antony marked a turning point in the history of the ancient world. For nearly a century the city of Rome, which controlled the destinies of most of the

Western world, had been torn by the most vicious and incredible civil wars, as a succession of would-be tyrants fought between themselves to make her their private possession. This long-drawn-out civil war had drained the whole of Italy of its blood, destroyed the economy, ravaged the farms, and made of Roman grandeur a mockery.

But by this sea battle of Actium the young man, who was later to be known as Caesar Augustus, made himself sole master of the world. There were no more opposing strong men; the Republic was dead; it was the beginning of the Roman Empire and a time to pick up the pieces. For the rest of his life—a total of forty-four years—Caesar Augustus tried as best he could to revive what was workable of Republican Rome and to create throughout the empire's vast complex of lands and cultures a solid stability where there would be no room for a Pompey, or an Antony, a Caesar, or an Octavian. It is perhaps a testimony to his greatness that the Roman Empire endured in the West for five hundred years, and in the East for a thousand, only in the end, as a recent historian has remarked, not to sicken and to die, but to be assassinated by the invading barbarians.

This was the world in which Publius Vergilius Maro lived and died. In his youth and early manhood he was witness to the misery and the chaos that spread over Italy, the blood baths, the purgings, the cynical denial of humanity, first by Pompey, then by Caesar, then Antony, and finally by the youthful Octavian, who until he had secured the position that enabled him to live out his years as a paragon of benignity and clemency, was as ruthless as the rest. In his maturity Virgil was one of those who shared intimately in the exciting new experience of peace and empire that Augustus envisioned. For the Emperor Augustus was Virgil's patron and had made him an intimate of the imperial circle. In 29 B.C., two years after Actium, Virgil began the *Aeneid*, on which he was to spend the last decade of his life and which he left unfinished when he died.

He took an old Roman legend that identified the surviving Trojans with the Romans and established Aeneas as the founder of Rome. With this he set out to glorify and to celebrate the concept of *Romanitas* through its early history, and to sing of the dawn of a new age of peace and prosperity, and incidentally to praise the creator of this *pax romana*, that Emperor Augustus, who through his adoptive great-uncle, the deified Julius Caesar, traced his ancestry back directly to the legendary Aeneas, and to his mother, the goddess Venus.

The revolution that Augustus achieved seemed to contemporaries to be, as all revolutions do seem, a turning point in history, and so created by destiny. Rome's whole history encourages a belief in destiny, being the story of a small city of people who time and again were asked to enter into foreign power struggles and who found themselves at war's end successively a greater power and overseer of more and more territory. This reading of the known events is at once nationalistic and naïve, but it is a common first century B.C. Roman version. Rome then was the child of destiny; her every step, each one unconscious and disinterested, toward world mastery was guided by this relentless destiny. For Virgil, who was attempting to give his epic the sense of vast scale that remoteness in time and a large saga tradition give to the Homeric epic, the Roman idea of destiny in their history was an exactly suitable background to his immediate narrative. Aeneas' actions become actually giant historical movements, the human drama becomes merged in the historical. What we so often mean by the word "epic" today comes from this fusion.

The *Aeneid* begins with the well-known phrase, "Of arms and the man I sing"; it is Virgil's intent to indicate that his poem is in some way to be an amalgam of his two Homeric models. "Arms" as symbol of warfare is a program note to the last six books of the *Aeneid* in which Aeneas distinguishes himself in the fashion of the Greek *aristeia*, both as general of the army and as combatant in duels—

this is the atmosphere of the *Iliad.* "The man," which implies psychological portraiture or ethical drama, points to the first six books, which document Aeneas' wandering, his reception at the court of Dido, and his lengthy narration of the fall of Troy—clearly, although in miniature, echoing scenes of the *Odyssey* where descriptions of intellect and personality keep the focus on humankind.

The *Aeneid* in its entirety, however, is a nationalized *Odyssey,* being a wandering, a change, and a progress toward a goal, that is home and settled life for the wanderer. Here is a brief summary of the plot:

The goddess Juno, ever hateful toward Troy and Trojans, causes a storm at sea which drives Aeneas together with his band of survivors from the Greek destruction of Troy to the coast of Africa, where they are eventually received at the court of Queen Dido, in the city of Carthage. Aeneas, after a great welcoming banquet, is asked to tell of the misfortunes that have brought him to Africa, and he answers with a lengthy narrative describing the fall of Troy (beginning with the Greek's contrivance of the wooden horse, the Greek Sinon's treachery in pretending to the Trojans that all the Greeks were departed, the amazing death of Laocoön by the mysterious serpent as well as a number of events after the Greeks had forced their way into the city, set it on fire, and begun to kill the citizens). He then continues with the description of the survivors' wanderings (to Crete, Greece) and the fabulous things they have seen. He concludes by mentioning that his father, Anchises, had died shortly before when the storm came up that blew them to Africa.

By the machinations of the goddesses Juno (who wants him to forget his destiny) and Venus (Aeneas' mother with the typical mother's limited notion of a son's happiness) and the latter's son Cupid, Dido proceeds to fall in love with Aeneas. On the occasion of a royal hunt they meet in a cave, consummate their love, and soon their ensuing love affair obliterates her legitimate concerns as queen and his as leader of his band, until Jupiter sends Mercury to remind Aeneas sternly of his destined mission of leading the remaining Trojans to Italy. Aeneas with heavy heart leaves after an agonizing confrontation with Dido; she in grief commits suicide.

Before Aeneas sets out in earnest to obey Jupiter's commands he returns to Sicily to conduct elaborate funeral games in honor of his father who had died there shortly before Aeneas went to Africa. He is then told by the Sibyl that he must proceed to the Underworld to consult his father about the future. In the Underworld, he meets his father, and after seeing the customary marvels of the place is shown the souls of Rome's future heroes where they are assembled to await the fated moment to re-enter this world. He leaves his father and the Underworld and when once again in the mortal world sails to Italy which he recognizes as the destined land by an omen that had been prophesied to him. His attempts to settle peacefully among the indigenous population are frustrated by the ever malicious goddess Juno (her actions are to an extent a divine reflection of the natural human situation). King Latinus, the ruler in Italy who has promised his daughter Lavinia to a young prince, Turnus, changes his mind upon meeting a delegation from Aeneas and decides that this foreign prince is the suitor actually decreed by fate. A fury sent by Juno rouses up the jealous Turnus and his supporter in the royal family, Queen Mother Amata. King Latinus is compelled for political reasons to follow the course set by Turnus, war begins, and the Italians gather their forces. The course of the war is developed largely through vignettes—Aeneas acquiring as allies King Evander and his gallant, noble young son, Pallas; Venus urging her husband Vulcan to create a heroic beautifully adorned shield for Aeneas; the sad adventures of two young heroes, Nisus and Euryalus, almost lovers in an elegant, aristocratic fashion who attempt a sortie into one Latin camp and are killed; the death of Pallas in battle at the hands of Turnus; the

killing of the evil old king, Mezentius, and his loyal en-
dearing young son, Lausus, by Aeneas, and finally the duel
between Turnus and Aeneas in which Turnus is killed.

The whole poem is definitely reminiscent of the *Odyssey.* Even the latter half of the poem which is supposed to
be specifically like the *Iliad* in tone, to the very end re-
tains the major theme of the *Odyssey.* For Aeneas in fighting Turnus is fighting a suitor, and winning the woman; in
achieving victory he is winning his homeland, and so his
home, for because it was destined the land was in some
sense his already. All these ideas are components of the
Odyssey. In the earlier part of the poem Juno's hostility
reflects Poseidon's; until he finally reaches Italy, Aeneas
roams the Mediterranean; he is beset by the temptation to
stop; he makes mistakes; it takes a messenger from Jupiter
to get him out of Carthage. He encounters fabulous creatures and sees the Underworld. He even manages to narrate part of his adventures. And in the end there is fulfillment, the goal is reached, the prize won. Structurally at
least, the poem is optimistic and in the hands of Virgil's
successors this epic form of struggle and progress became a
natural vehicle for Christian mythologies.

Perhaps the most important element of the opening
phrase of the poem is "I sing." The Homeric poet sang
only through the Muse, or rather was the instrument
through which the Muse created and sang. While I have
remarked that this is simply symbol for the large role of
tradition in oral epic, this conception of the relationship
between the poet and the Muse certainly puts the poet at
one remove from his work. Virgil, the literate poet, is quick
to indicate his own responsibility for the material that follows. He clearly wishes to emphasize his personal authority, for he illogically returns immediately to the epic
convention in an apostrophe to the Muse (line 8). The
juxtaposition of the two, "I sing" and the Muse establishes
his literary individuality.

Certainly he could not have been further removed from

the oral epic tradition of Homer. Through the selective process of conservatism and destruction, Virgil set out to re-create something long dead. The peculiar looseness, the anecdotal and digressive nature of oral poetry that remained in the literate Greek epic poets well into the Christian era was not permitted. The poet built his lines from words; his choice was always rigorous. One feels that Virgil wanted to ensure that every word extended the poem's meaning in the economical manner of lyric poetry. The repetitive nature of Homeric epic that gave to the narrative the secure sense of the normative had to be replaced with an equivalent that would not have the boring effect that direct repetition must produce in a literate audience. Everywhere the poem shows intense concern for structure. For a period of ten years Virgil, we are told, worked slowly dictating daily only a very few lines, then fashioning and refashioning each one, having first composed the entire work in prose and divided it into twelve books. Every line shows wide reading in Greek and Latin literature. When he lay dying at Brindisi in 19 B.C., he was so dissatisfied with his progress that he asked his literary executors to burn the manuscript. Such was the cautious, deliberate, and sensitive psyche that created the *Aeneid*.

Augustus sensibly countermanded Virgil's request to his executors, thereby preserving for the Western world what it has in most epochs held to be its greatest literary treasure. The twentieth century is rather disenchanted with the *Aeneid* for many reasons, first because we no longer find the Roman world that Virgil was celebrating very appealing. Then, his elaborately developed symbolism through the persons in the story tend to make the poem seem to us somewhat wooden. His vision of a cultural ambience, complete and self-contained, that is, the Graeco-Roman heritage worked out in paradigm, seems in this free-wheeling, experimental epoch parochial, if not provincial. For these reasons we moderns resist him, although Virgil ought to ring true to us immediately. For the *Aeneid* is a middle-

class epic and its hero goes through a spiritual crisis that
is essentially the bourgeois agony.

Virgil's care in establishing an ordered structure for his
poem is reflected in the point of view, the philosophy that
informs every part of the poem. The *Aeneid* has a unity
more pervasive than the Homeric epics show, which springs
from the intellect rather than an instinctual apprehension
of persons and situations. In addition Virgil has managed
a rather well-fashioned cosmic view. The literature of antiquity has been criticized as being too limited in scope,
because it is too much centered upon man, hence all things
become anthropomorphic in one way or another. The view
of man as a self-contained terrestrial phenomenon of the
here and now ignores the kind of implications that traditional theological and modern scientific speculations have
raised in the ensuing centuries. Virgil of all ancient writers
acts against the simple anthropomorphic view, perhaps the
reason why his characters seem something other than simply human. He has, in fact, developed a view of history,
destiny, and human action that far transcends the narrative moment.

The spirit of his age was revolution, a change in government and political philosophy that was destined to bring
forth a period of relative stability longer than the Western
world has otherwise known. Critics of the *pax romana* talk
of the spiritual torpor, the lack of significant cultural enterprise in the first centuries of the Christian era; they are
often correct. The atmosphere of the time, however, enabled mankind to prosper in the advancement of human-
ism, a state of mind, a philosophical position peculiarly
Roman, having a metaphysical and spiritual significance of
its own, and influencing greatly the entire course of Western Europe. *Humanitas* as the Romans conceived it was an
outgrowth of many things, principally a heritage from the
Greek culture of deifying man and his activity and from
the Stoics of identifying all men as brothers under the
skin. This, combined with the Roman propensity to tech-

nological skills and a peasant's drive toward material well-being (not splendor), produced the means for spreading over the known world a homogeneous culture in which everyone was educated and in which everyone participated, in which the central concern was humankind. The Romans created civilization as we know it, they invented the social and political modes by which it could spread. Stability gave vast numbers of men a chance to achieve a full identity. Eventually, centuries later, it was lost as men became members of a lumpen proletariat under the groaning weight and expanse of imperial bureaucratic structure. But in Virgil's time that was far in the future. What was in the immediate future, a tantalizing hope still, was that relaxation, peace, would bring the impulse to creativity that stable, strong government could give. Virgil uses civilization and government everywhere as a leitmotiv in the *Aeneid*. For instance, in a simile in the first book he compares the quieting of a storm at sea to the beneficent control a powerful ruler can have amid a turbulent crowd. Again in the simile of the bees toward the end of Book One, Virgil ignores the nonhuman elements and concentrates specifically on the social qualities of the hive, its mutuality and sense of commonweal. From the very first speech of Jupiter (1.257 ff), when he rehearses and outlines the destinies of imperial Rome, of "Romans, masters of the universe, the togaed race," we are reminded of the peculiar gift that Rome brought to the world—the continuing process of civilization within the structure and in terms of the structure of an established polity. Even if often only an ideal rather than an actuality, it remains a proud legacy; the vision of its potential animates the *Aeneid*. This world view is something Virgil brought to the traditional epic form and by so doing transformed it.

But Virgil has saved much from traditional epic and turned it to his own account. At times these reflections of the older epic are formal, at times sudden, unexpected but organically developed. For example, twice Virgil employs the idea of someone reaching out futilely three times to embrace the ghost of a dead person. In the *Odyssey* Odysseus tries three times to embrace his mother, Antikleia, in the Underworld. Virgil has reproduced this scene formally when Aeneas meets his father in the Underworld. But in Book Two Aeneas describes how his wife, Creusa, who was lost and died in the conflagration at Troy, appeared to him as a wraith which three times he tried to embrace. Here the recollection of the emotional depth of the Odyssean source for this gives an immediately stronger emotional quality to the relationship of Aeneas and Creusa, which Virgil otherwise does not have time to develop.

There are larger formal recollections of the Homeric epics as, for instance, the Catalogue of Italian troops in Book Seven which Virgil turns into a melodious and gently nationalistic hymn of place names; or, the funeral games in Book Five where Virgil gives to the participants names taken from the noble families of Rome's historical times, thereby endowing the formal, stock and routine athletic contests with marvelous social tension; or, the journey to the Underworld, the description of the shield, the assemblage of the gods—the list is long. In imitation great or small Virgil continually demonstrates his superiority to the other poets in the tradition of pedantic, allusive poetry begun in Greece in the Hellenistic era and much copied at Rome, for, although the knowledgeable reader is able to find considerable additional meaning in the ramifications of every learned allusion or imitation, Virgil so well adapts them to his own poem that they have immediate point for any reader.

Virgil's knowledge of his literary antecedents however seems at times to get the better of him. For instance, in his poem Venus is poorly developed, because she is too many things at once. She is the goddess of love, sexual pleasure, Aeneas' mother (hence, in a sense, a Roman matron), and the founder of the Roman race. In the *Iliad* Achilles' mother is the minor goddess, Thetis, who from time to time appears to comfort him in his wrath. In the *Odyssey*, of course, it is Athene who is always at hand to help out the hero; she is, however, bound to him neither by relationship, nor sensual instinct—she being the virgin goddess. Virgil has tried to combine the Thetis-Achilles relationship with the Athene-Odysseus relationship and ends up with a highy overprotective mother. The two most embarrassing moments for the reader are when the essentially puritanical Aeneas comes face to face with Helen, his mother's special protégé, and when Venus decides to enchant Dido into love by sending her divine son, Cupid, to make the queen fall into a passion. The love goddess, the mother figure, and the helper figure do not naturally associate themselves, especially in the Roman frame of reference.

On a smaller scale there are imitations of lines in other poets, some of which are very awkward. When Aeneas meets Dido in the Underworld (6.460) he says to her, "Unwilling, O Queen, I left your shore" (*invitus regina tuo de litore cessi*). This is derived from Catullus, who lived a generation before Virgil and was much caught up in the Alexandrian literary styles and fashions that were sweeping Rome. He translated into Latin a very pretty poem by the Greek poet, Callimachus, called the "Lock of Berenice" in which a lock of hair that has been cut from Queen Berenice's head laments the separation. All rather silly, especially since the poem is rather heavily burdened with mythological pedantries and courtly conceits. At one point the lock says to the queen, "Unwilling, O Queen, I left your head" (*invita, o regina, tuo de vertice cessi*). Since Catullus' poem deals with the agony and lament of separation, Virgil's learned reader may perhaps be able to invest Aeneas' quiet remark with the range of feeling that Catullus developed in ninety-two lines. On the other hand, perhaps the unlearned reader has the advantage here. Catullus' poem is at best an artificial, clever, rococo tour de force. This brief moment in the *Aeneid* is agonized and melancholy; the imitated line seems suddenly to charge the scene with a cynical frivolity. Perhaps Virgil used it as a stopgap which he would have removed had he lived to revise the whole poem.

Generally Virgil is successful in his use of the literary tradition, and he uses it, as he does history, to create the vast scale that is a hallmark of epic. Homer's continual brief allusions to mythological details well known to his auditors helped to create the sense of depth and dimension to the epic saga world that could not even be estimated by the reader. With his learned allusions Virgil achieves the same effect creating the image of a unified culture of immeasurable ramifications.

The poem is the story of death and rebirth as it occurs in the soul of Aeneas. This spiritual crisis is both developed in the action of the narrative and reflected in the history of Rome that is prospective to the dramatic moment but retrospective for the narrator. Four events within the poem significantly convey this theme: the scene of Aeneas carrying his father, Anchises, from burning Troy (Book Two); the scene of Aeneas picking up the shield embossed with famous moments in Roman history (Book Eight); Aeneas' confrontation of the past and the future in the Underworld (Book Six); and the duel between Turnus and Aeneas (Book Twelve). The emotional depth to the struggle in Aeneas' soul which this crisis produces throughout the poem is conveyed in the almost tragic story of the love affair between Dido and Aeneas, where she offers almost every conceivable temptation and is finally denied.

Anchises functions in the poem as a typal father. Roman culture centered on the *pater familias,* "father of the family," who was the keystone in Roman social structure. Tradition oriented, the Romans looked to the father figure whether in the family (*pater familias*) or the imperial throne (*pater patrias,* father of the country), or in the senate (*patres conscripti,* senatorial fathers), as repository of ancestral attitudes and customs. The attention which

Aeneas pays his father gives to the *Aeneid* a consciously Roman flavor. Aeneas' sense of responsibility to other persons, his humanistic piety, is born in the love which he bears his father. Anchises is, however, also a symbol of tradition; so Aeneas must bear the weight of the past when he carries Anchises from Troy.

Anchises dies early in the narrative. In part this is a mechanical necessity, since at Dido's court he could only have played something like a very heavy older Germant in a situation already dangerously melodramatic. The obvious reason is not, however, the important one. Psychologically Aeneas comes to act as a hero in his own right upon the death of his father. Greek saga tradition quite rightly suppressed the father but for Roman Virgil Anchises was important. For Virgil, the poet, Anchises was also important as a symbol. From being considered a son in the early part of the story, Aeneas is himself called "father" in the last few books. Since the action of the *Aeneid* is also a drama of history, the death of Anchises allows Aeneas to put down the burden of Troy's past before entering into the future, before becoming, as father par excellence, creator of Rome's destiny.

The Romans held it as an article of faith that they were descendants of the Trojans, but like the notion that the Irish are one of the lost tribes of Israel, the idea excited both repulsion and fascination. The inherent depravity in things Trojan was a constant theme in Latin literature. Figures out of saga offered the inspiration—Laomedon who cheated the gods of their earnings, Ganymede whose soft boyish sensuality caused Zeus to steal him away from Troy to be cupbearer at Olympos, and Paris, the effete seducer of a married woman, the beautiful young man who brought down the whole of the heroic world with his carelessness. The Romans could never, even in their extreme puritan exertions, erase the stain of their Trojan ancestry, probably because it so well subconsciously symbolized in their culture the nervousness of a poor and agrarian people, sud-

denly grown strong, masters of an empire, possessors of almost all the treasuries of the Mediterranean.

The failures of tradition and of the past are dramatized
in Anchises' general feebleness, but especially in his mis-
interpretation of the prophecies in Delos (Book Three).
The sense of failure in the past is also relevant to Virgil's
own time. All the agonies, stupidities, and cruelties of the
preceding century of civil wars at Rome are remembered
in Anchises. When after the mistaken trip to Crete the
Roman household gods tell prophecies to Aeneas, and not
to Anchises, Virgil implies as well that a new future has
been told to Augustus Caesar alone.

Although Troy was defeated, and perhaps owed some of
this defeat to a faulted tradition, the city possessed, on the
other hand, grandeur, richness, and glory: it held a central
place in the heroic tradition as it was created by Homer
and inherited by Virgil. The Roman poet is always nostal-
gic, sometimes self-consciously so—in keeping with the
elegiac tone one sometimes finds in epic. Anchises as Trojan often suggests a backward glance to that heroic grandeur, Greek or Trojan, that came into being before the
walls of Troy. For Virgil the death of Anchises suggests
the departure from this world of high heroics. Virgil, like
Apollonios Rhodios, has to account for the hero in the
structure of his epic, and, like the Alexandrian, finds that
the traditional epic hero is no longer viable. Anchises'
death, then, on this level frees Virgil from having to impose upon Aeneas a false traditional heroic personality.

Anchises' death leaves a vacuum. For a time Aeneas is
free and without burdens. The symmetrical pendant to
Anchises becomes the shield in Book Eight, for here
Aeneas resumes a burden, although of another order. What
he has set down in the burden of Anchises is now clear;
what he seems to be assuming with the shield is the whole
of Roman destiny. To be sure, sculptured upon that shield
is the marvelous span of time, from Romulus and Remus
being suckled by the wolf to an extended description of

Augustus' triumph at the battle of Actium. Virgil has chosen episodes representing the theme of empire which culminate in a list of the captive peoples following in the sway of Augustus upon his entry into Rome following Actium. The earlier episodes contrast brave selfless devotion to Rome (e.g., Cocles and Cloelia) with treachery derived from selfishness (Cataline), all prelude to the contest of these opposing ideologies at Actium.

Aeneas is not only shouldering the destiny of his people, becoming in fact its creator. He is also assuming an idea of state as the all-absorbing pervasive conception apart from which man has no identity. The destiny of Rome becomes the destiny of each man. Here individual heroism of the Homeric kind has no place, a personality such as Antony's has no place, nor will there be a place for Turnus. The assumption of the shield in terms of its symbolic meaning is a moment of triumph and rebirth for Aeneas; it follows psychologically upon his journey to the Underworld in Book Six where he immolated himself in Roman destiny after having symbolically died as an individual personality.

Virgil has rather thoroughly removed the fabulous from his story. It is a logical and direct inheritance of the *Odyssey*, yet Virgil cannot have a flesh and blood historic Aeneas encounter the Sirens, Scylla and Charybdis, or the Lotus Eaters, so he must content himself with allusions to these fairy tale creatures. He does, however, bring Aeneas to the Underworld, for, although it, too, is fabulous, the inherent symbolic potential in such a journey makes the Underworld visit important. Virgil's description of this event is completely serious: in contrast to the manner of the poet of the *Odyssey* who is appealing primarily to curiosity in representing the Underworld.

Aeneas' visit to the Underworld is in two parts, the first being a view of the traditional figures in the Underworld and persons from the Trojan saga, who are out of Aeneas'

own past, and the second a review of prominent souls in
Rome's history yet to be born. These episodes are bridged
by Anchises' explanation of reincarnation of souls. The
whole is a representation of the change in Aeneas' own
soul.

Anchises' discussion of the purification of souls and
their rebirth has a style all its own in the Underworld story.
It smacks of the lecture room, it is almost prosy, it resembles very much the Latinity of *De Rerum Natura* by
Lucretius. Because the passage here is so Lucretian and because Virgil owed such a debt to Lucretius' experiments
with Latin dactylic hexameters, many critics are tempted
to assume that this is a mere bijou, a tribute to the earlier
master. This is a continual critical problem in any style
made up of the embroidery of pedantic allusions. Once
we acknowledge, however, the suggestion of a Lucretian
tribute here, we can then remark that the description
boldly assaults us with its peculiar style. Emphatic, it
means something in the poem. Surely it is describing in
philosophic language what is presently happening to
Aeneas as he turns from his past, as he experiences a final
rejection from Dido here in the Underworld, whom he
in turn had rejected on earth. Purified now of his old
heroic interests, his former romantic interests, he turns to
see the souls of Rome's future, becoming one himself. He
is dead and is reborn in that short moment in which
Anchises expounds upon the souls.

The transformed Aeneas, while being shown the souls
of Rome's future, is charged by Anchises with a mandate
that sums up Rome's purpose:

> Others, I doubt not, shall more subtly make bronze
>   into breathing creatures
> others will draw our living faces from marble
> others will plead better their cases, with the rod
> shall discover the motions of the heavens
> and learn to tell the rising of the stars.

But you, O Roman, remember to rule with your
 power—
these are your arts—and to impose the law of peace;
to be merciful to the conquered, and to cast down the
 proud. (6.847–853)

From this moment on he can be nothing but victorious;
destiny must prevail. The second half of the *Aeneid* suffers
inevitably from the absolute inexorability of the events.
Virgil, it seems to me, grows confused in his attempts to
alleviate the stress of the narrative. In an effort to stall the
obvious conclusion, he introduces a variety of delaying
actions, some of them actually highly successful for the
story as a whole. Surely the Catalogue of Italian troops is
of that order, because it rehearses the names and places of
Italy, making of the *Aeneid* an intensely local and true
story. Of the same order is the visit with Evander in Rome
that kindles in the reader awe and curiosity as Aeneas
walks over sites later to become familiar and famous in the
final years of the pre-Christian era. Virgil, however, portrays human beings in this part who constitute a problem
in his story. The major figures are, with one exception,
beautiful, young, high-spirited and terribly vulnerable—
such persons as Camilla, Pallas, Euryalus, and Lausus.
Which cause they espouse—Aeneas' or Turnus'—doesn't
matter. They are all portrayed as victims of war. The *Iliad*
almost never dwells on this aspect of war, although the
feeling for it lies behind a number of small descriptions of
fallen heroes, and very clearly goes to make up the type
figure that is Andromache. In the *Aeneid* this melancholic,
aching view of war is forever being reinforced, and, of
course, it works against any expression of empathy or sympathy for Aeneas. His is the juggernaut, the war machine,
the depersonalized instrument of destiny before whom at
the very end of the poem falls Turnus, the one really well-
delineated personality of the *Aeneid*. We seem to see here
the same tragedy of history that Shakespeare saw when he

described two brilliant, glorious living individuals, Antony and Cleopatra, destroyed by the impersonal force of historical necessity that was Octavian.

In contrast to Aeneas, Turnus is well delineated because he is conceived as a single human being rather than a symbol. He is sympathetic because he acts on emotions that we well understand: grievance at being forced to give up his intended bride, Lavinia; hot anger at having to yield his lands and power to an invading force; and mad fury enveloping him at god's command. He is at once an epic hero and a tragic figure; his death is an emotional calamity no matter how logically necessary it is. Aeneas has dimmed the light of something much esteemed, and he gains no luster from it.

For any epic poet this is a major fault; Virgil had reason in wanting the poem destroyed. What he had tried for he had failed in achieving. Augustus very likely saved the poem because it is so clearly intended to praise Rome and the new era that Augustus was attempting to bring about. Later ages have continually responded to the poem, although the first half has always been the more popular part. The entire work, however, rings true, perhaps for many people only as a subconscious impression, if we understand the tragic struggle that the death of Turnus represents. For the last time Aeneas is putting away personal heroism, individual conscience, before the all-powerful need to act out the destiny of country, to forswear himself in obedience to his concern for others. He is always known as *pius*, not "pious," but "responsible." Responsibility makes Aeneas the grand historical figure, but it destroys him as an individual.

This is a reading of the poem with which many would disagree. But read any other way, the adventures of the hero become remote as he grows progressively more wooden. Everyone acknowledges that Aeneas lacks something that the other characters seem to possess. Everyone notices the melancholia of the poem. Aeneas seems to lack

humanity, and that, certainly, is a melancholy fact. He
seems warm enough in getting his family out of Troy; he
certainly responds initially to Dido. There is a change in
him that the poem develops; this is the central fact of
the narrative, making the *Aeneid* an ethical story like the
Iliad. In the winning there is a losing, a rebirth which
evolves from death.

Aeneas is most sympathetically portrayed in the fourth
book—perennially the most popular. In our own time however the affair of Dido and Aeneas has not found favor.
Especially in the schools, young Latin scholars (but who
else reads the *Aeneid?*) find Aeneas a hopelessly selfish
man in his dealings with the Carthaginian queen. In a
sense this is true. Yet there is considerably more to the
episode that should excite the imagination of the young
because it is a story of temptation, victory, and defeat that
has a peculiarly modern ring to it. The story involves
fateful choice, not, however, the sort that Achilles faced.
To die gloriously or to live on into an anonymous old age
is a dilemma that is totally personal. Achilles does not
indicate that external forces are operative on his motives
until much later in the epic. In the *Aeneid* the hero faces
a social choice—either alternative involves other people.
Social responsibility has to be exercised, the choice involves a degree of personal commitment.

The episode dealing with the love affair of Dido and
Aeneas is at once the most Roman and the most foreign
of the entire work. Aeneas' behavior seems always to leave
the modern reader with a certain uneasiness. He seems to
be at the least insensitive. And from this disenchantment
with Aeneas has sprung the theory that if Aeneas is to be
understood as the symbol of Augustus, or *Romanitas*, then
Virgil is indeed using his epic to praise the achievements
of the Roman race, but at the same time is subtly criticiz-
ing the mentality and morality that has brought forth these
achievements. However that theory is romantic nonsense.

The figure of Dido and this episode have so many liter-

ary antecedents that there is probably no end to possibilities of elucidating its several layers of meaning. Dido's
court is meant to recall the tempting, provocative court
at Scheria in the *Odyssey,* where Odysseus was lavishly
entertained and where he related the tale of his wanderings. In this sense Dido is meant to recall and to contrast
with the sensible young Nausikaa, who wanted Odysseus for
a husband, but resigned herself to the impossibility of such
a marriage. When Mercury comes to remind Aeneas of his
true destiny and to force him to leave Carthage, we are
back on Kalypso's isle, but with a difference. In the
Odyssey Kalypso was ordered to give up her love, who as
a matter of fact was pining to return home. In the *Aeneid*
the situation is harsher. Aeneas is forced to reject the passionate queen and their mutual love, with no pleasing prospect ahead, and the rupture is unavoidably ugly.

Aeneas, when he has become used to Carthage, dresses
himself in the luxurious oriental clothing of Dido's court.
In this sense Dido is made to represent, on the mythological level, the foreign enchantress, Circe, who turned
men into swine; but on the historical level, and probably
more poignantly to the Roman of Virgil's time, Dido becomes Cleopatra, the most feared foreigner save for Hannibal ever to come upon the Roman scene. All of Rome
trembled before the figure of this Greek queen of Egypt
who through her sensuousness, high intelligence, and sense
of splendor, had controlled from her bed much of Rome's
Eastern policies. In this sense Aeneas must remind the
reader of a potential Marc Antony; but there would have
been a special significance in this episode for the high officials around the emperor, who would have remembered
how Queen Cleopatra had tried after Actium once again
to enchant a Roman leader and how miserably she had
failed to excite Augustus. My reference to Hannibal should
also remind us that Dido, as queen of the Carthaginians,
was the ancestress of that hated general who led his army
over the Alps and once almost brought Rome to her knees.

This then is what Dido means in terms of Homer and history. The passionate love of which she is victim, however, is something quite un-Homeric, and indeed unusual in most ancient epic. For this Virgil turned to another model, namely the lovesick heroine of Apollonios Rhodios' *Argonautika*, the Asian sorceress, Medea. When Apollonios Rhodios was composing his epic, while naturally following Homer in most things he turned to the tragedies of Euripides to introduce something radically new in epic, the psychology of a woman in love. Romantic love was always something of an embarrassment to the dignity of grand ancient literature. Apollonios succeeded brilliantly in capturing the feelings of the woman involved; this Virgil has utilized. But there remained the problem of indicating the masculine love in a manner that would not be disconsonant with the majesty of epic.

Let us try to read the sad story of the jilted queen from Virgil's point of view. In the first twenty lines of the *Aeneid* the hostility between Carthage and Rome is brought to the reader's attention, which would remind any Roman of a fact already well known to him. Although the final battle of the Punic Wars and the destruction of Carthage had occurred over a century before this time, that mighty conflict was kept alive in the Roman mind as part of traditional nationalistic propaganda. Dido was a Carthaginian, and therefore an enemy.

Virgil goes at some detail into the lavishness of Dido's court; he details carefully the richness of its appointments, not only for the sake of spelling out their mythological symbols to delight the learned, but to suggest the vast luxury of an oriental court. The traditional Roman believed that simplicity and barren living was a moral necessity, and during the last few decades before Actium had viewed with disgust the appearance of elegance and material splendor in the lives of the aristocratic houses in the city of Rome. These were the same aristocrats who loved things Greek; from among their number had come Marc

Antony, who betrayed Rome for a foreign queen. Against such a background of luxuriousness Dido appears decidedly to be un-Roman.

In addition, the first three books of the *Aeneid* have made it abundantly clear that Aeneas must submit altogether to the destiny that calls him to Italy. To the workings of this destiny Dido is an obstacle. All of these objections to Dido are playing just below the surface of the narrative—to us, perhaps, they are inconsequential, to a Roman they were not.

In the earlier books Virgil has rehearsed temptations and travels for Aeneas that are similar to those found in the *Odyssey.* In the fourth book he embarks upon an episode that in one sense has no real parallel in the *Odyssey.* For throughout his long journey to Ithaka Odysseus remains disengaged; he is devoted completely to his return. Aeneas, on the contrary, who is always in part resisting the destiny that is forcing him to Italy, in part ignorant of it, becomes swallowed up in a monumental passion that consumes for a time completely his whole being, his intellect, his soul, and his body. We see this passion mostly from Dido's point of view, but in the tradition in which Virgil was working, this was the only course of good taste. A heroic man cannot become romantically passionate in dactylic hexameters.

Dido is a widow, Aeneas a widower; both are rulers, and neither is young. Virgil makes clear that the earlier marriage of each had been a love match. The phantom image of Creusa in Book Two, when bidding farewell to Aeneas, reminds him that although a dynastic marriage awaits him in the future in Italy, theirs had been a marriage of love. Dido, for her part, at the beginning of Book Four, swears eternal love for her dead husband, Sychaeus. There is then a certain shopworn quality to Dido and Aeneas that we would do well to bear in mind. This element is another example of Virgil's mastery of his materials. When Apollonios Rhodios drew the picture of Medea in love in his

epic, he had introduced something new: a passion grand
enough for Italian opera, as was the situation. A virgin
princess, indeed, a sorceress, falls wildly in love with the
visiting adventurer, Jason, and secretly marries him with
elaborate rites in a cave, to avoid her parents' disapproval.
Virgil has achieved the same monumental passion in his
work, but at the same time he has introduced enough safe-
guards so that his reader ought not to rebel when Aeneas
regretfully declines.

Everything has combined beforehand to indicate to the
reader that this affair cannot last. Dido's oath to her dead
husband, Sychaeus, is obviously the beginning of the end.
When that ponderous destiny in the form of Mercury
comes to goad Aeneas, there is nothing more to be said.
Aeneas stifles the last remnant of humanity that he has,
his love, in order to submerge himself completely into that
greater force which moves the world. He had wanted to be
a Trojan hero, fighting gloriously in the fall of his city;
that was denied him. He had wanted to be a dutiful son,
not a leader; that was denied him. When he was weary of
traveling, and wanted a resting place in Greece, that was
denied him. Now finally he has exercised his individuality
in that one, glorious, all-consuming emotion. For the last
time he is a personality with private human values. And
this too is denied him.

Dido's suicide is the traditional Greek reaction to a loss
of individual freedom. The traditional Greek literary response to the conflicts that man in his finest moment has
created is death. Virgil consciously chose to juxtapose the
fact of Dido's suicide with Aeneas wearily continuing to
live. Even as the thoroughly Roman Augustus was to pick
up the pieces, to deal with the aftermath, and to compromise (that pedestrian word) with the conflicts of this
world, so Aeneas was to go on living, now become a servant
of the higher good. And this is the pathos of *pietas*.

Aeneas, like any other human being, wants to deny his
fate, or is ignorant of it, and succumbs to temptation until

he is finally so thwarted, so humbled, that he sheds his humanity and immolates himself to this higher force, his destiny, but still more, the destiny of imperial Rome. A man in the clutch of destiny cannot be the heroic being as it was conceived by the archaic Homeric mind. Achilles, faced with a choice, could exercise a certain amount of free will. Aeneas, less so.

Western Europe has had a relatively unbroken cultural tradition for the past twenty-five centuries. Much is owed to Augustus Caesar's creation, the Roman Empire, which ensured that this culture would spread, take seed, and be protected for several centuries from hostile and alien forces. The colossal nervelessness that characterizes the later empire is an open indication of the effort of spirit and will that was required to keep the culture somehow living.

This mighty effort in *pietas* took a toll that we may see reflected in Aeneas' own agony; everything that made him a unique, sensitive, quickening human being was sacrificed to the dictates of Roman destiny. As he bound himself more firmly to this abstract, otherworldly and hence un-human force, he lost altogether his own humanity. And therein perhaps lies our disenchantment with the poem, for the civilization which we have inherited no longer really seems worth preserving. But if we will pause to read the poem as tragic in its underlying assumptions, then the life of Aeneas becomes a passion that has unassailable stature.

FURTHER READING

. . . the Homeric poems conceal nothing, they contain
no teaching and no secret second meaning. Homer can
be analyzed . . . but he cannot be interpreted.
    Erich Auerbach in an essay entitled
    "Odysseus' Scar" translated by Willard Trask

For those who are curious about the background to the
subject of this book, this chapter offers a brief indication
of where they may turn to enlarge their knowledge.
Luckily, many of the books which are mentioned are now
in paperback. Luckier still, almost all significant and informative books and articles that have to do with Homer's
poems are written in English. This is a development of
the past fifty years; before then, almost everything of consequence on the subject of Homer came from Germany.
The relatively brief number of books discussed in this
section ought to enable the interested reader to discover
where to go for still more information since all these books
contain bibliographies of one sort or another. If the reader
wishes, however, a detailed exposition of the trends and
innovations in Homeric research, he had best consult the
essay by E. R. Dodds, entitled "Homer" in *Fifty Years of
Classical Scholarship*, edited by Maurice Platnauer (Oxford, 1954). There is also a very witty and penetrating
article by F. M. Combellack, called "Contemporary

Homeric Scholarship" in the forty-ninth volume (1955) of the journal *Classical Weekly* (now renamed *Classical World*).

The discussion which follows is based on the books that I find particularly useful, and its order is based on the arrangement of the chapters of this book. At the start, however, I should remark that recently there has appeared a large handbook designed to cover every major topic of Homeric research. Entitled A *Companion to Homer*, edited by A. J. B. Wace and F. H. Stubbings (London, 1963), this book is scholarly and authoritative. Every kind of topic is covered—from oral poetic technique to archaeological excavation. One quickly sees from only a glance at the table of contents that the Homeric epics are frequently the starting point for research that has nothing to do with the poems as poems. Much the same material which this handbook presents in difficult professional essays is simplified and made more readable in G. S. Kirk's *The Songs of Homer* (Cambridge, 1962), recently revised and abridged and retitled *Homer and the Epic* for the Cambridge University Press paperback series.

The Homeric epics have surely motivated more research than any other piece of ancient literature. The reasons for this, while many, have little to do with the superior quality of the poems. The *Iliad* and *Odyssey* stand as valuable, illuminating documents for historians, archaeologists, and students of comparative literature. Moreover these poems form the basis for one of the more elaborate and enduring games of classical scholarship. Known as "the Homeric question," it flourished in the nineteenth century, principally in Germany, and, indeed, continued active until Germany's eclipse in the Second World War. While the majority of English-speaking Homeric scholars no longer take its tenets too seriously, almost every writer still speaks subconsciously to those tough, arrogant German scholars of long ago who set the tone of much Homeric research.

Therefore, it is worth while to learn something of these men and their ideas.

"The Homeric question" arose principally because nineteenth-century scholars were convinced that no one man could compose and remember, without the aid of writing, poems as long as the *Iliad* and *Odyssey*. They knew that a system of writing appeared not to exist at the time the poems were created. They sought, therefore, on the basis of their evidence to create reasonable hypotheses for the existence of these poems. The obvious conclusion was that each poem was an amalgam of smaller poems. The task then turned to attempting theories which would explain the process of growth and development, a process that supposedly transformed these small poetic bits and pieces into two long epic poems. There were almost as many theories as there were men studying the poems; a hint, perhaps, of the instability of the assumptions upon which the theories were built. Two, however, grew to dominate, one explaining the *Iliad*, and the other, the *Odyssey*.

The most popular theory that explained the growth of the *Iliad* is often called the "Kernel" theory. In English, it is best developed in the introduction and commentary by Walter Leaf to the Greek text of the *Iliad* (London, 2nd edition, 1900). To put it briefly, Mr. Leaf suggests that at an early time there was an epic poem recounting the quarrel of Agamemnon and Achilles and the latter's subsequent angry behavior. In the passage of time, there came to be added to this kernel various episodes from other epics until finally the full *Iliad* as we know it was assembled. Proof for this hypothesis was sought in a close examination of the text, a search for awkwardness, inconsistencies, contradictions, illogical repetitions, and the like that would demonstrate that various episodes were in origin alien to each other. In the same manner, attempts were made to discover which passages seemed to presuppose others in the story in order to demonstrate the newness or antiquity of any given episode. The theory advanced for the *Odyssey* held that essentially three poems were welded together, the Telemachia, the travel stories, and the narrative of most of the last twelve books of the poem. (Considerable scholarly opinion since the Alexandrian period has insisted that the last part of the twenty-third book and the whole of the twenty-fourth are definitely a very late addition to the original poem.) In demonstrating that these three sections were not originally kindred, scholars established a similar set of criteria as they had for the *Iliad.*

Any thorough understanding of these theories or related ones depends upon a knowledge of German because naturally their best exposition is in that language. Various English scholars have discussed (if often only to attack) them. Andrew Lang, in his *Homer and the Epic* (London, 1893), gives a useful survey of major nineteenth-century scholarly judgments. He then proceeds to discuss their improbability. He argues that only by thinking of the *Iliad* and *Odyssey* as poetry and not as prose exercises in logic can one truly grasp their unity. He further remarks that those who would deny the unity of each poem spend their energies examining *minutiae* so that they have no way to consider each epic in its entirety. He then challenges in considerable detail a number of these German arguments, always keeping his eye on the poems' integrity. The book is a wise review of a number of important, though often strange, opinions, several of which are still held in some countries to this day. Lang's discussion also shows the way in which men were affected by notions of the scientific method and of scholarship as a thing apart from traditional humanistic pursuits.

J. L. Myres, in *Homer and His Critics* (edited by D. Gray, London, 1958), outlines various critical ideas about Homer from antiquity down to the beginning of the twentieth century. Professor Myres, an archaeologist, was a very old man when he wrote so that he can create for us

a sense of the excitement in his youth following the discovery that Troy and Mycenae actually did once exist.
Before Schliemann excavated these sites in the nineteenth
century, the *Iliad* and the *Odyssey* were generally considered to be fables. When these heroic cities turned out
in fact to have existed, suddenly Homer's poems were
true, fact not fiction. In their enthusiasm, some scholars
saw the two poems at least subconsciously as eyewitness
accounts of the Minoan and Mycenaean civilizations.
Homer became a historian not a poet. Archaeology came
to depend upon Homer, and Homer upon archaeology in
a peculiarly close way. Myres's book is most interesting as
an insight into the climate of archaeology and as an appraisal of the more important men who formed connections between the poems and the archaeological work in
the field. He, too, inherited an interest in the question
of the unity of the two poems; his approach to defining and
solving the problem is that of an archaeologist. Criteria
of apparent truth or falsehood are important to him, as
though in point of fact the poems were bona fide historical
documents. Any critical understanding of poetry, however,
even traditional poetry that may have been inspired by
real events, must be based on an understanding of the
fictionalizing intent of the poet, the operation of his free
will and personal control over the material. This fact is
usually a stumbling block for historians and archaeologists
when they approach Homer.

A sometimes hilarious, sometimes irresponsible attack
on German Homeric studies is mounted by J. A. Scott in
his *The Unity of Homer* (Berkeley, 1921). He sets out to
prove by statistical evidence that the poems show throughout common characteristics of style and language that
would imply unity. He furthermore points out that any
number of supposed inconsistencies and contradictions are
based on almost ludicrous conceptions of poetic creation
as well as a complete misunderstanding of the mentality
either of poets or of editors (who in several theories were

presumed to have put the poems together). A great deal of nineteenth-century research into Homer was colored by the growing prominence of science. Homeric scholars wanted their work to show a lucidity, objectivity, and tightness similar to that exhibited by scientific studies. Hence came the unblinking, unthinking logic that Scott finds so odious. Logic and propriety of the sort which these scholars sought are the properties of prose. Poetry, on the other hand, shares in a kind of mystical ambiguity. Poetic analysis, especially of poems so remote as the *Iliad* and *Odyssey,* is perhaps better managed with tentativeness, suggestion and implication as the only possible means of arriving at a proper understanding.

The faults of the scholarship of the late nineteenth and early twentieth centuries are sometimes seen in D. L. Page's *History and the Homeric Iliad* (Berkeley, 1959; also a University of California paperback). An example is the appendix that is occupied with the question of multiple authorship for the *Iliad.* Professor Page, for example, says in this appendix that the fact Achilles in the eleventh and sixteenth books fails to acknowledge that the Greeks in the ninth book have made considerable efforts at conciliation proves that two versions of the story, or two authors, are in evidence here. Professor Page argues that so short a time has in fact elapsed between the scenes that any man could not keep silent about these details from Book Nine. But this is to assume that Achilles is a real person who must exhibit everywhere every last subtlety of normal human behavior. Further, it is to assume that a real span of time exists in the story of the *Iliad.* Neither of these assumptions is likely or relevant. Achilles is a creation of the poet and he will be manipulated like a marionette. He has no other existence. As long as what he does is conventionally human, he is believable and we can overlook what he does not do. Likewise, time is the poet's creation—the distance between the ninth and eleventh books, however small mathematically and logically, is great by virtue of the interruption which the tenth book provides, for that episode changes the focus and mood significantly. Page understands the theory of oral poetry, but he seems to be overlooking the special emphasis in such poetry upon the present moment. Furthermore, he seems to ignore the special way in which long poetry must be read, which is so well described by C. S. Lewis in *A Preface to Paradise Lost* (Oxford, 1942). Still more crucial is the apparent inability of Page or his school to accept what seem to him inconsistencies and contradictions, as in fact *intended* by the poet himself. It is far more intelligent and realistic to accept the poems as they are and proceed to interpret them on that basis. For whether such passages are by our poet or another is not the question. No one introduces or lets stand marked absurdities or anomalies; to believe so is to misapprehend creation.

Nonetheless, much of this sort of research has had in the end a salutary effect upon Homeric scholarship in general. Men of this school have had generally so profound a knowledge of the texts of the *Iliad* and *Odyssey* that they inevitably increase our awareness of the extraordinarily variegated and cunning texture of the two poems. By emphasizing anomalies in the text, they have forced everyone who is concerned with the poems to examine the texts more closely, to avoid simple generalizations. More specifically, they have motivated the attempts to formulate an aesthetic for oral poetry, peculiar to itself and not dependent upon written literature. For their objections to the integrity of either Homeric poem usually were and are based upon literate usage—often, it seems, novels of the realistic school. While these epics do tell a story as novels do, they are, on the other hand, uniquely poetic. Their special nature has been much better understood as a result of these earlier investigations and theories.

The oral nature of the *Iliad* and *Odyssey* was first statistically surveyed by the American Milman Parry in two French theses. His ideas were introduced into English in two articles appearing in the *Harvard Studies in Classical Philology* entitled "Studies in the Epic Technique of Oral Verse-Making." Part I, "Homer and the Homeric Style," appeared in volume 41 (1930), and Part II, "The Homeric Language of an Oral Poetry," in volume 43 (1932). Here, Parry presented exciting proofs that the oral poets created out of phrases, rather than words, that they created new phrases on the model of others, metrically similar, semantically different. Their technique of narration was shown to be based upon an elaborate special language, as it were, whose elements were so much larger than the individual words of normal speech that the composition of an over fifteen-thousand-line poem was considerably simplified on the mechanical level. In sum, Parry demonstrated how it would be possible for a poet to create a poem of the *Iliad's* length out of a poet's memory without a verbatim memory of any previously heard text. He set out to Yugoslavia to study the living tradition of oral poetry there, because he needed actual proofs for his statistical and theoretical conceptions. By means of dictation and recordings, he was beginning to acquire a large body of Yugoslavian epic when he most unfortunately died at an early age. Parry's assistant, A. B. Lord, continued his work in the field. The fruit of his intimate knowledge of oral poetic practice in Yugoslavia is contained in a very informative book, called *The Singer of Tales* (Cambridge, Massachusetts, 1960; also an Atheneum paperback). Professor Lord first describes the Yugoslavian oral poetic technique and then attempts to apply this knowledge to the Homeric epics. This book is a source, as well, to articles by Lord and others written over the years which take up detailed problems of the oral poetic technique of Homer, almost all of which are highly illuminating.

One may object, however, to Mr. Lord's insistence on parallels between Yugoslavian poetry and the Homeric epics, or to the rigidity with which he has established his theories. There is a singular point of difference between the Homeric poems and the Yugoslavian materials so far translated into English; that is, the overwhelming superiority of the *Iliad* and *Odyssey*. Yugoslavian epic does indeed betray the essentially mechanical and somewhat primitive mode of composition that the oral theory suggests when carried to its logical conclusions. The Homeric epics, on the other hand, are full of surprises and seem far more sophisticated in their conception. Then, too, since we truly know nothing about the composition of the Greek poems, any one-for-one relationship between the two literatures cannot be sustained. The Parry-Lord theory of oral versemaking is, however, the fashion today. It has been called the new orthodoxy by M. W. M. Pope in an article in the sixth volume (1964) of the *Proceedings of the Classical Association of South Africa,* entitled "The Parry-Lord Theory of Homeric Composition." This is a corrective essay. Professor Pope addresses himself to questioning with example and statistic the inexorable truths of the theory upon which Mr. Lord insists. The article is an important reminder that in many ways the theory remains just that, theory. The fervor of its adherents makes it seem at times an article of faith.

Since almost every culture possesses an oral epic tradition, it is instructive to compare these with the Homeric poems. Such comparisons sustain a belief in the universal manner of oral poetry while, at the same time, enlarging our notions of the manifold possibilities inherent in the technique. H. M. and N. K. Chadwick have created an invaluable treasure house of facts about these various oral literatures in their monumental three-volume *The Growth of Literature* (Cambridge, 1932–40). The book not only surveys every area in the world, but also distinguishes between different types of creation within each tradition. Reading anywhere in this vast work is instructive, but for those whose time is limited, the third volume contains at the end a very useful two-hundred-page "General Survey." Still more specifically useful is C. M. Bowra's

Heroic Poetry (London, 1952; also a St. Martin's Library paperback) which is in some ways a distillation of the Chadwicks' three volumes. Professor Bowra's orientation is to Homer; moreover, his fine literary critical sensibilities keep the emphasis on the truly relevant features of comparative study.

One of the more tantalizing questions of Homeric research concerns the centuries which elapsed between the Mycenaean period and the time when Homer, or whoever, composed the *Iliad* and *Odyssey.* How did the saga tradition develop? How did the poetic tradition grow? Invariably the answers to these questions will be speculative, but they help in defining such notions as "originality" when applied to the authors of this kind of poetry. Gilbert Murray in *The Rise of the Greek Epic* (Oxford, 4th edition, 1934; also a Galaxy Books paperback) has an excellent discussion of what he calls the traditional book. His examples are the Bible, the *Song of Roland,* and, somewhat less appositely, various script alterations in early English theater. Since he does not utilize the studies of Milman Parry, he discusses the growth of the epics more as changing written texts. Nevertheless, he has well described the psychology that lies behind the making of traditional poetry. Rhys Carpenter in *Folk Tale, Fiction and Saga in the Homeric Epics* (Berkeley, 1956; also a University of California paperback) has, as the title indicates, attempted to sort out the various disparate elements that went into making the poems. His definition of folk tale or fairy tale is highly instructive; his arguments for labeling certain episodes as created by our poet, the last poet, are very convincing. Professor Carpenter also turns to comparative study. One of the more interesting chapters, not too persuasive, is "The Folk Tale of the Bear's Son," in which Carpenter attempts to demonstrate that the essential story of the *Odyssey* derives from a story that is also ancestor to *Beowulf.* What relevance this has to our *Odyssey* is unclear except that it perhaps helps to explain Odysseus'

peculiar personality. The way in which Homer recasts a
common story for his own purposes is explained in D. L.
Page's account of the Polyphemus episode, "Odysseus and
Polyphemus," in his *The Homeric Odyssey* (Oxford,
1955). The episode is common to folk tales throughout
Europe. Professor Page subtly examines the way in which
Homer has employed it with modifications and accretions
that are specifically suitable to his over-all story. The chap-
ter is a valuable exposition of the personal control which
Homer exercised over his material.

A major effort to hypothesize the Mycenaean poetry
that is presumed to lie behind the *Iliad* and *Odyssey* has
been undertaken by T. B. L. Webster in *From Myceneae to
Homer* (London, 1958; also a Norton paperback). The
book is especially valuable because its author combines a
knowledge of history and archaeology with literary critical
skills. Naturally, the book is highly speculative since we
do not possess the slightest specimens of Greek epic poetry
prior to Homer. Of particular importance is the full use
which Professor Webster makes of the remains of Eastern
poetry, particularly the epic of *Gilgamesh*, which bears
strong affinities with the *Iliad* and *Odyssey*. A similar attempt to relate the East and the Greek world is C. H.
Gordon's "Homer and the Bible" in volume 26 (1955)
of the *Hebrew Union College Annual*. In the main, the
article is a list of parallel passages, motifs, and attitudes
drawn from the Bible and the Homeric epics. Another
important source for Professor Webster's formulation of
an idea of pre-Homeric poetry lies in the material remains
of the earlier periods. He is inclined toward the belief
that the stylistic principles of poetry will not differ much
from those that inform the plastic arts. Therefore, he is
able to use the considerable remains of works of art to
derive some notion of this hypothetical poetry, as well as
to analyze the Homeric epics. It is dubious, however, to
impute too much to a relationship between the two aesthetics. In creation, one is manual while the other is oral;

in reception, one is visual, the other heard, and the senses do not seem to have a common denominator, but rather each creates its own shape.

An excellent survey of all that is known of the Mycenaean age is found in E. Vermeule's *Greece in the Bronze Age* (Chicago, 1964). Professor Vermeule covers all aspects of the period as we now know them from the archaeological remains. She will not employ Homer as evidence since the fluid nature of oral poetry makes the *Iliad* and the *Odyssey* less than reliable as evidence. There are, therefore, no direct references to Homer's poems in her book. Still, the book offers a fine background to the poems, although at times the author conjures up images of life in Mycenaean times when the facts are not really there. The archaeologist's role is hard, for he must use his imagination enough to transform his mute and fragmentary evidence into reflections of their original state, while at the same time accepting the inhibitions against any such transformation that his materials present. Joseph Alsop's account of the Pylos excavation in *From the Silent Earth* (New York, 1964) is an interesting study of the mentality and the passion which lead the archaeologist on. The book has, in addition, a series of provocative speculations about the evidence for the Bronze Age which archaeologists have uncovered.

The historian M. I. Finley uses the Homeric texts as evidence in his *The World of Odysseus* (New York, 1954; also a Meridian Books paperback) for creating a portrait of Homer's contemporary era. He goes beyond the tangibles to try to re-create the ethos of that world, in discussing ideas of justice, politics, the family, etc., as they are to be found in the *Odyssey.* Professor Finley speaks as a historian with an understanding of sociology. Quite another re-creation of the mood of that time is contained in the first four chapters of W. W. Jaeger's *Paideia* (New York, 2nd edition, 1945; also a Galaxy Books paperback). Professor Jaeger was a student of philosophy, particularly

Aristotle; his conceptions of the *Iliad* and *Odyssey* are markedly philosophical, idealized and abstracted. His treatment of some of the cultural concepts in the two poems, particularly *aretē*, the act or moment of the fulfillment of a man's potential, is impressive and underlies most present-day interpretations of Achilles. At some remove from *Paideia* is H. L. Lorimer's *Homer and the Monuments* (London, 1950), an exhaustive account of the material evidence found by archaeologists for the artifacts which Homer describes. The book offers lavish descriptions of armor, eating utensils and all the other sometimes perplexing elements of Homer's material world. The final section, entitled "Conclusions," is an extremely thoughtful appraisal of the date of the poems. Naturally, the book is continually compromised by the new finds from excavations, but it is sensibly written and remains thought provoking and informative. For an account of the religious practices of the time, M. P. Nilsson is the final authority in *The Mycenaean Origin of Greek Mythology* (Berkeley, 1932; also a Norton paperback) and in *The Minoan-Mycenaean Religion and Its Survival in Greek Religion* (Lund, 2nd edition, 1950).

Although any number of books take up at some point the subject of the Homeric style, almost invariably this is to illustrate something else. On the other hand, C. M. Bowra's *Tradition and Design in the Iliad* (Oxford, 1930) is an attempt to define and assess the poet's materials and his control over them from the view of the creating of poetry. The book is subtle, learned, and thorough. At times, however, it suffers when Professor Bowra seems defensive or when, capitulating to the historian's mentality, he enters upon discussions that are not relevant to his purpose. The single best book on Homer's poetic technique is *The Poetry of Homer* by S. E. Bassett (Berkeley, 1938). Bassett is not altogether indifferent to the tiresome questions raised by the Homeric problem. He quickly lays them to rest, however, in his first chapter. Then having established his belief in treating the poems as poetry, he proceeds to an excellent discussion of what he calls the epic illusion, that is, the kind of mood and image of reality that oral epic poetry creates. This is followed by a sensitive account of the way in which we may assume Homer manipulated his audience. Thereafter, Bassett discusses details of the poetic language, endowing individual words and phrases with far more meaning than Parry or, in fact, most students of epic would have allowed. Yet his exposition is always illuminating and provocative.

One of the few books devoted essentially to the *Iliad* is C. H. Whitman's *Homer and the Heroic Tradition* (Cambridge, Massachusetts, 1958; also a Norton paperback). The book is almost always stimulating except for some unnecessary introductory essays attempting to prove various hypotheses relevant to the place and date of the composition of the two poems. When Professor Whitman turns from these to discuss the language of Homer, especially when he is under the influence of Susanne Langer's *Philosophy in a New Key,* the book is exciting. The best chapter, "Image, Symbol and Formula," describes the inherently symbolic quality of formulaic phrases, and discusses as well the unity of Homeric imagery. Strangely enough, the chapter, "Fire and Other Elements," in which Whitman attempts to demonstrate the importance of fire as a symbol which unifies the poem is self-defeating: it succeeds rather in suggesting that the fire motif is so much a cliché and pervasive that it symbolizes everything and therefore nothing. Another important chapter is Whitman's attempt to demonstrate a rigidly symmetrical structure to the *Iliad* ("Geometric Structure of the Iliad"), an attempt that fails for me, but which suggests far more order than one usually divines in the *Iliad.*

Whitman takes up, among other things, the idea of Homeric heroism. As for Jaeger and others, this concept is for him an ennobled and ennobling one which dominates the *Iliad.* Quite the reverse is maintained in a well-known,

thoughtful and philosophic essay by Simone Weil entitled
The Iliad, or The Poem of Force (now published in
pamphlet form by Pendle Hill Publications). She sees the
Iliad as a story of force, hate, horror, desolation and brutality that is saved from a monstrous nihilism by brief
vignettes of human beings still with souls intact, and capable of love. In our era, when war has ceased to be
romanticized, this interpretation of the *Iliad* seems attractive and logical. There is more to the poem, however. Certainly, Mlle. Weil offers an important corrective to overly
romantic inclinations which exalt heroism. On the other
hand, she only examines the *Iliad's* background. The story
of Achilles with which the description of war is completely
bound is considerably more complex and humanized than
the episodes she offers as proofs for her theory.

The *Odyssey*, perhaps because it is so much more enigmatic, has been treated by a number of interesting minds
in original ways. Samuel Butler's *The Authoress of the
Odyssey* (London, 2nd edition, 1922) is without exception
the best book on the poem. Butler's thesis—that a young
woman wrote the *Odyssey*—is probably nonsense and, in
any case, cannot be proved. His observations on the feminine psychology, however, which he finds everywhere in
the poem illumine the *Odyssey* in a new way. Suddenly
the poem's subtlety, the depth of characterization, the
poet's self-consciousness become real. Above all, Butler
shows the peculiar importance—threatening and not be-
nign—which women possess in the *Odyssey*. W. J. Wood-
house's *The Composition of Homer's Odyssey* (Oxford,
1930) offers a further revelation of the unique quality of
this epic. He singles out a number of common techniques
of storytelling which he traces to folk tale or fairy tale
origin. His demonstration of the prevalence of these folk
tale motifs helps to establish the essential difference between the *Iliad* and *Odyssey*.

Odysseus, in turn, because he is the most complex
character in the epics, has been the most studied. The

gentle and veiled malevolence of the hero becomes clearer upon reading an excellent article by G. E. Dimock, Jr., "The Name of Odysseus," in the *Hudson Review,* volume nine, number one (Spring 1963)—also to be found in a Spectrum Books paperback, *Homer (Twentieth Century Views)* edited by G. Steiner and R. Fagles, in which Dimock plays with the connection between Odysseus, anger, hatred, and his name as it is given him by his grandfather Autolykos. W. B. Stanford has four chapters on the Homeric Odysseus in *The Ulysses Theme* (Oxford, 1954), a book that stands out as one of the finest written by a professional classicist. Professor Stanford's aim is to relate the manner in which a figure from myth, Odysseus (or Ulysses as he is known in Latin), can be used and transformed throughout Western literature. To begin, he presents a detailed portrait of Odysseus as he appears in the *Iliad* and *Odyssey.* The analysis is profound and leaves little room for doubt that the Homeric Odysseus is truly one of the most complex literary personages. Stanford's discussion, in turn, demonstrates how far more subtle than the *Iliad* the *Odyssey* seems to be.

Most early epics, the *Iliad* among them, do not encourage the search for subtleties or underlying meanings. If the poet does not clearly state a fact of the narrative, we may not presume that it is there. Yet again and again the *Odyssey* shows a more complicated structure and a deeper texture. By the effective repetition of motifs and by playing the *Odyssey* against the *Iliad,* or, at least, the mood of the *Iliad,* the poet suggests relationships that the story line does not advertise. A convincing elucidation of one of the subtler moments of the *Odyssey* is an article by P. W. Harsh, entitled "Penelope and Odysseus in Odyssey XIX," *American Journal of Philology,* volume 71 (1950). Professor Harsh shows that Penelope is aware of Odysseus' true identity soon after their meeting when he is disguised as a beggar. The careful analysis of the language and emotion of Penelope, the parallel between the increase in tension and the increase of veiled hints leaves no doubt of the episode's true meaning. Since antiquity, the idea has been suggested from time to time, but critical standards for epic did not allow such interpretations. The finest expression of the traditional point of view is Erich Auerbach's essay "Odysseus' Scar," reprinted in *Mimesis* (Princeton, 1953; also a Doubleday Anchor Book paperback), in which Auerbach contrasts the clarity of Homeric exposition with the ambiguity of Old Testament narration, calling the former objective and the latter subjective. His approach seems, however, not valid for the *Odyssey*, in particular. In any case, such men as those whose works I have just cited are admirably penetrating the Odyssean enigma.

Although Virgil's *Aeneid* is a small part of the present book, and the emphasis of the discussion of the *Aeneid* was upon its relevance to the *Iliad* and *Odyssey*, the reader very likely would appreciate some bibliographical aides here as well. The bibliography of Virgilian studies is as vast as the Homeric, so that any selection will seem arbitrary. Viktor Pöschl's *The Art of Vergil: Image and Symbol in the Aeneid* (Ann Arbor, 1962) is an investigation of the elaborate movement of the *Aeneid* in terms of its symbols. Professor Pöschl takes up the basic themes of the poem, shows how they all appear in the first book and suggests that every scene in the poem in some way plays out these main themes. His discussion of the central figures in the poem rightly brings out their symbolic quality, a quality which tends to inhibit their delineation as human beings in a story on human scale. Most recently the subject has been treated again by Brooks Otis in *Virgil: A Study in Civilized Poetry* (Oxford, 1963). Professor Otis is committed to structural analysis as a means to elucidate the sense of the *Aeneid*. Otis also consistently insists upon a spiritual depth to the *Aeneid* (perhaps a little awkwardly Christian)—an important balance to those who admire Virgil only for his style. He believes as well that Virgil so far rose above or left behind his many models and sources that we may almost dismiss them in interpretation. This is a healthy position if one can believe that Virgil was not enchanted in the spell of reflection and derivation, was not indeed caught in the amber of tradition. Virgil is important as a part of a tradition, however. His sources were many, some quite unclear to us. Some notion of these sources may be had in H. W. Prescott's *The Development of Virgil's Art* (Chicago, 1936). In turn, Virgil shaped the epic genre, influencing all epic poets who succeeded him—as may be seen in C. M. Bowra's account of the successive attempts at epic in *From Virgil to Milton* (London, 1945; also a St. Martin's Library paperback).

Most people today read the *Iliad* and *Odyssey* in translation. Perhaps if they realized how relatively easy Homeric Greek is, how after at most an academic year of grammatical study, most persons can read some of the epics, albeit haltingly, then they too would try their hand at it. The enormous amount of repetition and the formulaic nature of the language allows the student to grow accustomed to Homeric Greek rather quickly. Once read in Greek, the *Iliad* and the *Odyssey* become a habit. They can be read over for a lifetime, like Shakespeare—never to be exhausted of their meanings.

Both poems have often been translated into English. In an earlier era the translator's motive was generally to attempt poetry in what is essentially another genre. That is to say, a translation is neither the original poem nor altogether the translator's creation. It falls somewhere in between and must be judged as something unique. A Chapman or a Pope could expect most of his readers to be able to judge the translation against the original Greek of Homer as well as against contemporary English poetic usage. In our time, the translator often feels that he must assume the far harder task of conveying everything in the poem to his reader, who cannot manage the original. As a result, he often imagines himself to be performing a

service rather than creating a work of art. Such is the motive and quality of my own translations throughout this
book, or those of A. T. Murray who translated both poems
for the Loeb Classical Library (Harvard University Press).
Mr. Murray's translations have the original Greek text fac-
ing each page. As is so often the case with volumes of the
Loeb Library translations, this seems to act as an in-
hibiting rather than a liberating factor. Mr. Murray sus-
pects his readers of knowing some Greek, and being a
scholar rather than a poet, he achieves in his translation a
timid fidelity.

Naturally, no translation can suffice when it is expected
to re-create the original poem. Language cannot be so
transformed. No word in any tongue is anything more
than a vague approximation of a word in another language.
The uniqueness of phrases and grammatical usage com-
pound the problem of achieving parallel meanings in two
distinct languages. Finally, there is the formidable barrier which the denotative qualities of words set up to any
true representation of foreign speech.

Few attempts have been made to systematize the criteria for judging translations, since they are not generally
held to be a separate genre, or a unique kind of literary
expression. A comparison and discussion of modern translations, of the Homeric poems, therefore, is somewhat of a
problem. The best statement of what one may expect of a
translation of Homer is Matthew Arnold's *On Translating
Homer* (London, revised with introduction, 1905). Arnold
manages in addition to convey the feeling one gets from
reading Homer's Greek as he describes how translations
known to him convey—or do not convey—the sense of various lines or the diction as a whole. Arnold addresses himself particularly to nineteenth-century translators, but the
problems of translation he brings up are valid for any time.
What he has to say is too long and involved to summarize
here. Anyone, however, who wishes to read the Homeric

poems in translation seriously should consult Arnold before choosing his translation.

Since translators cannot bring everything from the original into their translation, they must choose. Homer is remarkable for his elevated poetic diction and for the rapid
lucidity of his narrative. The two, which might seem to
conflict in any poetic enterprise, actually establish a marvelous tension in Homer and succeed in combination. This
success, however, is Homer's secret and no translation
manages to bring it off. It is between these two poles of
Homer's art that most translators perform.

At the turn of the century, A. Lang, W. Leaf, and E.
Myers translated the *Iliad* and S. H. Butcher and A. Lang
translated the *Odyssey* into King James English prose (currently available in the Modern Library). Recognizing the
impossibility for men who are not poets to write poetry,
they chose prose. They sought, however, to reproduce the
grandeur, the remoteness and what they felt must have
been the quaintness of Homeric Greek. For anyone raised
on the King James version of the Bible, these translations
do convey the sense of ritualized activity, of things handed
down immutably. On the other hand, King James English
belongs to scripture and not to secular narrative; Homeric
King James English produces an awkward effect on the
reader. Moreover, in the latter half of the twentieth century, few can rapidly comprehend King James English although they may feel they know the Bible well. This un-
familiarity slows the narrative, making a pedantic exercise
of what is essentially a story. Beyond this, the very quaintness achieved is perhaps untrue to the original. The Greeks
throughout their history continued to learn Homer by
rote and much of his diction was absorbed into other
literary forms, so that while they did not speak Homeric
Greek, it was familiar to them in a way King James English can never be to us.

A far more successful use of prose has been achieved by
E. V. Rieu in his translations of the two poems (available

in the Penguin series paperbacks). His diction is the vernacular of British English as spoken by cultivated people with large vocabularies and refined sensibilities who will not let their education intrude too much on their speech. His English is therefore neither common or trivial nor, on the other hand, stuffy. This allows him to keep the pace of his narrative rapid and at the same time introduce Homer's ornamental epithets and repetitious phrases without awkwardness. Curiously enough, the style is far less successful in the *Iliad* than in the *Odyssey*, which again only serves to emphasize the essential difference between the poems. The *Odyssey* has an amused tone throughout in Mr. Rieu's translation whereas the *Iliad* seems somewhat heavy and pretentious. Somehow, he has not got the original tone, nor has he made a contemporary one. The *Odyssey*, on the other hand, sparkles with wit. For instance, in the thirteenth book when Athene reveals herself to Odysseus, she says in Mr. Rieu's translation, "What a cunning knave it would take to beat you at your tricks," and later, "How like you to be so wary! And that is why I cannot desert you in your misfortunes: you are so civilized, so intelligent, so self-possessed." Mr. Rieu has created dialogue for the stage, natural enough to move rapidly, but at the same time not the simplest vernacular.

There are two important poetic translations, one of the *Iliad* by Richmond Lattimore (Chicago, 1961; also a Phoenix Books paperback) and one of the *Odyssey* by Robert Fitzgerald (New York, 1961; also a Doubleday Anchor Book paperback). Both are successful; both are written by poets. Professor Lattimore is very faithful to his original, even to the point of maintaining an almost line for line translation. The formal, stately, ritualized quality of the *Iliad* comes across by straining the natural word order of English and by allowing the natural dimensions of the line to offer a counterpoint to the sense and rhythm of the sentences which frequently do not correspond to the line. Because, as he says, we possess no poetic

diction today he has used the simplest language of prose
to keep the lucid and plain Homeric style. He is true to
the Greek and avoids the pretentious. But his translation is
far too sparse. There is no exaltation to his translation;
when the story is not dramatic, merely descriptive, Professor Lattimore's language does not carry the narrative.
Sometimes his translation seems to be merely prose set in
lines, as:

> one of these [springs] runs hot water and the steam
>   on all sides
> of it rises as if from a fire that was burning
>   inside it.
>
> *(Iliad* 22.149–150)

Sometimes he reproduces Homer with immediacy, as:

> They ran beside these, one escaping, the other one
>   after him.
> It was a great man who fled, but far better he who
>   pursued him . . .
>
> *(Iliad* 22.157–158)

Professor Fitzgerald's *Odyssey* is much better poetry
and stands as a poem independent of its original. Naturally, therefore, one's interest is more quickly engaged and
more easily retained. Fitzgerald the poet, however, maintains a control that is sometimes difficult for anyone who
wants to know more precisely what Homer said. For instance, when Telemachos says:

> Men prefer the song which is newest to them listening
>
> *(Odyssey* 1.351–352)

Mr. Fitzgerald translates:

> Men like best a song that rings like morning on the ear.

Homer rarely employs brief similes such as this. The expression suggests lyric poetry, and there is in fact a lyrical

quality to the whole of Fitzgerald's translation. This delicacy, while pleasing, is not really epic. Moreover, Fitzgerald is not afraid to omit lines or passages which some scholars have considered misplaced. He omits, for instance, the parts of Athene's speech in the first book of the *Odyssey* that make her directions contradictory. Again, he omits the spirited remonstrance which Telemachos makes to his mother when she objects to Phemios' song. To do so with no indication seems unfair, although perhaps we may say that Mr. Fitzgerald stands in the limbo of the translator's craft more to the side of his creation than to the original poem. This is legitimate, but I do not agree with him, especially since he has created the finest translation in a long time, one that is a true poem and will inevitably be read by everyone.

FURTHER READING UPDATED

Homeric scholarship, as is often remarked, constitutes a separatate industry of itself in the entire spectrum of the study of antiquity. Recently, the later part of the vast bibliography of this subject was listed and categorized by means of computer in David W. Packard and Tania Meyers *A Bibliography of Homeric Scholarship Preliminary Edition 1930-1970* (Undena Publications, Malibu California, 1974). The more important aspect to this listing is the subject index although, as the editors caution, the computer has listed everything quite impartially so that one cannot know what are the more important essays.

The never ending spate of books and articles sometimes develops significant new directions in our understanding of the *Iliad* and *Odyssey*. The most important work done in the past decade is an assessment of the artistry of oral poetry, or more precisely what appears to be oral poetry as we find it in the *Iliad* and *Odyssey*. Adam Parry the lamented brilliant son of Milman Parry edited the collected papers of his famous father (*The Making of Homeric Verse* [Oxford at the Clarendon Press 1971]) including translating his French dissertations. He begins with a magisterial essay surveying the so-called Homeric Question. It is an illuminating discussion of the study of Homer in the nineteenth century, Milman Parry's intellectual background and development and his successors. Then Parry *fils* points out the need for an analysis of the *art* of the oral style and the oral tradition, arguing that "our Homer" was its master. He himself has written beautifully on this very subject in "Have We Homer's

'Iliad'?" *Yale Classical Studies* volume 20 (1966) pp. 177-216. Parry is concerned to demonstrate the propriety of Homeric verse. Nothing can be removed, nothing added; everywhere we observe a just measure as Parry shows in detail for certain passages arguing thereby that we observe one man's control over the formulary style.

Milman Parry's effort was to define and describe a technique whereby a poet could create *ex tempore* line after line of poetry. Parry concentrated on the *mechanics* of this technique. His approach often implied that any given poet was the servant of the technique. The contempory reaction has been to look for the ways in which the poet controls the technique and transcends its mechanics. Necessarily, most studies work closely from the text; much Greek is quoted. Some of the best, howver, do not depend so much upon the Greek so that they are not incomprehensible to the Greekless.

An orthodox Parry-ist essay on devising an aesthetic for oral poetry is contained in J.A. Notopoulos "Studies in Early Greek Oral Poetry" *Harvard Studies in Classical Philology* volume 68 1964 pp. 45-78. Notopoulos more than most contemporaries adheres to the notion that the poets were using a relatively rigid system which did not allow for individual variation. Nonetheless he raises some valuable questions, how the poet takes his audience into the poem by his allusions, the nature of the recitations (several singers spelling each other over a few days? one singer singing over several weeks?), the manner of recitation, the importance of *parataxis* (see pp. 36-37 of this book) and Homer's originality.

Diametrically opposed to Notopoulos' emphasis upon the mechanical is D. Young "Never Blotted a Line? Formula and Premeditation in Homer and Hesiod" *Arion* volume 6 (1967) pp. 279-324. The followers of Milman Parry stress that the poet was able to create anew each time, that he was not memorizing and repeating his poem or parts of it. Young thinks otherwise. First, he discounts the pervasiveness of the formulary system, arguing that what many classify as similar phrases, hence formulaic, are not so, second he claims that contemporary illiterate Scots poets can carry poems in their

memories for years *verbatim*, that examples from medieval
epic show it could have been possible that the Homeric epics
were written from the start. Young argues for the uniqueness
of Homer's language and for the possibility that Homer's
formulae are all of them his creation. The essay is
stimulating and remains a rallying point for those who insist
upon a relatively great poetic freedom and control. See also
A.B. Lord "Homer as Oral Poet" *Harvard Studies in
Classical Philology* volume 72 (1967) pp. 1-46 who challenges
some of the revisionist notions; and W. Sale "Literary Values
and the Homeric Question" *Arion* volume 2 (1963) pp.
86-100 which is another approach to the problem of an
aesthetic for oral art.

One of the best of the young Homerists, a student of Parry
fils, J.A. Russo, has written, "Homer is not the perfection of
all that went before him but the eruption of a mighty and
singular talent into wholly new realms of expression." The
essay from which that sentence is taken "Homer Against his
Tradition" *Arion* volume 7 (1968) pp. 275-295 is Russo's
attempt to distinguish between what seems traditional and
what seems to be Homer's innovation. He makes four
categories; 1) *verbatim* repetition, 2) the repeated typical
scene with qualitative additions where he compares for
example the arming of Agamemnon (*Iliad*, Book 12) with
other more routine descriptions of arming, 3) the very loose
use of stock material, similes, for instance, which may seem
to be on a theme but which are real variations and 4) scenes
showing significant distortions. The problem, of course, is to
gain some control over the text so as to be able to see what is
traditional and what is innovative. In every case, we must
establish a suitable definition of a formula.

J.B. Hainsworth *The Flexibilty of the Homeric Formula*
(Oxford at the Clarendon Press 1968) tries to go beyond
Parry's use of the noun-epithet combination for a definition
of a formula. Chapter 1, "Composition with Formulae" pp.
1-22, has important questions leading us to understand that
more work must be done with common nouns. Chapter 3,
"What is a Formula?" pp. 33-45, is valuable although it
contains a good deal of Greek. Most recently a dazzling book
has appeared, M.N. Nagler *Spontaneity and Tradition*

(University of California Press Berkely 1974), in which the author presents a very radical thesis using the latest ideas of linguistics, anthropology, folk lore and psychology. Unfortunately the prose is almost impenetrable. Nagler claims that all the chapters after the first are accessible to the Greek-less; but what about those who read English? In any case, Nagler disclaims the necessity for the poet's having to think in remembered formulae, arguing quite mystically for transcendent phonemic, grammatic shapes, in the sub-liminal unconscious, phrases that replicate themselves, it seems to me, after the manner of "word association" as it is understood on the analyst's couch. The book is exciting and my instinct tells me that it is on the right track but it is hard to master.

On a far less exalted level is Bernard Fenik's *Typical Battle Scenes in the Iliad (Hermes Einzelschriften Heft 21* Steiner Weisbaden 1968). The battle narrative has the most seemingly formulaic language in the Homeric corpus; the action is the most cliched. For Fenik, anything repeated at least twice is considered to be typical. This makes the discussion at time unmanageable since so loose a criterion proliferates the instances of presumed typicality. He has in his own words "tried to write a kind of 'Poetics' for the *Iliad's* battle scenes." Whether he has actually succeeded in this is doubtful. But he has extended our knowledge of these very common passages, looking at the repeated details of description and their variation, the necessary prelude to seeking significance or assessing the poet's intent.

The battle narrative is particularly valid for this sort of investigation because the language is indeed so typical. It has seemed to me, in fact, very like the catalogue style which we find in the Catalogue of Ships (see my "Homeric Battle Narrative and Catalogues" *Harvard Studies in Classical Philology* volume 68 [1964] pp. 345-374). C.P. Segal has written a monograph, *The Theme of the Mutilation of the Corpse in the Iliad (Mnemosyne Suppl.* 17 E.J. Brill Leyden 1971) which again deals with battle narrative. Segal has taken one theme—mutilation—to show what he considers to be the poet's conscious manipulation and development of the theme to underscore the meaning of the action. As one expects with Segal's pieces, the footnotes are as valuable as the text. His argument shows us a poet firmly in control of his narrative idea down to the details.

J.N.H. Austin "The Function of Digression in the *Iliad*" *Greek, Roman and Byzantine Studies* volume 7 (1966) pp. 295-312 raises all the question of unity, in particular the problem of *parataxis* or the 'strung-on style.' (*lexis eiromene* as it is called). Does the *Iliad* represent an artistic unity? or is it just pieces strung together mechanically until we reach the end? Austin looks to the digression as indicative of the narrator's habit of mind. He first discusses whether we may legitimately, in fact, speak of any passages as digressions. He then discusses digressions as examples of the well-known Homeric (and in general Greek) penchant for instruction through example (*paradeigma*, as it is called in Greek). Material directly relevant to the Trojan War is told in the merest allusion, he points out, whereas far less relevant material (as for instance the exploits of Nestor's youth) is told in great detail in digression. The poet can scarcely be retrospective about an event which is taking place so he must turn to other saga material for his examples. But the so-called digressions relate directly to the moment at hand. "[The digression] brings time to a complete standstill and locks our attention unremittingly on the celebration of the present moment" (p. 312).

There have been few major works of interpretation in the intervening years. S. Bernadette "The Aristeia of Diomedes and the Plot of the *Iliad*" *Agon* volume 1 (1968) pp. 10-38 focuses on Homer's gods. The plot according to Bernadette depends upon Homer's revealing gradually the relations between gods and men; the first revelation is contained in the *aristeia* of Diomedes in the fifth book. Why Bernadette ignores the close of book one seems unclear to me except that it would argue against his thesis, I believe. Bernadette stresses the importance of the gods in the *Iliad*. His essay is full of good insights, for instance: "The general absence of moral indignation in the *Iliad* would thus be the other side of Homer's reticence about pain." J.A. Russo and B. Simon have written a very stimulating essay "Homeric Psychology

and the Oral Epic Tradition" *Journal of the History of Ideas*
volume 29 (1968) pp. 483-98 in which they discuss differing
views of the Homeric sense of self. They stress the Homeric
emphasis upon the external as opposed to the internal self.
Homer portrays the inner self with exterior description,
similes particularly. For instance, the inner contemplation
by Achilles about killing Agamemnon takes place in the
external dialogue with Athena (compare Odysseus addressing his own soul in external dialogue). The authors relate
this to the psychology of oral performance, to the way in
which the poem is external to the poet who is quite literally
inspired. They ponder the question to what degree the poet's
language may constitute the way of thinking and speaking
among his contemporary audience. The essay is in the same
mode of speculation as B. Snell *The Discovery of the Mind*
(Harper Torchbook 101: New York 1960), pages 1-41 of
which might be read as a complement. I myself have written
on the strong emphasis upon women in the *Odyssey* and on
sexual roles in general in "Male and Female in the Homeric
Poems" *Ramus* volume 3 (1974) pp. 87-101. In addition, I
have written two chapters on Homer in my *Ancient Greek
Literature and Society* (Doubleday Garden City 1975) pp.
30-94, some of which repeats the ideas contained in this
book. See also C.S. Littleton "Some Possible Indo-European
Themes in the *Iliad*" in *Myth and Law Among the
Indo-Europeans* J. Puhel, ed. (Berkely University of California Press 1970).

D.M. Gaunt *Surge and Thunder: Critical Reading in
Homer's Odyssey* (Oxford University Press 1971) has made an
interesting and on the whole successful experiment at
conveying the aesthetics of Homer's style and diction to
Greek-less readers. He translates twenty important passages
from the *Odyssey* which are followed by his critical comments.
Transliterated Greek throughout allows the reader to approach, at least a little bit, the sound of the poem. Gaunt has
valuable insights of his own as well as bringing in relevant
allusions to other literatures and in turn drawing attention to
important published scholarship and criticism. There is
much cross referencing which keeps the whole poem in

mind, although he deals only with passages. A Thornton *People and Themes in Homers Odyssey* (London Methuen 1970) is a book with which I have little sympathy, yet as a source book to recover various ideas of the character of Odysseus and Penelope or some commonplaces on the themes of the poem the book may be valuable to the student. The discussion of the possible shamanistic background to the story of Odysseus' wandering is interesting, but I am not convinced that it has much bearing on Homer's Odysseus.

The *Odyssey* seems to have received more treatment recently since it had been so much more neglected earlier on. H.W. Clarke's *The Art of the Odyssey* (Prentice-Hall Englewood Cliffs 1967) is a modest but valuable account by a man of demonstrable critical talents. Clarke discusses the source of the poem's overall structure; this he finds in cult and in Jungian archetypes. So he can relate the poem to a variety of western literary motifs which helps to explain how the *Odyssey* can be so profound and influential although its surface plot and value seem relatively light. See further his chapter on comparative epic. Nowhere are Clarke's sensitivity and perception more apparent than in the second appendix "Translation and translations." One would like an entire book on this subject from Clarke. As it is, Clarke should be read in conjunction with Gabriel Gemain's *Homer* (New York Grove Press 1960); they complement each other nicely.

Sir Maurice Bowra died while finishing writing *Homer* (Scribner New York 1972), a general discussion of the poet and the poems, which shows the same literary civility and sensitivity which his earlier works reveal. (see pp. 243 f., 247 of this book). The work is essentially retrospective, not innovative.

Paolo Vivant *The Homeric Imagination: A Study of Homer's Poetic Perception of Reality* (Bloomington, Indiana University Press, 1970) is a curious book, almost an anachronistic one in which Vivante seeks to recover the style and intent of a very individual poet. Vivante does not mention traditional poetry, oral technique or formulaic language, scene and character. He is at pains to disassociate himself from such figures as Bassett or Whitman (see pp. 248 f. of this book) who create "works of literary criticism and history" but "seem to disregard the individual poet." Vivante prefers a "purely speculative point of view, as if we were reading him [Homer] for the first time." This point of view is not really new, but may seem so since it is nowadays so unfamiliar; it is essentially the view which preceded the nineteenth century Homeric question and the twentieth century response to it. So it seems most curious when Vivante talks of the poet deliberately ignoring the specifics of locales (pp. 72 ff.). One does not need to accept a mechanistic theory of oral poetry to see these features as relating to a long developed and pervasive technique.

The pieces of epic poetry which were created after the period of the Homeric epics survive in the merest fragments. There is little we can know about them. G.L. Huxley *Greek Epic Poetry* (Cambridge Harvard University Press 1969) is a survey of these remains, or what passes for a survey given the slim pickings available to him. Little is said about the genre, about literary critical problems, too much on dating the epics and their political nuances. In trying to recover the skeletal outline of the stories of these epics, however, Huxley is at his best, and students of the literary use of myth will profit.   Some of the ideas which I presented on Apollonius Rhodius' *Argonautical* in this book, especially the role of Jason as a hero whose *arete* is the capacity for romantic love have been more fully developed and published in "Jason as Love-Hero in Apollonios' *Argonautika*" *Greek, Roman and Byzantine Studies* volume 10 (1969) pp. 31-55. The material is now further reworked and included in the chapter on Alexandrian poetry, pp. 368 ff. in my *Ancient Greek Literature and Society.*

The epic genre is treated by Albert Cook *The Classic Line: A study in Epic Poetry* (Bloomington Indiana University Press 1966). His study of the *Iliad* concentrates on the demands which a long poem makes, how complexity, simplicity and variety are achieved together, how the poet balances the general and the particular. His discussion of the *Odyssey* relates particularly to that in this book, being on the remarkable way in which Homer has confined the subject. He begins the book with remarks on Beowulf and medieval epic; he also treats Virgil, Dante and Milton. One of the virtues of Cook's work is his attention to the details of language reminding us that the story line is only a small part of what makes an epic poem.

Since 1966 Mr. Lattimore has translated the *Odyssey* (Harper Torchbook New York 1968) and Mr. Fitzgerald, the *Iliad* (Doubleday Garden City 1974). I review the latter in a forthcoming issue of *Parnassus: Poetry in Review*. I am not pleased with any of these translations. They are pallid, perhaps because the translators were trying to follow the Greek. One cannot, of course, bring over the Homeric manner exactly into English. Most of all, one misses the authority which the Homeric diction and style give to the Iliad, that stability and security of a narrative that acknowledges nothing tentative and no alternative. By contrast, Christoper Logue has translated the sixteenth book of the *Iliad* (*The Patrokleia of Homer* [U. Michigan Press Ann Arbor 1963]) in a handsome way, perhaps because he knows no Greek. Logue made his poem from what he was told the Greek meant. Perhaps, in these Greekless days that is the better way, for then the poet stands together with his audience, mouth agape, receiving Homer as thing unknown, all *impression*.

INDEX

Achilles, 7, 14, 20–21, 23, 33–34, 81, 82, 111, 161, 163, 240; similarity to *Gilgamesh*, 16–17; relationship to Patroklos, 55, 84–86; in the Underworld (*Odyssey*), 190–91; Chapter IV *passim*
Actium, 211–12, 225
Aeneas, 151; Chapter VI *passim*. See also Aineias
Aeneid, 19; Chapter VI *passim*
Agamemnon, 7, 28–32, 82, 87, 92, 100, 161, 163, 190; his quarrel with Achilles, 26, 33–34; his political power, 51–54; Chapter IV *passim*
Aigisthos, 24–25, 164, 179
Aigyptios, 84
Aineias, 41. See also Aeneas
Ajax son of Telamon, 99, 190; entreating Achilles, 131–32, 136
Alexander the Great, 210
Alexandrian age, 208–10; scholarship, 114
Alkinoos, 7, 77, 160, 184–85, 187; his political power, 55–57; similar to Menelaos, 177; his politeness, 197–98
Anchises as father figure, 222–24; in the Underworld

(*Aeneid*), 226–27
Andromache, 28–32, 94, 117; symbol of woman, 149–51; lamenting Hektor, 154–55
anecdotes, 94–96
Antikleia, 220
Antinoos, 83, 179
Aphrodite, 66–70, 196–97. See also Venus
Apollo, 66, 69
Apollonios Rhodios, 209–10, 224, 231–33
Archilochos, 194
Ares, 66, 71, 108, 116–17
Arete, 177–78, 198
aretē, 120–21
Argonautika, 209–10, 231
Argos, 41
aristeia, 126, 193–94, 213
Artemis, 66; Nausikaa compared to, 196, 199
Ascanius, 167
Athene, 34–36, 63–64, 66, 69, 100, 159, 174, 181–82, 196, 221; symbol of common sense, 70, 119; function in *Odyssey*, 71–73
Augustus Caesar, 211–13, 217, 224–25, 228, 230, 234
Autolykos, 182–83

272 THE *Iliad, Odyssey,* AND EPIC TRADITION